T5-AFS-902

THE IMPACT OF VECTOR AND PARALLEL ARCHITECTURES ON THE GAUSSIAN ELIMINATION ALGORITHM

Algorithms and architectures for advanced scientific computing

Advanced scientific computing is a rapid evolving discipline. Dramatic progress has been made recently as a result of two major advances:

- the advent of vector and parallel computers, which has led to a complete reformulation of the standard methods for their efficient use on new machines

- the development of new algorithms and techniques, some of which relate to parallelism, and some of which are due to the emergence of new methods in applied mathematics.

Algorithms and architectures for advanced scientific computing is a new series of monographs that reflects these exciting developments. The series concentrates on recent advances in scientific computing and has a special emphasis on new algorithmic methods and computer architectures. These structured books of international current research interest will be essential reading for all postgraduates and researchers, and important to all whose work is involved with the rapid developments in these areas.

YVES ROBERT

THE IMPACT OF VECTOR AND PARALLEL ARCHITECTURES ON THE GAUSSIAN ELIMINATION ALGORITHM

MANCHESTER UNIVERSITY PRESS

HALSTED PRESS

a division of JOHN WILEY & SONS

New York Brisbane Toronto

Published by
Manchester University Press
Oxford Road, Manchester M13 9PL, UK

Copublished in the Western Hemisphere, Australia, and New Zealand by HALSTED PRESS, an imprint of JOHN WILEY & SONS, Inc.
605 Third Ave, New York, NY 10158

British Library cataloguing in publication data
Robert, Yves
The impact of vector and parallel architectures on the Gaussian elimination algorithm.——(Algorithms and architectures for advanced scientific computing).
1. Computer systems. Parallel-processor systems. Use of algorithms
I. Title II. Series
004.35

UK ISBN 0 7190 3365 9 *hardback*

Library of Congress Cataloging in Publication data
The Impact of vector and parallel architectures on the Gaussian elimination algorithm/edited by Yves Robert.
p. cm. — (Algorithms and architectures for advanced scientific computing)
Includes bibliographical references and index.
ISBN 0–470–21703–0
1. Computer architecture. 2. Vector processing (Computer science). 3. Parallel processing (Electronic computers). 4. Algorithms. 5. Gaussian processes.
I. Robert, Yves, 1938– . II. Series.
QA76.9.A73155 1990
519.2—dc20 90–47463
CIP

US ISBN 0 470 21703 0

Printed in Great Britain
by Biddles Limited, Guildford and King's Lynn

CONTENTS

PREFACE

No, this is not just another book on parallel processing ! Many general textbooks are already available, and they survey all aspects of this new discipline, from algorithms and architectures to languages, software and programming tools, including computational models and complexity results.

A single algorithm ...

Rather than presenting several parallel algorithms and their implementation on several machines, we deal in this book with a single algorithm, namely Gaussian elimination.

For many researchers of the Computer Science community, Gaussian elimination means three interleaved loops, which can be interchanged. Pivoting is usually needed, but that does not complicate matters too much. We explain in the first chapter why we have chosen Gaussian elimination rather than several other classics.

... implemented on several parallel architectures

So why a book on parallel Gaussian elimination ? The thesis of this book is that the target architecture has a tremendous impact on the design of the parallel algorithm. The idea is to keep the same algorithm throughout the book and to move from one class of architectures to another to see what we should change if we want an efficient implementation. In the first part of the book we analyse shared memory vector multiprocessors, distributed memory machines and systolic arrays. We change a lot for each case.

We describe each implementation in great detail. Not too much, however. The life-span of a parallel architecture is (at most) a few years nowadays. We take care to extract the key ideas and concepts, and we review the tools (scheduling algorithms, performance models, methods for automatic synthesis) in the second part of the book. See section 1.1 for a complete overview of the book.

In a word, we believe that *efficient programming* and *architecture-independent programming* are still incompatible activities. Although we should tend to the goal of unity,[1] we are far from achieving it.

[1] See Chandy and Misra [1988].

Who should use this book ?

The principal audience for this book is intended to be graduate students in Computer Science. The book also contains useful ideas for any programmer wishing to efficiently implement his preferred algorithm on his preferred parallel machine.

Acknowledgements

I have devoted several years of my (professional) life to the study of parallel Gaussian elimination, and this was a rewarding experience due to the collaboration of many friends. I owe a lot to my colleagues in the following list:
• I have learned much on vector multiprocessors from all the staff at the IBM European Center in Rome (ECSEC). Giuseppe Radicati and Piero Sguazzero deserve special thanks.
• A lot of work has been done with the TIM3-IMAG hypercube in Grenoble, with Michel Cosnard, Pierre Fraigniaud, Serge Miguet, Bernard Tourancheau, and Gilles Villard. I have also been influenced by Youcef Saad.
• I have designed systolic algorithms in cooperation with Abdelhamid Benaini, Patrice Quinton, Maurice Tchuente and Denis Trystram.

I would like to extend these thanks to the Parallel Processing Community, and to the students in Grenoble and Lyon who have been taught various parts of this book.

I have been supported by grants from the Research Programme C3 (Cooperation, Concurrency and Communication) of the French National Council for Research (CNRS) and by the European Economic Community (Esprit Basic Research Action 3280). I also thank my institutions, the Institut National Polytechnique de Grenoble and the Ecole Normale Supérieure de Lyon, for providing excellent working conditions.

Finally, I dedicate this book to my friend Michel Cosnard, who could have written it with me if he were not so administratively loaded with the direction of our laboratory LIP-IMAG. Note that LIP means "Laboratory for Parallelism in Computer Science": could I dream of a better research environment ?

Credits

This book has been written with Microsoft Word 4 (Microsoft Corporation) on a Macintosh IIx (Apple Computer, Inc.). The figures have been drawn using Superpaint (Silicon Beach Software), Mac Draw (Claris Corporation), Cricket Draw and Cricket Graph (Cricket Software).

CHAPTER
ONE

INTRODUCTION

The thesis of this book is that the design of efficient parallel algorithms is heavily dependent upon a deep knowledge of the underlying parallel architecture. Of course the key word in the previous sentence is *efficient* . When implementing a parallel algorithm, our aim is to squeeze the most out of the target computer that faces us and resists our efforts. To achieve this goal, we need to fully reformulate the well-known sequential schemes. The techniques involved are quite different for shared memory vector multiprocessors and for hypercubes or systolic arrays. In order to illustrate these techniques, we choose the same target example—namely Gaussian elimination—throughout the book. Our aim is to capture the key features of each main class of parallel architectures, and to deduce the best way to match the algorithm design with the architectural constraints.

To summarize in a sentence, this book is neither a general textbook on parallel architectures, nor a general textbook on parallel algorithm design. Rather, it is a tutorial on the impact of the former upon the latter.

The first part of the book is implementation oriented, whereas the second part is devoted to design tools and methodologies. A substantial portion of the material presented has not been covered in other textbooks

Our basic assumption is that the reader is convinced that parallel processing is upon us. Parallel processing seems to be the only viable, cost-effective solution to fulfilling the ever-increasing need of more CPU performance. The concept of parallel processing is a departure from the trend of achieving increases in speed by performing single operations faster. Rather, it achieves increases in speed by performing several operations concurrently. Dozens of parallel architectures are commercially available, at every price, from low-cost workstations up to the most powerful supercomputers. Several textbooks explain the reasons that led to the departure from the sequential von Neumann computer. See the bibliographic notes at the end of the chapter for a list of references on parallel architectures and algorithms.

Before moving to a brief overview of the contents of the book, we must explain why we have chosen Gaussian elimination as a case study. As already said, we want to concentrate on a single algorithm rather than deal with several classics, such as matrix-matrix multiplication, sorting, or FFT transforms. But why Gaussian elimination, and not another of these classics ? First, Gaussian elimination is a *useful* algorithm. It is certainly the most used method for solving dense linear systems of equations, and therefore it is at the very heart

of numerous scientific computing applications. Its implementation in a vector and/or parallel environment has been extensively studied in the literature. Here are some *pros* of Gaussian elimination:
• it can be expressed in a very compact form, that of three interleaved loops. Interchanging the loops evidences the impact of memory accessing and operation chaining on vector supercomputers;
• it requires a number of arithmetic operations which is an order of magnitude higher than the number of input/output requirements. In other words, it is a compute-bound algorithm, and as such offers good promise for massive parallelism;
• depending upon the pivoting strategy, local or global information will be required at each step, leading to various communication and synchronization problems in a distributed memory environment;
• there are many precedence constraints during the execution of the algorithm, so that scheduling techniques must be introduced;
• as the elimination progresses, the amount of work decreases, so that tuned data allocation strategies will be needed to achieve a good workload balancing among the processors.
We are already anticipating the contents of the next chapters.

In summary we primarily chose Gaussian elimination just because it is an ideal algorithm to illustrate the basic concepts of vector and parallel processing ! Also, Gaussian elimination is complicated enough to motivate a thorough analysis, but the techniques involved for its parallel implementation are simple and general enough to be re-usable in other situations. Our hope is that the reader who wishes to implement his own favourite algorithm on his own favourite parallel architecture will find useful guidelines in the following pages ...

1.1. Book overview

The following sections of this chapter are devoted to some background material on Gaussian elimination and parallel processing terminology. Chapter 2 is an introduction to pipeline, vector and parallel architectures. Special emphasis is put upon the distinction between shared and local memory systems. Three case studies complete the presentation.

The next three chapters (part 1 of the book) are implementation oriented. We describe the restructuring techniques needed for shared memory vector multiprocessors, distributed memory systems and systolic arrays. In chapter 3 we describe the recasting of the Gaussian elimination algorithm in terms of vector-vector, vector-matrix and matrix-matrix kernels (three levels of the so-called Basic Linear Algebra Subroutines). The target architecture here is a vector multiprocessor with a hierarchical memory system, such as a Cray 2, an ALLIANT/FX8, or an IBM 3090. In chapter 4 we discuss hypercube computing, and we give real-life examples of implementations on message-passing distributed memory systems. We choose the systolic array model in chapter 5 as a representative example of special-purpose VLSI-oriented massively parallel architectures.

Chapters 6 to 8 (part 2 of the book) are more theoretical. Task graph scheduling is the subject of chapter 6. Complexity results and speedup evaluation in a distributed memory environment are presented in chapter 7. Automatic synthesis methods for systolic arrays are introduced in chapter 8. There is a one-to-one correspondence between the chapters of the two parts of the book, as illustrated in table 1.1.

Target architecture	**Part 1** *Parallel algorithm design*	**Part 2** *Models and tools*
Shared memory	Chapter 3	Chapter 6
Distributed memory	Chapter 4	Chapter 7
Systolic array	Chapter 5	Chapter 8

Table 1.1 : Organization of the chapters

1.2. Background: Gaussian elimination

Throughout the book we use Gaussian elimination as a target example. Let $A x = b$ (1) be a linear system of equations, where A is a dense square matrix of order n, and b a vector with n components. We consider the matrix A augmented with the right-hand side b, that is, we let $A := (A,b)$ be an $n \times (n+1)$ matrix.

To solve the system $A x = b$, we transform it into an equivalent triangular system $U x = c$ (2). Then we easily solve the triangular system (2) by back-substitution. The transformation from system (1) to system (2) consists of n-1 steps. At each step k, we zero out the elements of column k which are below the main diagonal. To this purpose, we add a multiple of row k to each row i, $k+1 \le i \le n$. For instance, at step 1, we add a multiple of row 1 to all other rows so as to annihilate all the coefficients in column 1 except the first one, a_{11}. Thus the elementary operation is a row update: for $2 \le i \le n$, we let

$$\begin{pmatrix} \text{row } 1 \\ \text{row } i \end{pmatrix} := M_{i1} \cdot \begin{pmatrix} \text{row } 1 \\ \text{row } i \end{pmatrix}$$

where M_{i1} is the following 2×2 matrix:

$$M_{i1} := \begin{pmatrix} 1 & 0 \\ -\dfrac{a_{i1}}{a_{11}} & 1 \end{pmatrix}$$

As a consequence, the element in position (i,1) is updated into

$$a_{i1} := -\frac{a_{i1}}{a_{11}} \cdot a_{11} + a_{i1} = 0$$

Let $A^{(0)} = A$ be the original matrix. The first step of the algorithm is to pre-multiply $A^{(0)}$ by a unit lower triangular matrix L^1 such that the first column of $A^{(1)} := L^1 A^{(0)}$ has only zeros in positions 2 to n. L^1 differs from the identity matrix only in its first column, whose elements are $l^1_{i1} = -\dfrac{a_{i1}}{a_{11}}$ for $i \ge 2$. More generally, at step k, we add a multiple of row k to each row i, $k+1 \le i \le n$, so as to annihilate elements in the k-column below the diagonal. Equivalently, we update $A^{(k-1)}$ into $A^{(k)} := L^k A^{(k-1)}$, where L^k is unit lower triangular and

$l_{ik}^{k} = -\dfrac{a_{ik}^{(k-1)}}{a_{kk}^{(k-1)}}$ for $i \geq k+1$ (L^k differs from the identity matrix only in its k-th column).

Note that at step k, the first k-1 rows and columns of $A^{(k-1)}$ are left unchanged.

After n-1 steps we obtain an upper triangular matrix $A^{(n-1)} = L^{n-1} L^{n-2} \ldots L^2 L^1 A$. Let $U := A^{(n-1)}$ and $L := (L^{n-1} L^{n-2} \ldots L^2 L^1)^{-1}$. We have $A = L\,U$, where L is a unit lower triangular matrix whose entries are magically given by $l_{ij} = -l_{ij}^{j}$ for $i \geq j+1$. Overwriting the first n columns of A by L and U, we obtain the generic formulation of the Gaussian elimination algorithm:

```
for k = 1 to n-1 do
          { step k }
          for i = k+1 to n do
                    { add a multiple of row k to row i }
                    a_ik := a_ik / a_kk
                    for j = k+1 to n+1 do
                              a_ij := a_ij - a_ik * a_kj
```

The arithmetic cost of the algorithm is $\frac{2n^3}{3} + o(n^3)$ floating-point operations.[1] If there are many systems to solve (with the same coefficient matrix A but with different right-hand sides), it is important to keep track of L and U, because solving another system A x = b' only requires $O(n^2)$ operations once the decomposition A = LU has been computed.

1.2.1. Column-oriented versions

In the generic formulation of the algorithm, the innermost loop accesses the matrix by rows, which is not suitable in a FORTRAN programming environment, where matrices are stored by columns. We develop hereafter two column-oriented versions:

```
{ KJI-outside version }
for k = 1 to n-1 do
          for i = k+1 to n do
                    a_ik := a_ik / a_kk
          for j = k+1 to n+1 do
                    for i = k+1 to n do
                              a_ij := a_ij - a_ik * a_kj

{ KJI-inside version }
for k = 1 to n-1 do
          for j = k+1 to n+1 do
                    a_kj := a_kj / a_kk
                    for i = k+1 to n do
                              a_ij := a_ij - a_ik * a_kj
```

[1] We say that $f = O(g)$ if $\frac{f}{g}$ is bounded, and that $f = o(g)$ if $\frac{f}{g} \to 0$.

The KJI notation refers to the order of the three main loops and is due to Dongarra, Gustavson and Karp [1984]. Note that in the KJI-inside version, we do not exactly compute the LU decomposition of A, because we normalize row k at step k. Let D be the diagonal of U and V be such that U = D V. Rather than computing the factorization A = L U, we compute the factorization A = L D V, with L and V unit diagonal.

In both versions, the innermost loop accesses elements of the matrix by columns. We discuss the importance of accessing vectors stored in contiguous memory locations (with stride[1] 1) in chapter 3.

There is an important difference between the inside and outside versions. The outside version can be concisely expressed as:

```
{ KJI-outside version }
for k = 1 to n-1 do
        prep(k)
        for j = k+1 to n+1 do
                update(k,j)
```

Similarly for the inside version:

```
{ KJI-inside version }
for k = 1 to n-1 do
        for j = k+1 to n+1 do
                update(k,j)
```

In both procedures, given k, the tasks update(k,j) of updating the columns j≥k+1 are independent and can be executed in parallel. However, in the outside form, the task of preparing column k is a predecessor to all the updating tasks and must be executed serially. We will analyse these intuitive notions in depth in chapter 6.

1.2.2. Partial pivoting

In fact the real motivation for considering the outside form is pivoting. The generic Gaussian algorithm is known to be numerically stable for only a few classes of matrices, such as diagonally dominant and symmetric positive definite. For general matrices we need to use a technique to avoid the occurrence of small pivots: at step k in the preceding versions, we perform a division by $a_{kk}^{(k-1)}$, called the pivot, which is safe only if its absolute value is large enough. A widely used technique, called partial pivoting, is the following: at step k, we search in column k of $A^{(k-1)}$, from rows k to n, for the largest element in absolute value. Let $a_{lk}^{(k-1)}$ be this element. If $l \neq k$, we interchange row k and row l before beginning the computations of step k. Owing to this interchange, we perform the division by a large element in the task prep(k), and all the multiplicative coefficients in the elimination matrix L^k will be smaller than 1 in absolute value. It is widely accepted that Gaussian elimination with partial pivoting can be used with confidence in practical

[1] The stride of a vector is the address increment between two consecutive components

problems (Golub and van Loan [1983]). To include partial pivoting in the KJI-outside version, we modify the procedure prep(k) as:

```
{ prep(k) for partial pivoting - KJI outside }
find l such that |a_lk| = max { |a_kk|, ..., |a_nk| }
pivot(k) := l
swap(a_pivot(k),k, a_kk)
for i = k+1 to n do
    a_ik := a_ik / a_kk
```

And for update(k,j):

```
{ update(k,j) for partial pivoting - KJI outside }
swap(a_pivot(k),j, a_kj)
for i = k+1 to n do
    a_ij := a_ij - a_ik * a_kj
```

Note that with partial pivoting, the distinction between the KJI-inside and KJI-outside forms is no longer meaningful: at step k, we must search for a pivot in the whole column k below the diagonal, and this is a synchronization bottleneck anyhow.

A last word: we have selected column-oriented algorithms because they are suited to a FORTRAN-oriented environment. For the versions without pivoting, this is not important, and row-oriented versions can be written very similarly. However, when partial pivoting must be included, column-oriented versions are more natural: we need to interchange rows so as to generate a good pivot, and this is done through a scanning of the pivot column. Interchanging columns is still possible, but it amounts to post-multiplying the coefficient matrix by some permutation matrix, and the resulting procedure becomes less natural.

1.2.3. Loop interchanging

The Gaussian elimination algorithm can be concisely expressed with three interleaved loops. In this section we discuss new versions obtained by reordering the loops. There are six possible variations, but since we choose to deal with column-oriented versions, we obtain only three of them, which are characterized by the position of the k-loop: note that for column-oriented versions, the index i on rows always follows the index j on columns. For the sake of simplicity, we do not take pivoting into account and compute the LU decomposition of the matrix A without processing the right-hand side.

The first version is the KJI-outside form, already introduced. Figure 1.1 summarizes the access pattern for this version. At step k, we perform a scaling of column k to generate the k-th column $l^{(k)}$ of L, and then a rank-1 update $A^{(k)} := A^{(k-1)} - l^{(k)} u^{(k)}$, where $u^{(k)}$ is the k-th row of U. In the column-oriented version, the rank-1 update is performed as a collection of AXPY operations $y_j := y_j + \alpha_j x$, where y_j is a column of $A^{(k)}$, α_j the element above y_j and $x = l^{(k)}$ (see figure 1.1). An AXPY operation is thus a scalar-vector multiply followed by a vector-vector add: AXPY stands for A times X Plus Y.

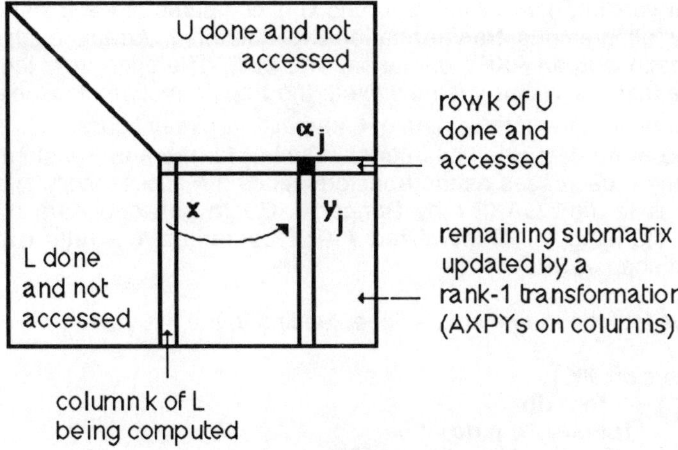

Figure 1.1 : Access pattern for the KJI version

Note that in the KJI form, the rank-1 transformation generated at step k is immediately applied on the lower right corner of the matrix, hence the name "immediate update form" given by Ortega [1988].

In the second version, we let k be the middle-loop index. We obtain the JKI algorithm:

```
{ version JKI }
for j = 1 to n do
        for k = 1 to j-1 do
                for i = k+1 to n do
                        a_ij := a_ij - a_ik * a_kj
        for i = j+1 to n do
                a_ij := a_ij / a_jj
```

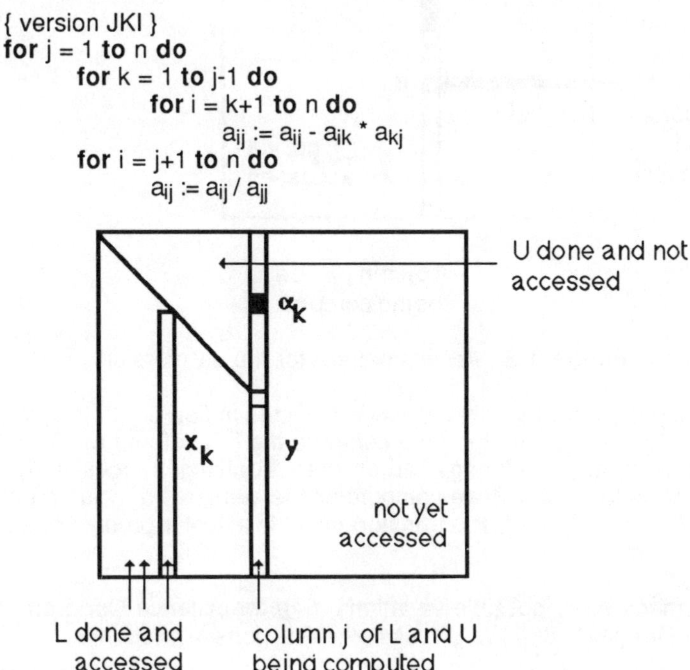

Figure 1.2 : Access pattern for the JKI version

In the JKI version, one column of L and U is computed at each step. At step j we apply all previous transformations to column j. Again, each of these transformations is an AXPY operation. The main difference from the previous version is that the vector y is now fixed: the transformations look like $y := y + \alpha_k x_k$, where x_k is the k-th column of L and $\alpha_k = a_{kj}$ (see figure 1.2). Vector y is composed of the last n-k elements of column j for the k-th transformation, so that its length decreases as the transformations are successively applied. The JKI form is termed GAXPY by Dongarra, Gustavson and Karp [1984], the acronym standing for Generalized AXPY operation. We return to the JKI version in chapter 3.

Finally, we let k be the innermost loop, leading to the JIK version:

```
{ version JIK }
for j = 1 to n do
    for i = 1 to n do
        for k = 1 to min(i,j)-1 do
            a_ij := a_ij - a_ik * a_kj
    for i = j+1 to n do
        a_ij := a_ij / a_jj
```

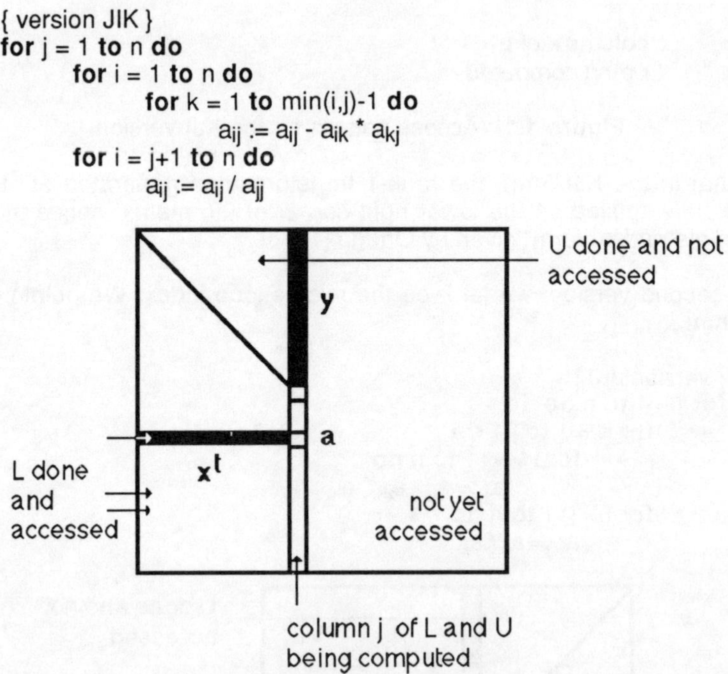

Figure 1.3 : Access pattern for the JIK version

The access pattern for the JIK version is depicted in figure 1.3. In fact, it is like the JKI version, in that at step j we compute the j-th column of L and U. The difference is in the updating: rather than applying successively all the transformations to column j, we compute all the elements of column j one after the other. As a result, the basic transformation is a scalar product of a row of L and a column of U.

There are many other possible variations. See for instance Oppe and Kincaid [1988] and Ortega [1988]. We discuss other versions in chapter 3.

1.3. Background: speedup and efficiency

Two important measures of the quality of parallel algorithms are speedup and efficiency. The speedup S_p achieved by a parallel algorithm running on p (identical) processors is the ratio of the time T_1 taken for the serial execution of the algorithm on a single processor to the time T_p taken for the parallel execution of the algorithm on p processors:

$$S_p = \frac{T_1}{T_p} = \frac{\text{execution time with 1 processor}}{\text{execution time with p processors}}$$

This formula is ambiguous, because parallel algorithms frequently contain extra arithmetic operations and additional communication overhead to accommodate parallelism. Hence it is not fair to compute the speedup with this formula, because it exaggerates the speedup. To give a more realistic appraisal of performance, we should define speedup more precisely by the formula

$$S_p = \frac{\text{time of best serial algorithm}}{\text{time of parallel algorithm}}$$

Unfortunately, the best serial algorithm is rarely known; however, speedup is still bounded by

$$S_p \leq \frac{\text{time of emulated parallel algorithm with 1 processor}}{\text{time of parallel algorithm with p processors}}$$

A possible way for simulating the parallel algorithm on a single processor is given by Faber, Lubeck and White [1986]. The program on processor i is called D_i. First execute the first instruction of D_1, then the first instruction of D_2, ..., then the first instruction of D_p. Now execute the second instruction of D_1, then the second instruction of D_2, etc. Continue in this way until the problem is solved. Here we assume that each instruction requires the same amount of time to execute. If not, we can clump instructions together into equal running time units and execute these units.

Assume that the parallel algorithm has an execution time T_p using p processors. Its simulation on a single processor obviously has an execution time $p.T_p$, so that $S_p \leq p$. In other words, superlinear speedup is not possible.

Several authors have argued against this conclusion. The following point of view is given in Quinn [1987]: fairness dictates that the best sequential algorithm and the parallel algorithm be chosen before the particular problem be chosen. If we happen to design a parallel algorithm that exhibits superlinear speedup, then, according to the previous discussion, its simulation on a single processor is better than the currently best serial algorithm. It is going too far to allow the definition of *best* to change every time. Indeed, the literature abounds with examples of algorithms specially designed for a parallel implementation and that perform better on a single processor than the well-known standard scheme from which they have been derived. To quote but one experience, complicated preconditioners for the conjugate gradient method tuned for an actual parallel implementation have revealed themselves more efficient on a single processor than the standard incomplete factorization scheme (Radicati and Robert [1989]). Nobody would have imagined such preconditioners in the absence of parallel machines.

From a theoretical point of view, the previous argument does not hold, because in the evaluation of the speedup the sequential algorithm must be the *optimal* one. However, the hypotheses have not been fully stated. In particular, the cost of memory access is totally neglected in the simulation process. See the discussion in Janssen [1987], which includes a complexity result from the CREW PRAM model (Concurrent Read Exclusive Write, Parallel Random Access Memory). Generally speaking, the hardware limitations are not taken into account when simulating the parallel algorithm. For instance, consider a shared-memory machine with 2 processors, and assume that each processor has a cache memory. Then an algorithm whose memory access management is tuned for 2 caches may run more than twice as fast as any algorithm implemented on a single processor.

Several authors have tried to bound the speedup factor. Amdahl [1967] proposes considering the fraction *f* of the computation which is inherently sequential, and hence which can be executed by a single processor alone. The serial time is $T_1 = T_{seq} + T_{par}$, where $T_{seq} = f\,T_1$ is the inherently sequential part and T_{par} is the part that can be parallelized. Using p processors, the best than can be achieved is to execute 1/p of the parallelizable part T_{par} simultaneously on each processor, so that $T_p \geq T_{seq} + T_{par}/p$. As a consequence:

$$S_p = \frac{T_1}{T_p} \leq \frac{1}{f + \frac{1-f}{p}} \leq \frac{1}{f}$$

and the speedup is smaller than the inverse of the inherently serial fraction, whatever the number of processors. For example, if 10% of the program is sequential, the speedup is smaller than 10 for any p. This result is known as Amdahl's law.

Amdahl's law has been generalized by Lee [1980], who considers the quantity of the sequential program which can be executed with i processors, i varying from 1 to p. Let $q_i T_1$ be this quantity: of course $\sum_{i=1}^{p} q_i = 1$. The parallel execution time is then $T_p \geq \sum_{i=1}^{p} \frac{q_i}{i} T_1$, so that $S_p \leq \frac{1}{\sum_{i=1}^{p} \frac{q_i}{i}}$. When all the fractions q_i are equal, we obtain $q_i = \frac{1}{p} \Rightarrow S_p \leq \frac{p}{\log p}$.

Minsky and Papert [1971] are even more pessimistic. They consider the execution of programs with conditional branch instructions and come up with the bound $S_p \leq \log p$. Stone [1973] proposes the classification of table 1.2, where the speedup is (empirically) evaluated for some common problems.

S_p	e_p	Examples
$k\,p$	k	matrix calculations, discretization
$\frac{k\,p}{\log p}$	$\frac{k}{\log p}$	sorting, tridiagonal linear systems, linear recurrences, evaluation of polynomials
$k \log p$	$\frac{k \log p}{p}$	searching
k	$\frac{k}{p}$	some nonlinear recurrences and compiler operations

Table 1.2 : Possible speedup for some usual problems

In table 1.2, k is a machine-dependent quantity such that $0<k<1$. We have also introduced the efficiency e_p, defined as the ratio of the speedup to the number of processors: $e_p = \frac{S_p}{p}$. Of course, saying that superlinear speedup is not possible is equivalent to saying that the relation $e_p \leq 1$ must always hold. In fact, the efficiency e_p measures the average utilization of each processor. The better the parallelization of the algorithm, the closer e_p to 1. Table 1.2 shows that a constant value of e_p as p goes to infinity is only possible for some particular problems.

We conclude our discussion on the speedup by reporting on a simple timing model for parallel processing that has been proposed by Flatt and Kennedy [1989]. Consider a program for which the execution time on a single processor is T_1. As above, we split T_1 into $T_1 = T_{seq} + T_{par}$. To be more realistic when evaluating the execution time T_p with p processors, we add a synchronization and communication overhead $T_o(p)$:

$$T_p = T_{seq} + \frac{T_{par}}{p} + T_o(p)$$

Given reasonable estimates for the overhead $T_o(p)$ such as a linear cost $T_o(p) = k_1\,(p-1)$ or a logarithmic cost $T_o(p) = k_2 \log p$, it is easy to show that there exists an optimal value p_o of the number of processors p that minimizes the execution time T_p:

$$T_o(p) = k_1\,(p-1) \Rightarrow p_o = \sqrt{\frac{T_{par}}{k_1}}$$

$$T_o(p) = k_2 \log p \Rightarrow p_o = \frac{T_{par}}{k_2}$$

In other words, it is useless to take more than p_o processors to solve the problem.

Up to now, we have considered only fixed-size problems. A virtue of parallel machines is that they make it possible to attack much larger problems, owing to the multiplication of hardware resources. When evaluating the performances with a large number of processors, it is not fair to be restricted to a problem small enough to be solved on a single processor. Gustafson [1988] has recently proposed considering the largest size problem and normalizing the execution time so as to compute a *scaled* speedup. We come back to this proposal in sections 4.5 and 7.2.

1.4. Bibliographic notes

There are several textbooks dealing with parallel architectures. Technological improvements that permit the building of modern multiprocessor systems are well described in Hockney and Jesshope [1988]. Major application domains of parallel architectures are extensively surveyed in Hwang and Briggs [1984], a reference survey on many aspects of parallel architectures. Information on recent machines is given in Hwang [1987]. See also Almasi and Gottlieb [1989].

There are also several textbooks devoted to the design of parallel algorithms. Quinn [1987] is a general survey. Bertsekas and Tsitsiklis [1989], Modi [1988] and Schendel [1984] are more oriented towards numerical methods. Fox et al. [1988] survey algorithms for distributed memory computers. Akl [1989], Gibbons and Rytter [1988] and Kronsjö [1985] contain theoretical material and complexity results.

Gaussian elimination is well documented in Stewart [1973] and Golub and van Loan [1983].

Our discussion of speedup has been inspired by a succession of short notes that appeared in Parallel Computing: see Faber, Lubeck and White [1986, 1987], Parkinson [1986] and Janssen [1987]. See also Helmbold and McDowell [1989].

CHAPTER
TWO

VECTOR AND PARALLEL ARCHITECTURES

In this chapter we introduce parallel architectures. We start with pipeline and vector computers. Next we discuss multiprocessors: shared memory systems and distributed memory machines. We study two commercial general-purpose computers, a vector multiprocessor (the IBM 3090) and a hypercube machine (the FPS T Series). We conclude with a presentation of systolic architectures, which are highly parallel processor arrays devoted to special-purpose computations.

2.1. Pipeline computers

Pipelining is a technique which is present in most serial computers. The basic principle is quite simple: given a task to be performed, we divide it into k distinct stages, to be executed successively. The pipeline is a hardware realization of this division into stages. Inputs of stage i are the outputs of stage i-1: see figure 2.1. Each stage is a pure combinational circuit, separated from its neighbours by latches, i.e. registers where intermediate results are held.

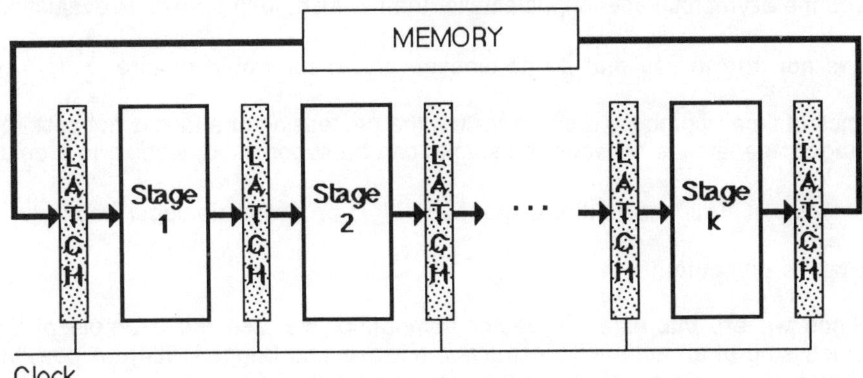

Figure 2.1: Basic structure of a pipeline processor

Assume that we have a uniform-delay pipeline: all stages have equal processing time τ_p. Let τ_l be the delay of the latch. The clock period τ of the pipeline is the minimal delay needed between two successive inputs fed into the pipe: $\tau = \tau_p + \tau_l$. Let $T_1, T_2, ..., T_n$ be a set of tasks to be executed on the pipeline. The inputs of T_i are loaded in the pipe τ units of time after those of

T_{i-1}, so that when stage i executes part i of T_m, stage i-1 executes part i-1 of T_{m-1}. The first result is delivered at time $k.\tau$: k cycles are used to fill up the pipeline (start-up time, or initialization delay). The total time to process the n tasks is $t_k = (k+n-1)\tau$: after that the first result is output, a new result is delivered every cycle.

The same number of tasks can be executed on a non-pipeline processor in time $t_1 = k\ n\ \tau$, hence the speedup due to the use of a k-stage pipeline is

$$S_k = \frac{t_1}{t_k} = \frac{k\ n\ \tau}{(k+n-1)\ \tau}$$

Note that $S_k \rightarrow k$ for large n: the asymptotic speedup is optimal. The efficiency e_k is defined as the ratio of the speedup to the number of stages:

$$e_k = \frac{t_1}{k\ t_k} = \frac{n}{k+n-1}$$

Equivalently, e_k measures the percentage of activity of the stages of the pipeline. Note that $e_k \rightarrow 1$ for large n: the larger the number of tasks flowing through the pipeline, the better its efficiency.

In general, the stages do not have the same length, and S_k is always smaller than k, even for large n. If stage i has a time delay τ_i, then the clock period of the pipe is $\tau = \max_{1 \leq i \leq k}(\tau_i) + \tau_l$, because we need to operate at the period of the slowest stage. We obtain

$$S_k = \frac{n \sum_{i=1}^{k} (\tau_i + \tau_l)}{(k+n-1).(\max_{1 \leq i \leq k}(\tau_i) + \tau_l)}$$

and the asymptotic speedup is smaller than k. Also, in the previous evaluation, it is not true to say that a non-pipeline processor would require $\sum_{i=1}^{k} (\tau_i + \tau_l)$ units of time to process a single task: if the processing of a task is not split into stages, the latches between the stages can be suppressed, leading to a delay of $\sum_{i=1}^{k} \tau_i + \tau_l$. This shows that a speedup of k is an optimistic upper bound for a pipeline computer.

Since we are interested in vector computing, we take the example of the processing of an arithmetic instruction (Hwang and Briggs [1984]). A possible segmentation into six stages is the following (figure 2.2):

- fetch instruction
- decode
- compute the addresses of the operands
- fetch operands
- execute arithmetic operation
- store results

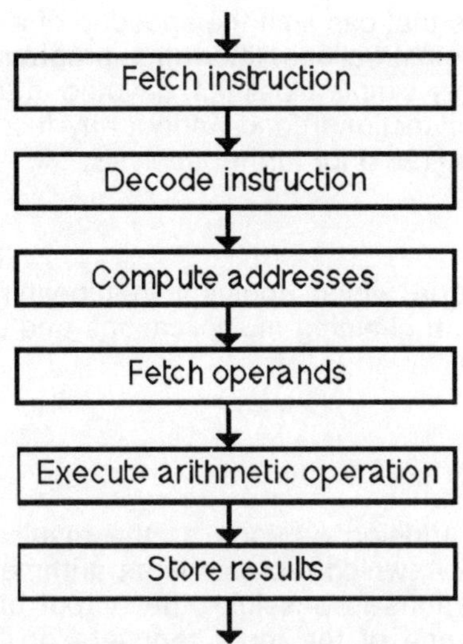

Figure 2.2: Pipeline for processing an arithmetic instruction

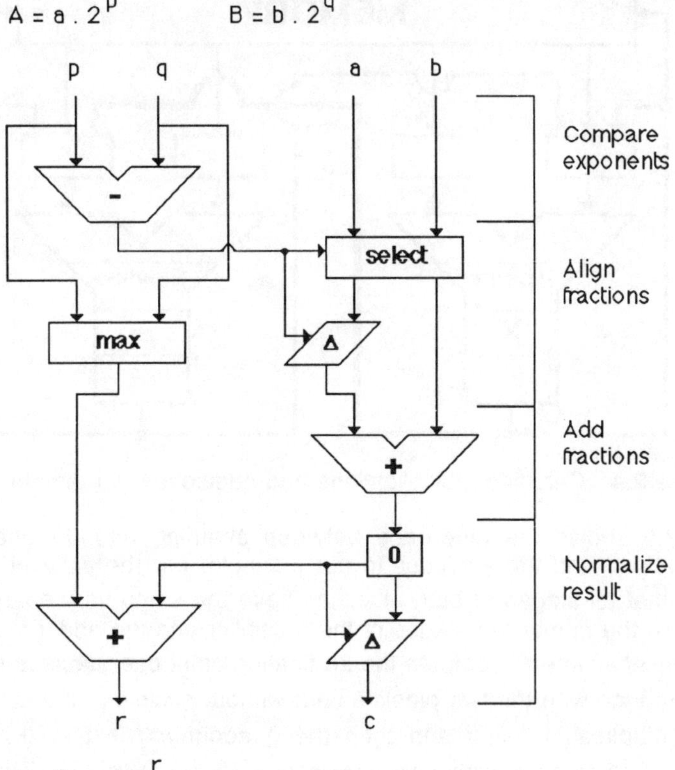

Figure 2.3: A pipelined floating-point adder

There are many factors that can limit the speedup of a pipeline, including data dependencies between instructions, interrupts, program branches, ... Also, we have dealt only with very simple pipelines, devoted to a single operation (such pipelines are called unifunctional) and without any feedback. See Hwang and Briggs [1984] or Kogge [1981] for further analysis.

2.1.1. Chaining

Chaining is a technique which consists in pipelining several pipelines ! Consider the example of chaining multiplications and additions. We have the loop:

for i = 1 **to** n **do**
    $a_i = S * b_i + c_i$

We want to start the addition as soon as the result of the multiplication is available. See figure 2.4, which represents an arithmetic unit where chaining of floating-point operations is possible: the output of the multiplier can be directly forwarded to one of the input registers of the adder, without any temporary store in the memory.

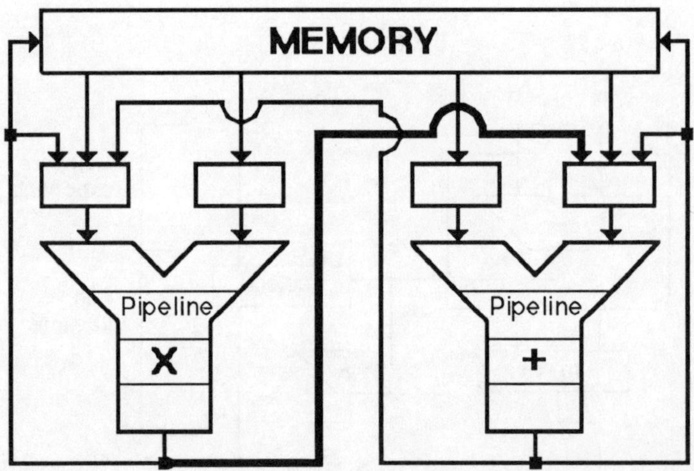

Figure 2.4 : Chaining multiplications and additions in an arithmetic unit

Figure 2.5 shows the difference between chaining and not-chaining the multiplications and the additions in our example. For the sake of simplicity, assume that all stages of both pipelines have the same time delay τ. Let k_x and k_+ be the number of stages of the multiplier and the adder respectively. The sequential time to compute the 2n floating-point operations is $t_1 = nk_x\tau + nk_+\tau$. The time with the two pipelines but without chaining, that is computing the n multiplications first and then the n additions, is $t_2 = (k_x+n-1)\ \tau + (k_++n-1)\ \tau$. The time with chaining is $t_3 = ((k_x+k_+)+n-1)\ \tau$. This clearly illustrates the gain due to chaining: the two chained pipelines are equivalent to a long pipeline of $k_x + k_+$ stages.

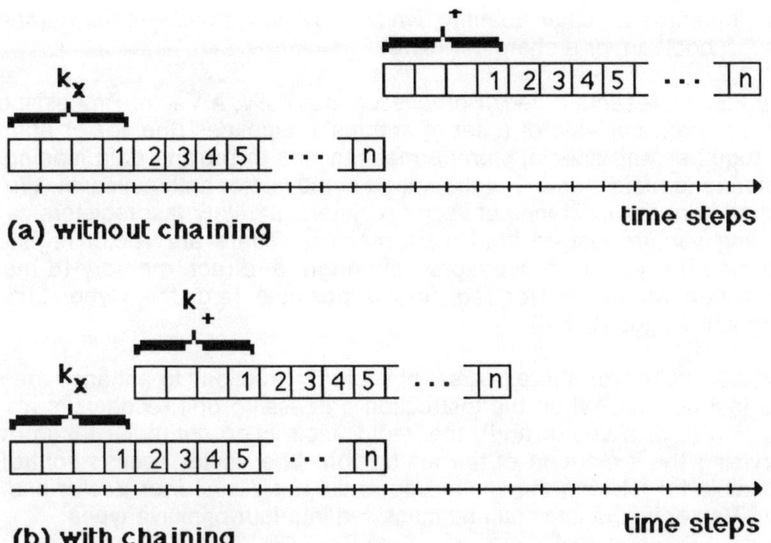

Figure 2.5 : The effect of chaining

2.2. Vector computers

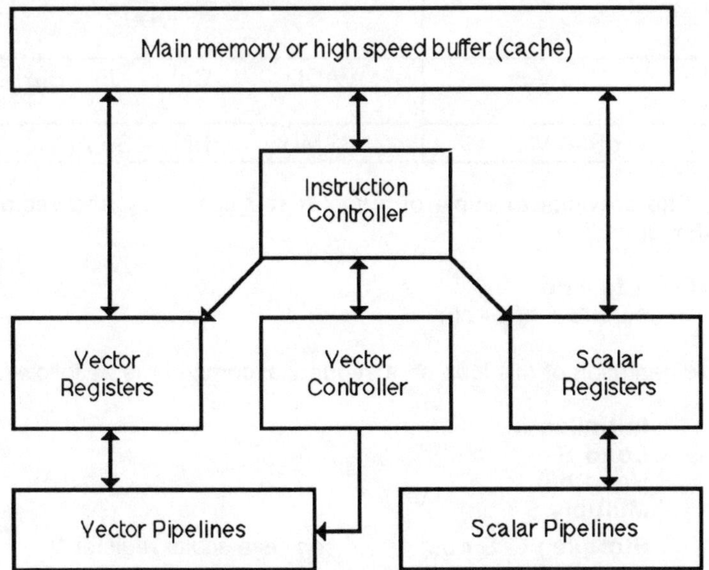

Figure 2.6 : Architecture of a vector processor

A vector processor is a computer with an instruction set that includes operations on vector as well as scalar operands. A vector operand is an ordered set of n homogeneous elements, where n is the length of the vector.

Each element is a scalar quantity, which may be a floating-point number, an integer, a boolean, or a character (byte).

Figure 2.6. represents a vector processor. Basically, a Vector Processing Unit (VPU for short) consists of a set of arithmetic pipelines (the vector arithmetic unit), together with special storage mechanisms to provide data loading from and storing to main memory at the speed of the vector arithmetic unit. We have assumed here the existence of vector registers, i.e. very fast registers capable of storing vectors loaded from main memory. There are vector registers in most modern vector processors, although a direct memory-to-memory organization without vector registers is possible (e.g. the Cyber 205, see Hwang and Briggs [1984]).

In a vector processor, there is a set of vector instructions to enhance the set of scalar instructions. When the instruction processing unit recognizes a vector instruction (e.g. a vector add), the vector instruction controller takes over in supervising the execution of the instruction. The vector access controller is responsible for fetching the vector operands. Let V stand for Vector and S for Scalar. Vector instructions can be classified into four primitive types:

Type	**Example**	
$V \rightarrow V$	VSIN	$B(i) \leftarrow \sin(A(i))$
$V \rightarrow S$	VSUM	$S \leftarrow \sum_{i=1}^{n} A(i)$
$V \times V \rightarrow V$	VADD	$C(i) \leftarrow A(i) + B(i)$
$V \times S \rightarrow V$	VSMU	$B(i) \leftarrow S * A(i)$

Consider the previous example of a vector-scalar multiply and vector-vector add (AXPY operation):

```
for i = 1 to n do
        a(i) = S * b(i) + c(i)
```

The implementation of this loop on a sequential computer is as follows:

```
        Initialize i=1
        Load S
10      Read b(i)
        Multiply S * b(i)
        Store reg ← S * b(i)        /* reg  is a scalar register */
        Read c(i)
        Add reg + c(i)
        Store a(i) ← reg + c(i)
        Increment i ← i + 1
        If i ≤ n goto 10
```

On a vector processor, we obtain the following program:

```
reg(1:n) = S * b(1:n)
a(1:n) = reg(1:n) + c(1:n)
```

where v(1:n) denotes elements 1 to n of vector v. Note that the scalar register *reg* has been expanded into a vector register of size n. A realization of this program with chaining is illustrated in figure 2.7.

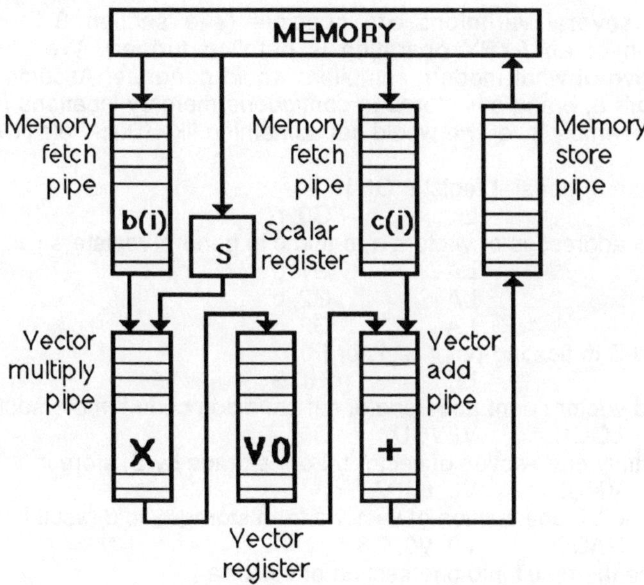

Figure 2.7 : Chaining the execution of the loop $a_i = S * b_i + c_i$

What happens if the size n of the vectors in the previous loop is greater than the size Z of the vector registers ? Loop sectioning is the answer. Basically, the original **for** loop is transformed from an iteration over n single elements to an iteration over groups or sections of Z elements. In other words, we have the conceptual second loop:

```
for ii = 1 to n step Z do
    for i = ii to min(n,ii+Z-1) do
        a(i) = S * b(i) + c(i)
```

The inner loop is replaced by a vector instruction at compile time. Assume that S is already loaded in a scalar register. The pseudo-code generated by the compiler can be expressed as:

```
for ii = 1 to n step Z do
        for i = ii to min(n,ii+Z-1) do
                { scalar reg. times memory, result stored in vector reg. 0 }
                Vector MUL:        vr0(i) = S * b(i)
                { memory plus vector reg., result in vector reg. }
                Vector ADD:        vr0(i) = vr0(i) + c(i)
                { store vector reg. back in memory }
                Vector STORE:      a(i) = vr0(i)
```

Of course several variations are possible (see section 3.1. where the vectorization of an AXPY operation is detailed further). We give a code representative of what modern compilers would generate. Assume that each of the vectors a, b and c is stored in contiguous memory locations (with stride 1). At the assembly level, we would get something like (Buchholz [1986]):

```
{ load n in general register G0 }
                L          G0, n
{ load addresses of vectors a, b and c in general registers }
                LA         G1, a
                LA         G2, b
                LA         G3, c
{ load S in floating-point register F0 }
                LE         F0, S
{ load vector count and update; set condition code if more sections }
        LOOP    VLVCU      G0
{ multiply one section of vector b from storage by S, store in V0 }
        VMUL    V0, F0, G2
{ add to V0 one section of vector c from storage, hold result in V0 }
        VADD    V0, V0, G3
{ store the result into one section of vector a }
        VSTO    V0, G1
{ branch to condition if there is still one more section to process }
        BC      2, LOOP
```

If the vectors a, b and c were not stored in consecutive memory locations, we would specify the address increment between their elements. Early vector computers restricted the elements of a vector to be consecutively stored in memory, but most current vector computers accept a constant (or even variable) increment between the elements of a vector.

2.3. Parallel computers

Numerous parallel computers are now commercially available. To make a classification, we emphasize the number of instruction streams and the distribution of the memory (global/local).

2.3.1. Flynn's taxonomy

From a programming point of view, the most important distinction to be made in a classification is that introduced by Flynn [1972], namely the number of instruction streams and data streams available. An instruction stream is a sequence of instructions performed by the computer. A data stream is a sequence of data used to execute an instruction stream. There are four possible classes of computer, according to the multiplicity of hardware used to manipulate instruction and data streams:

- SISD (single instruction stream, single data stream)
- SIMD (single instruction stream, multiple data stream)
- MISD (multiple instruction stream, single data stream)
- MIMD (multiple instruction stream, multiple data stream)

SISD organization

This is the well-known von Neumann computer. Instructions are executed sequentially, but can be pipelined, as in most serial computers available today. The SISD organization is represented in figure 2.8.

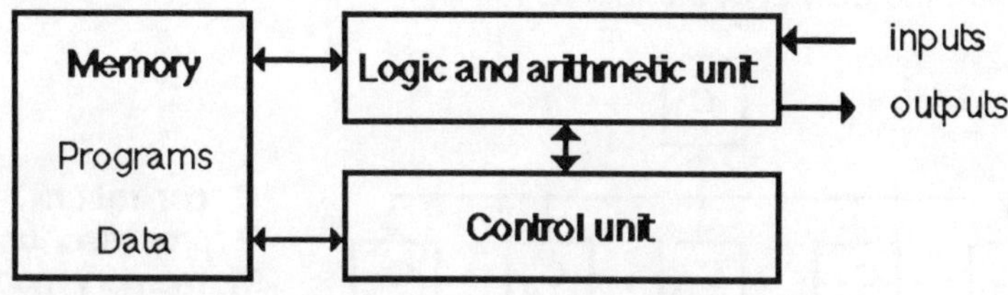

Figure 2.8 : SISD computer

SIMD organization

The SIMD organization is represented in figure 2.9. Several processing units (PU) are under the supervision of the same control unit (CU). All PUs receive the same instruction from the central CU but operate on distinct data sets from distinct data streams. Since each PU executes the same instruction at the same time, the operating mode is synchronous. The memory is shared by all PUs. However, for a large number of PUs, it is not realistic to assume that all PUs can access simultaneously any memory location. As outlined in figure 2.9, the shared memory can be subdivided into modules. The access to the different modules is through an interconnection network.

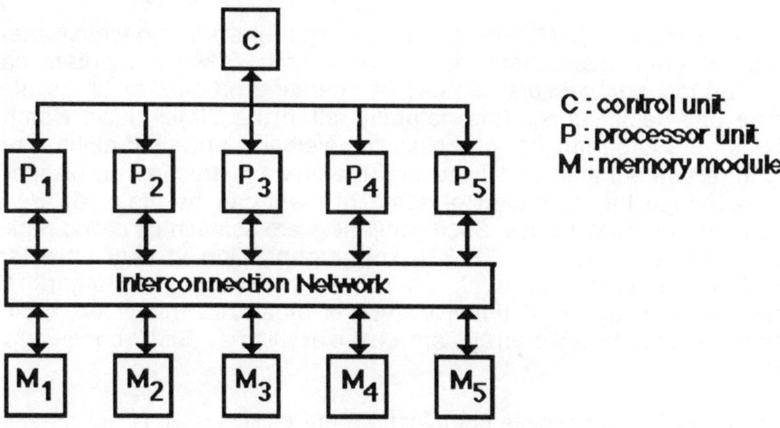

Figure 2.9 : SIMD computer

MIMD organization

The MIMD organization is represented in figure 2.10. The main difference from the SIMD model is that each PU now has its own control unit. Hence the processors can operate independently. In particular the operating mode is asynchronous. To be a real MIMD computer, the processors must interact, otherwise we would get a juxtaposition of multiple SISD computers. There are two possible ways of interaction: through the shared memory, if any, or through sending and receiving messages via the interconnection network. Depending on the degree of interaction, we have tightly coupled or loosely coupled MIMD machines. Most machines with few processing units devoted to a multi-user time-sharing environment are loosely coupled (e.g. the IBM 4381). On the other hand, vector multiprocessors are tightly coupled (e.g. the Cray X-MP, the Cray 2, or the IBM 3090).

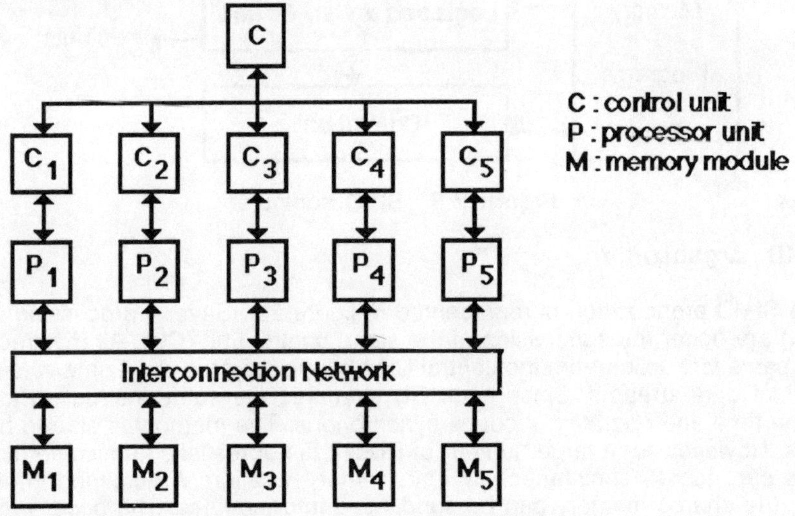

Figure 2.10 : MIMD computer

Generally speaking, MIMD computers are more powerful, because they can process different instructions at the same time. SIMD computers can be viewed as monoprocessors capable of operating on sets or slices of data. Pipeline and vector computers naturally fall in the SIMD class. Computers made out of a large number of processing elements arranged along a regular interconnection scheme and executing the same instruction on distinct data items (although the operation of some of them can be masked) are other members of the SIMD class. Such computers are sometimes called replicated SIMD computers (Hockney [1987]).This organization is very attractive for specialized applications such as image processing or digital signal processing. For instance, the ICL DAP is organized into a 64 x 64 two-dimensional grid. Systolic arrays are also classified as SIMD computers (see section 2.4.3).

Note that the fourth possible combination, the MISD class, is not attractive: if we are not rich enough to afford an MIMD computer, we prefer to have the same instruction on different data (SIMD) rather than different instructions on the same data (MISD).

In the middle between SIMD and MIMD computers, we find SPMD computers: Single Program Multiple Data. Apparently, the potential of SPMD computers is the same as that of SIMD ones, because each processor executes the same program loaded in its private memory by the centralized control unit. However, from a programming point of view, SPMD computers are very close to MIMD computers, due to the possibility of conditional execution in the common program. For instance if each PU knows its identity, it is able to switch to a portion of the code that it will be the only one to execute (think of a *case* statement at the beginning of the program). Therefore different instructions can be executed at the same time, and the operating mode can be asynchronous.

2.3.2. Shared versus local memory

An important feature for the programmer is the organization of the memory in the parallel architecture. We distinguish shared memory from local memory systems.

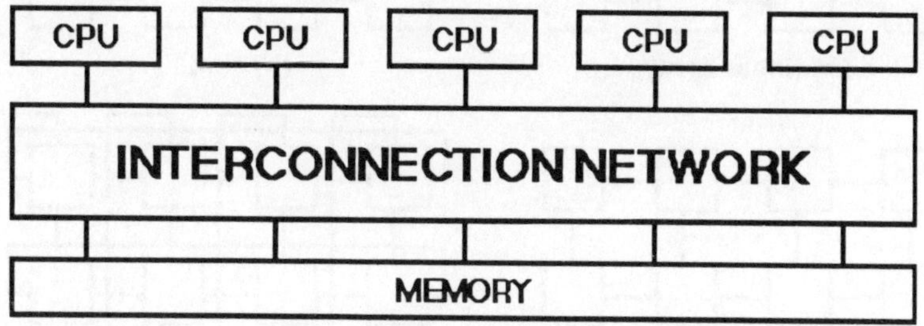

Figure 2.11 : Shared memory machine

In a shared memory system, there is a global memory accessible to all processors (figure 2.11). Each processor may have some local memory, such as a cache (e.g. the Cray 2 or the IBM 3090). But the key-feature is that the access time to a piece of data in the memory is independent of the processor making the request. Karp [1987] says that if the code running on two processors can be swapped without affecting performance, then the system is a true shared memory system.

Access to the shared memory becomes more and more a critical operation as the number of processors increases. A full crossbar interconnection network is no longer possible, and the performance of the interconnection network decreases as the number of its internal stages increases. Even though subdividing the memory into modules or banks (interleaved memory, as in the Cray 1) or using a hierarchical structure of the memory (with a cache) can help reduce the memory bottleneck, no full shared memory system with, say, 100 processors, has ever been built (see the discussion on the scalability of shared memory systems in Athas and Seitz [1988]).

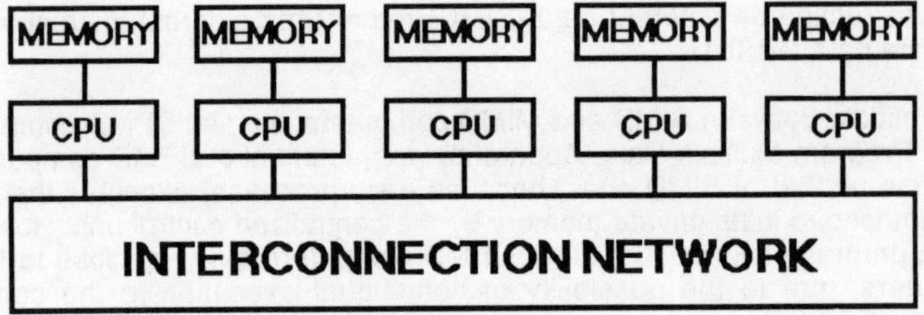

Figure 2.12 : Distributed memory machine

For the design of massively parallel machines, we need to use decentralized memory and reduced (local) connections between the processors. In a distributed memory system (figure 2.12), each processor has a small fast local memory and communicates with a few other processors via an interconnection network. Again a full crossbar interconnection network is not possible, and a reduced communication topology is used.

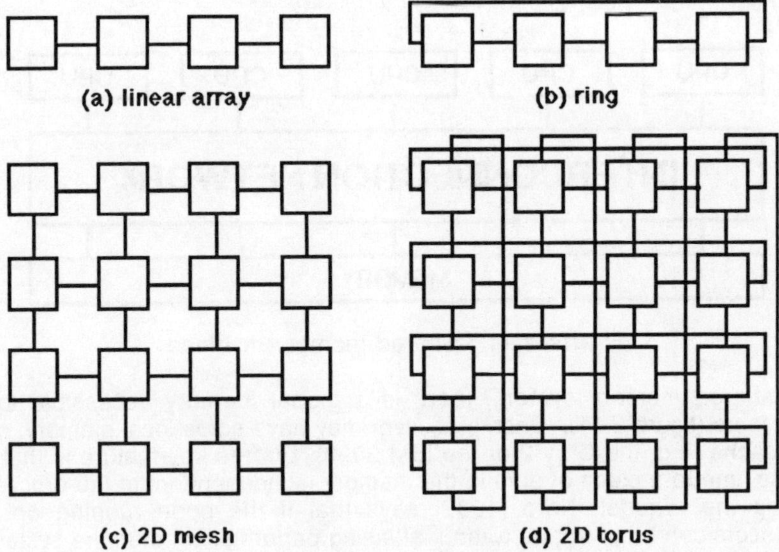

Figure 2.13 : Linear and two-dimensional arrays

In a distributed memory system, we seek for a compromise between the number of neighbours of each processor and the largest distance between two processors. The degree of the connection graph is defined as the maximum number of neighbours of a given processor. The smaller the degree of the connection graph, the easier the realization of the architecture under given technological constraints. The other factor to be minimized is the diameter of the connection graph, i.e. the largest distance between two processors. It takes a time proportional to the diameter of the connection graph to exchange information between two remote processors, thereby reducing the communication speed. The simplest topologies are the linear array and the ring (figure 2.13). For an array or a ring of p processors, the degree of the graph is $\delta = 2$, but the diameter Δ of the graph is proportional to p, making communications very slow. A denser wiring is that of mesh machines (figure 2.13): for a 2D mesh (with or without toroidal connections) of p processors, $\delta = 4$, while Δ is proportional to $\sqrt{p}$.

An architecture where $\delta = \Delta$ will achieve a good balance between the communication speed and the complexity of the topology network. Hypercubes achieve this equality, which explains why they are one of today's most popular design (e.g. iPSC of Intel Corp., T Series of FPS, n-CUBE, Connection Machine of Thinking Machines Corp).

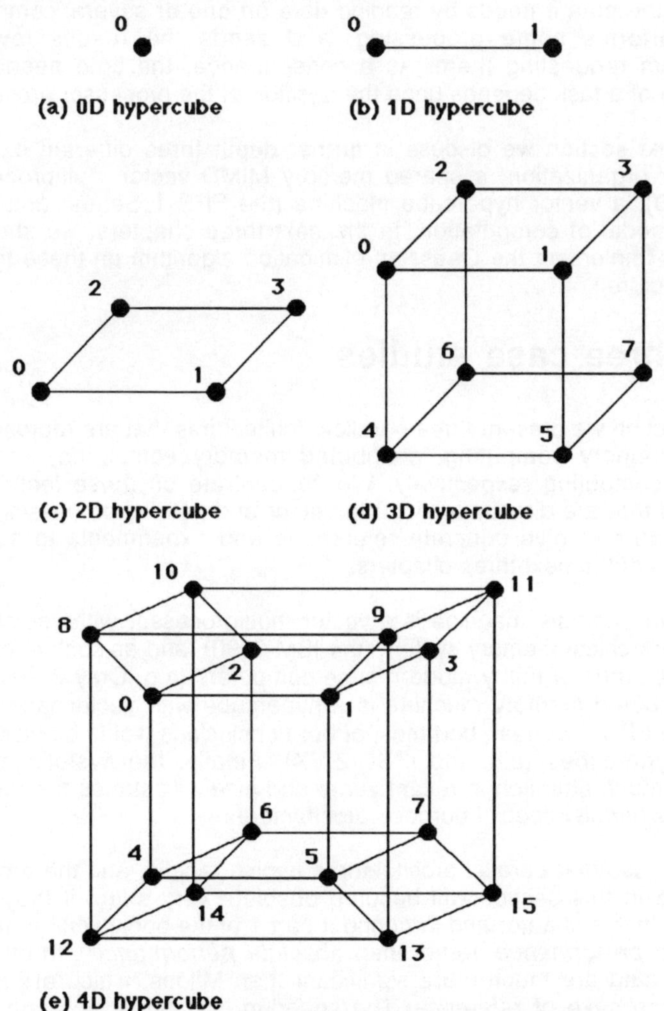

Figure 2.14 : Hypercubes grow by replication

Hypercubes (figure 2.14) grow by replication. Given two hypercubes of dimension n, i.e. with 2^n processors, we build a hypercube of dimension n+1, with 2^{n+1} processors, by connecting corresponding vertices of the two hypercubes. This process is illustrated in figure 2.14 for n=0 to n=4. For a hypercube of dimension n, we have $\delta = \Delta = \log_2 n$. In figure 2.14, we observe that two adjacent nodes are numbered in such a way that their binary representations only differ by one bit. We come back to hypercube node numbering in chapter 4.

In a shared memory system, processors operate on the data from the common memory. Each processor reads the data it needs, performs some processing, and writes the results back in memory. In a distributed memory system, processors operate by sending or receiving messages. Each processor receives the data it needs by reading data on one or several communication links, performs some processing, and sends the results towards the processors requesting them. As a consequence, the time needed for the execution of a task depends upon the position of the processor processing it.

In the next section we discuss in further depth three different examples of computer organization: a shared memory MIMD vector multiprocessor (the IBM 3090), a vector hypercube machine (the FPS T Series) and the SIMD systolic model of computation. In the next three chapters, we show how to efficiently implement the Gaussian elimination algorithm on these three types of architecture.

2.4. Three case studies

In this section we present three parallel architectures that are representative of shared memory computing, distributed memory computing, and special-purpose computing respectively. We concentrate on those features of the machines that are directly relevant to vector and parallel processing. Our aim is to be able to give concrete references and experiments to support the discussion of the next three chapters.

The shared memory machine is a vector multiprocessor with vector registers and a hierarchical memory system (the IBM 3090), and as such encompasses the key features of many modern supercomputers (e.g. Cray 2, Alliant FX/8). The distributed memory machine is a hypercube with vector facility at each node (the FPS T Series), and most of our conclusions would be valid for other vector hypercubes (e.g. the iPSC/2-VX). Finally, the systolic model has received much attention in recent years and nicely illustrates the principles of massively parallel special-purpose architectures.

A word of caution: parallel architectures evolve rapidly, and the architectures described in this section will become obsolete very soon, if they have not already.[1] In this chapter and throughout part 1 of the book, what really matters is *relative performance* rather than *absolute performance* . In other words, speedup data are much more significant than Mflops, which are mentioned only for the sake of reference. The speedup is obtained through algorithm

---

[1] In this section we give data for the IBM 3090 model E, which has been already replaced by the model F. Also, the FPS T Series is no longer manufactured. Finally, the forthcoming iWARP might influence the description of systolic arrays.

recasting, and the underlying concept remains valid as the architecture evolves.

2.4.1. A shared memory MIMD vector multiprocessor

We describe the architecture of the IBM 3090-600E, i.e. the largest configuration currently available, with six vector processors. Figure 2.15 describes the structure of the machine. The six processors share a common memory, divided into a central storage unit (from 64 to 256 Mbytes) and a very large expanded storage unit (up to 2 Gbytes, managed by the operating system as a temporary paging device). A system control element (SCE) serves to connect three central processors (with their vector facility) to an input/output channel subsystem, to the other SCE and to the central and expanded storage.

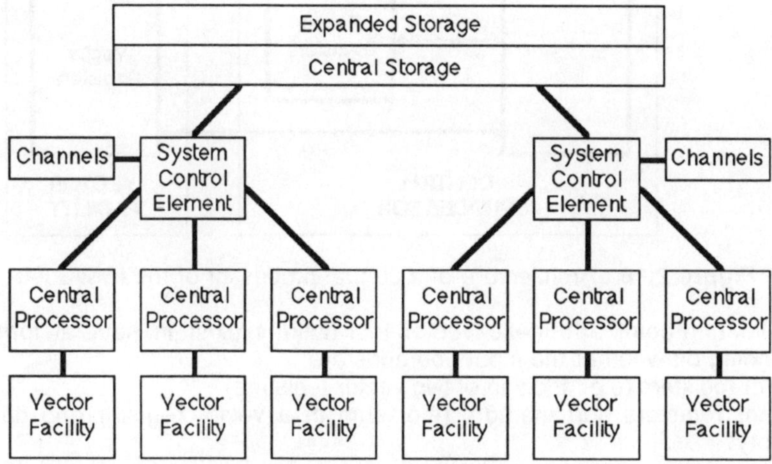

Figure 2.15 : Overview of the IBM 3090 with 6 vector processors

Each central processor (figure 2.16) consists of an instruction element and an execution element whose designs incorporate pipeline and overlap features, such as instruction prefetching. The vector facility provides a pipelined arithmetic unit. There are 16 vector registers of length Z = 128 (the vector section size).

The Vector Facility provides floating-point and integer arithmetic vector instructions, logical vector instructions, and load and store vector instructions. It allows the conditional execution of arithmetic and logical instructions depending on the vector mask register. No explicit chaining is available, but two floating-point compound instructions, *multiply-add* and *multiply-accumulate* , perform two flops (a multiplication and an addition) per cycle-time (17.2 ns). Also, most vector instructions can have one operand taken directly from memory: this feature is somewhat similar to the chaining provided on the Cray machines. For example, the vector instruction

VMAD: vector register ← vector register + scalar register * vector in memory

performs two flops per cycle once the corresponding pipeline is configured. Performing two flops per cycle time leads to a peak performance of 116 Mflops per central processor.

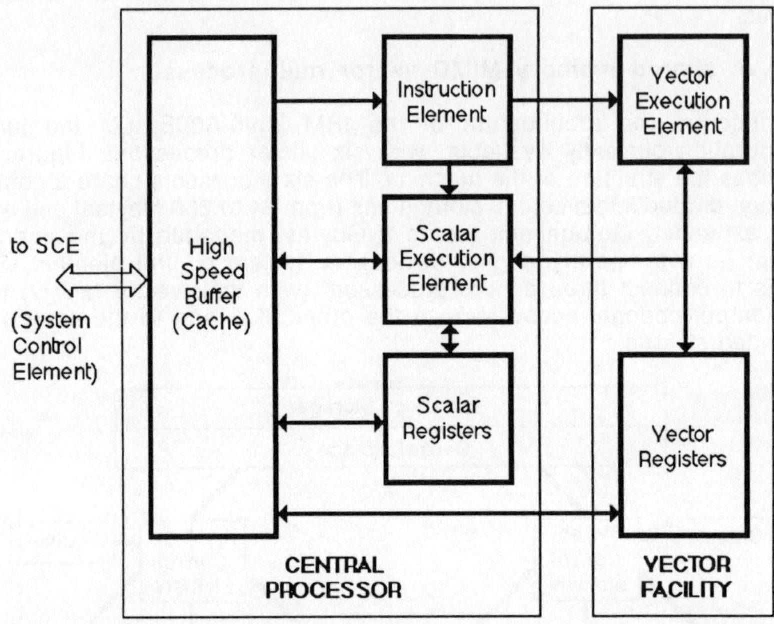

Figure 2.16 : Architecture of a central processor of the IBM 3090

The floating-point arithmetic vector instructions exist in several formats, depending on whether the input operands are:

• vector registers (e.g. addition of two vector registers)

• vector registers and memory (e.g. sum of a vector register and data in memory)

• vector register, memory and a scalar floating-point register (e.g. multiply a vector by a constant which is in a floating-point register)

In all cases the result of the vector instruction is in a vector register.

The instruction element, the execution element and the vector facility are connected to a cache, a 64-Kbyte high-speed memory. The memory system of the IBM 3090 is thus hierarchical: data from the main memory are available to a processor only after they have been brought into its cache. When a storage location which is not already in the cache (it can be in the system central storage or in the cache of another processor) is accessed by the CPU, a cache miss occurs. The operation that caused the cache miss will be completed only after one or more cache lines of 128 bytes, which contain the data, are transferred to the cache, where they displace the least recently referenced cache lines. The SCEs know where the last copy of any line resides and are responsible for finding it and transferring it to the requesting processor.

For example, a floating-point instruction that references a single word may cause an entire cache line of 128 bytes to be transferred to the cache. However, if the next instruction references another word in the same cache line, it will already be available. In particular a vector operation with an operand from memory delivers one result per machine cycle provided the data is in cache. Otherwise it may require approximately two machine cycles per vector element before the entire operation, data transfer to cache and vector operation, is completed.

Note that the cache cannot be directly programmed by the user, making the system look like it has a single, global memory. In other words, the user need not worry that a piece of data is in the cache of the wrong processor, since the operating system makes sure the correct value is delivered (cross-cache validation). However, performances are dramatically affected by the number of cache misses caused by non-local references (see the discussion in chapter 3).

2.4.2. A vector hypercube machine

In this paragraph, we briefly describe the architecture of the FPS T Series hypercube (see Gustafson et al. [1986]), with particular emphasis on the Vector Processing Unit (VPU) and the internode communication routines.

2.4.2.1. Architecture overview

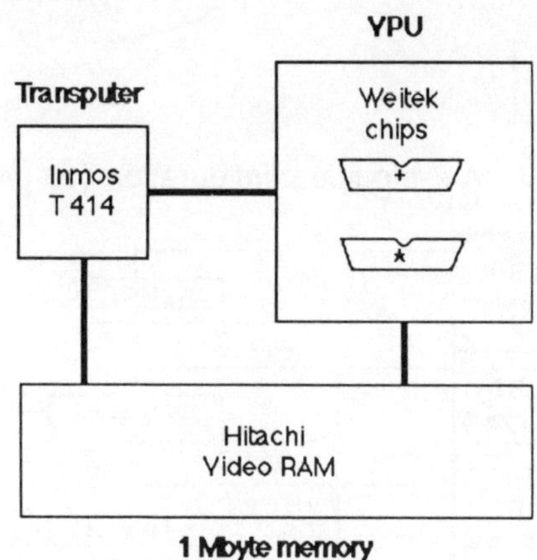

Figure 2.17 : A node of the FPS T Series

The FPS T series multiprocessor is an MIMD distributed memory machine whose communication network is a hypercube. A node consists of (figure 2.17):

• a microprocessor for handling communication and system control (Inmos Transputer T414)
• a vector pipelined unit for floating-point computation (Weitek chips)
• a memory of 1 Mbyte (Hitachi Video RAM)

Eight nodes arranged in a three dimensional subcube form a module. Each module has a system node with a disk and a link on the bus to the host (figure 2.18). The host is a μVAX running the Ultrix operating system for FORTRAN and C and VMS for Occam. It serves for program development and loads T-code on the system nodes for execution.

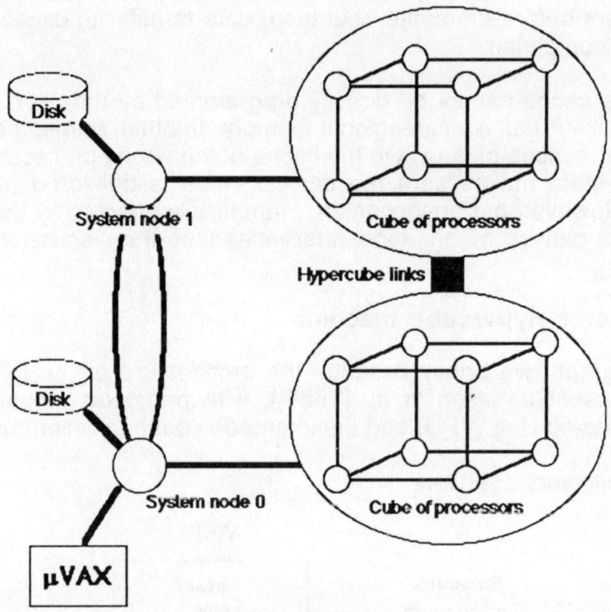

Figure 2.18 : A 2-module configuration (16 processors)

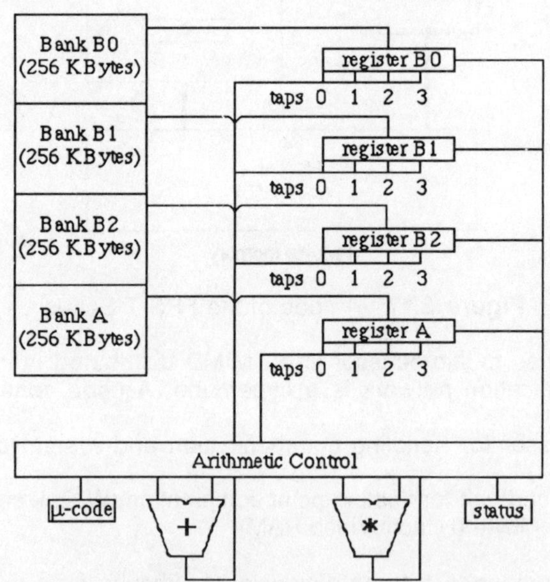

Figure 2.19 : The VPU and the memory

The VPU contains four registers and two pipelined arithmetic units for addition and multiplication (see figure 2.19). The floating-point calculation is done in double precision (64 bits). The peak performance is 12 Mflops. The memory is partitioned into four banks. Each bank is composed of 256 slices of 1024 bytes (or 128 double reals) that can be loaded in the vector registers within one cycle.

2.4.2.2. Single-node software

FORTRAN, C, or OCCAM programs are developed and compiled on the host. The object code is loaded at execution time to each node. Hence the machine operates in SPMD (Single Program Multiple Data) mode.

The code is executed on the Transputer. Access to the VPU is possible only through the call to routines and functions of the mathematical library (there is no vectorizing compiler).
There are three levels for programming the VPU :
• single-node routines are general high level routines
• generic routines are middle level routines. The vector arguments must be stored in consecutive memory locations (stride one). Maximum performance is obtained when vectors are aligned on taps boundary
• parameter block routines are low level routines which operate on vectors of size at most 128 (size of the registers) for a call. There is no automatic alignment of the input vectors on a tap boundary, and the result is aligned on the right of a memory slice, which requires some data shifting if the length is less than 128.

The user has the possibility of specifying where variables are located in memory. The *locator* software is invoked after compile time. This facility is a *sine qua non* when using parameter block routines. Aligning vector sources on the same tap of memory slices greatly improves performances of single-node and generic routines, because it avoids the memory moves required before loading into the VPU registers. Just to give an insight of the performances, we report in figure 2.20 the Mflops achieved for an operation $z \leftarrow y + \alpha x$, where x, y and z are vectors of length n, stride 1 and aligned on the same memory tap. Figure 2.20 shows the impact of start-up time on vector performance (see section 3.1.5).

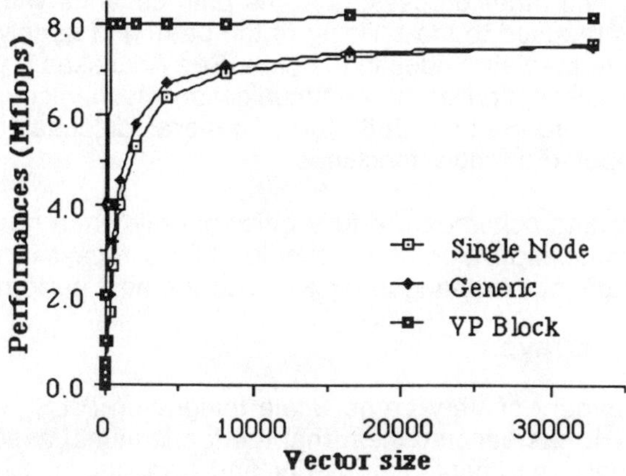

Figure 2.20 : Performances of an AXPY operation

2.4.2.3. Internode communication

The primitive operation for communicating messages between nodes is the send/receive procedure between neighbour nodes. The syntax for sending and receiving a message between two neighbours is the following:

```
{ receiving } receive(hypercube_link,receive_buffer,length) ;
{ sending }   send(hypercube_link,send_buffer,length) ;
```

The time to transfer L words between two adjacent processors can be modelled by $\beta + L\,\tau_c$, where β is the communication start-up and τ_c the elemental transfer time. It turns out that β is an order of magnitude higher than τ_c for most commercial hypercubes, which makes the transmission of short messages very expensive: see Dunigan [1987]. For the FPS T Series we obtained experimentally β = 750 µs and τ_c = 1.44 µsec per byte, or equivalently τ_c = 11.5 µsec per 64-bit word.

A collection of system routines for internode communication is available. The programmer can call not only direct neighbour-to-neighbour communication routines, but also more complex message passing procedures, such as the broadcast of a message from one node to all the other nodes. See chapter 4 for a detailed description of global communication procedures in hypercube systems.

The FPS T Series is a first-generation hypercube in that the store-and-forward routine technique is used for communicating between two remote nodes: each intermediate node in the communication path stores the message in its memory, and it is not available for other (useful) processing when handling the communication. Second-generation hypercubes such as the iPSC/2 include a routing facility: when one node wants to communicate with another, a series of switches are closed, and the communication path is established. Only the sending and receiving processors are then involved in the communication. The other processors in the path continue with their activity. The overhead is reduced to the building of the path, and largely insensitive to the number of intermediate nodes in the path. See Arlauskas [1988] or Nugent [1988] for a full description of the communication mechanism in the iPSC/2. See also Athas and Seitz [1988] for a general discussion on second-generation distributed memory machines.

Note that the routing schemes are fully efficient only when no conflict occur. Intensive communication algorithms should still be recast in terms of local neighbour-to-neighbour exchanges for attaining the best performances.

2.4.3. Systolic arrays

With the development of Very Large Scale Integration (VLSI, see Mead and Conway [1980]), it has become clear that the fundamental aspects of cellular structures, namely regularity, modularity and parallelism, can lead to the concrete realization of high-performance devices. The major contribution of Kung and Leiserson [1980] is to have realized that cellular networks should be conceived not as universal machines but rather as procedures on silicon.

Indeed, such parallel computing resources can be efficiently implemented with today's high circuit-density VLSI technology, provided that the two following conditions are satisfied:

• the resource is a special-purpose computing device which is attached to a host architecture (rather than a universal machine)

• the application run on the resource is a compute-bound application, where the number of arithmetic operations is much larger than the number of input and output elements. Front-end processing in radar, sonar, vision, or robotics yields typical examples of compute-bound applications (see Kung [1988]).

Systolic arrays, as defined by Kung and Leiserson [1980], are a useful tool for designing special-purpose VLSI chips. A chip based on a systolic design consists essentially of a few types of very simple cells which are mesh-interconnected in a regular and modular way, and achieves high performance through extensive concurrent and pipeline use of the cells. The most usual interconnection geometries of systolic arrays are depicted in figure 2.21.

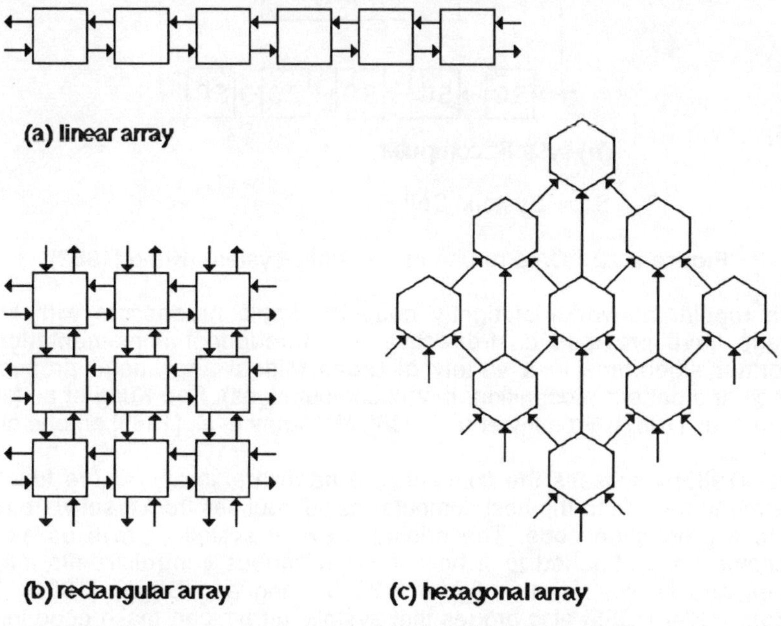

Figure 2.21 : Examples of communication geometries

The name systolic given by Kung and Leiserson is taken from the physiology of living beings. A systole is a contraction of the heart, by means of which blood is pumped to the different components of the organism. In a systolic system, the information (data and instructions) is rhythmically sent through a structure of elementary processors (cells), to be processed and passed to neighbouring cells until a result reaches some border of the system communicating with the host.

Kung [1982] carefully explains how systolic architectures should result in cost-effective and high-performance special-purpose systems, and he gives three main reasons to justify the advantages of the systolic model:

• systolic systems are easy to implement because of their simple and regular design
• they are easy to reconfigure because of their modularity
• they permit multiple computations for each memory access, which speeds up the execution without increasing I/O requirements.

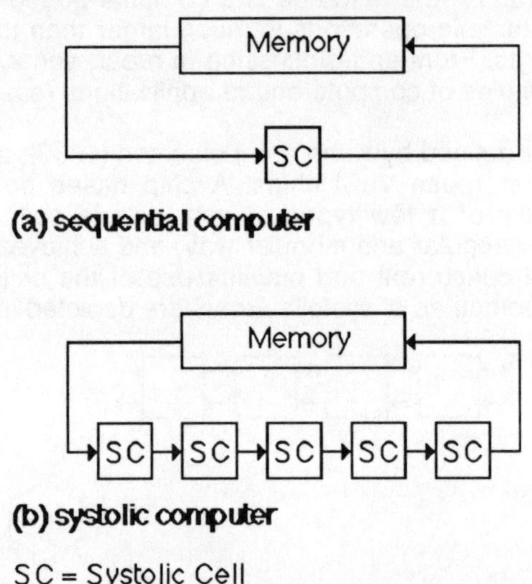

Figure 2.22 : Data re-use in a systolic system (Kung [1982])

Such regular networks of tightly coupled simple processors with limited storage have provided cost-effective high-throughput implementations of important algorithms in a variety of areas (signal and image processing, speech and pattern recognition, matrix computations). See Kung et al. [1985], Moore et al. [1987], Bromley et al. [1988], McCanny et al. [1989] among others.

Heller [1985] discusses the concept of a hardware library, where functional units are in relation to the host computer as subroutines from a software library are to a production code. The original view of systolic arrays as external functional units attached to a host through various controllers fits into this model, and is illustrated in figure 2.23 (Hwang and Briggs [1984], Kung [1988]). Heller [1985] also argues that systolic arrays can make good internal functional units, taking the role for simple matrix computations that vector pipelines now have for simple vector computations. We describe in chapter 5 some systolic arrays for the Gaussian elimination algorithm that can be viewed both as external units to speed up the execution of pieces of programs run on the host, and as functional elements of a "matrix" internal arithmetic unit.

It is important to provide designers of systolic algorithms and architectures with methods that help them explore various implementations of the same algorithm. Several alternatives may then be compared according to various criteria such as the size of the array, the complexity of the elementary cells, the throughput and the pipelining delay. We discuss automatic design methodologies and complexity results in chapter 8.

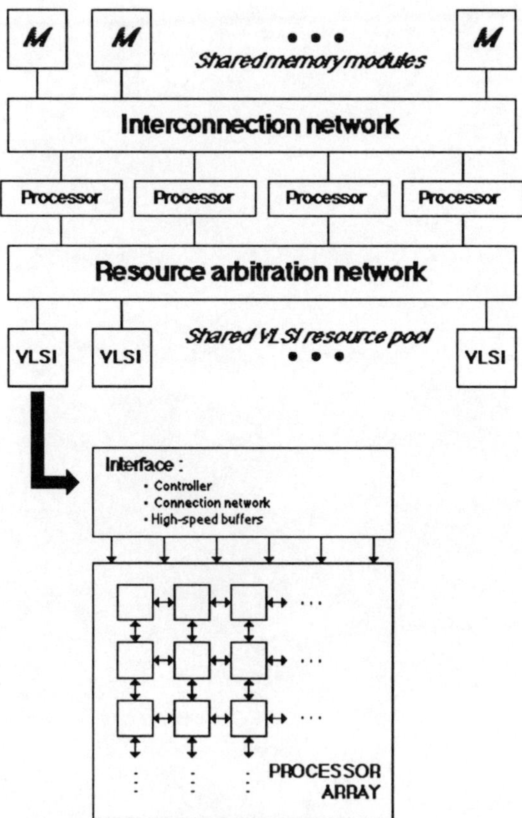

Figure 2.23 : Concept of a hardware library (Hwang and Briggs [1984], Kung [1988])

2.5. Bibliographic notes

Pipeline computers are described in Kogge [1981], Hwang and Briggs [1984] and Stone [1987]. For vector and parallel architectures, see the general textbooks mentioned in chapter 1. Basic references for the IBM 3090 are Buchholz [1986] and Tucker [1986]. More generally, volumes **25** number 1 (1986) and **27** number 4 (1988) of the IBM Systems Journal contain several papers on the IBM 3090 architecture and software. Further references on hypercube computers can be found in Heath [1986, 1987], Fox [1988] and André and Verjus [1989]. For systolic arrays, the basic reference is Kung [1982]. See also Kung [1988], Quinton and Robert [1989] and the proceedings quoted in the text

PART 1

Parallel algorithm design

CHAPTER

THREE

VECTOR MULTIPROCESSOR COMPUTING

In this chapter we discuss programming techniques for vector multiprocessors. We show that the vector hardware and memory hierarchy have a profound impact on the design of the algorithms. A complete restructuring of the algorithms is needed to achieve high performance on today's supercomputers. For vector processors like the Cyber 205, which are characterized by the fact that the CPU accesses operands directly from the main memory, it is generally sufficient to recast the algorithms in terms of elementary operations, such as the BLAS kernels, which we discuss in the first two sections. For processors like the Cray XMP, which are characterized by the presence of vector registers, it is necessary to intensively re-use the data which have been loaded in the vector registers. This has generated an effort to recast the algorithms in terms of matrix-vector operations, such as the Level 2 BLAS kernels. We discuss vector register re-use in section 3.3 and apply this to Gaussian elimination in section 3.4.

The recent advent of processors with a hierarchical memory structure coupled with vector and concurrent processing facilities (such as the Alliant FX/8, the Cray 2, the ETA 10 and the IBM 3090) has led us to move to a third level of granularity. The need for Level 3 BLAS kernels based on matrix-matrix operations has been demonstrated for optimizing data reference locality and cache re-use. We discuss matrix-matrix kernels in section 3.5 and apply this to Gaussian elimination in section 3.6.

We conclude this chapter (sections 3.7 and 3.8) with the multiprocessor implementation of the restructured vector algorithms. Section 3.7 briefly surveys the software tools that are available for the parallel execution of programs on shared memory multiprocessors. In section 3.8 we show that the recasting of the algorithms in terms of high level modules, which is essential for an efficient vectorization, also leads to better performance for parallel implementation.

3.1. Vectorization of vector-vector operations

In this section we show how the basic vector-vector operations (such as an AXPY or a scalar product) are vectorized.

3.1.1. AXPY operation

We have already considered in chapter 2 the vectorization of a scalar-vector multiply and vector add AXPY operation. Consider the loop:

```
for i = 1 to n do
        a(i) = S * b(i) + c(i)
```

For the implementation on a vector processor with vector registers of size Z, we have the following segmentation:

```
for ii = 1 to n step Z do
        for i = ii to min(n,ii+Z-1) do
                a(i) = S * b(i) + c(i)
```

Assume that S is already loaded in a scalar register. The simplest pseudo-code we can imagine is perhaps:

```
for ii = 1 to n step Z do
        for i = ii to min(n,ii+Z-1) do
                { load a section of b in vector register 0 }
                Vector LOAD:        vr0(i) =  b(i)
                { multiply vector register 0 by scalar S }
                Vector MUL:         vr0(i) = S * vr0(i)
                { load a section of c in vector register 1 }
                Vector LOAD:        vr1(i) = c(i)
                { add vector register 1 to vector register 0 }
                Vector ADD:         vr0(i) = vr0(i) + vr1(i)
                { store vector register 0 back in memory }
                Vector STORE:       a(i) = vr0(i)
```

Such an implementation requires 5 vector instructions to process a section, i.e., to compute Z elements of the result vector a. We already mentioned in chapter 2 that a modern compiler would typically generate a code with 3 vector instructions per section, such as:

```
for ii = 1 to n step Z do
        for i = ii to min(n,ii+Z-1) do
                { scalar times memory, store in vector register 0 }
                Vector MUL:         vr0(i) = S * b(i)
                { memory plus vector register, result in vector register }
                Vector ADD:         vr0(i) = vr0(i) + c(i)
                { store vector register back in memory }
                Vector STORE:       a(i) = vr0(i)
```

For instance, the code above could be generated on the IBM 3090. Several other solutions are possible. Among others:

```
for ii = 1 to n step  Z do
        for i = ii to min(n,ii+Z-1) do
                { load a section of b in vector register 0 }
                Vector LOAD:        vr0(i) =  b(i)
                { vector register times scalar plus memory }
                Vector MULADD:   vr0(i) = S * vr0(i) + c(i)
                { store vector register back in memory }
                Vector STORE:       a(i) = vr0(i)
```

The main point is that 3 vector instructions are needed to compute a section of the result. Note that this number is optimal in some sense, since at least two vector loads (for vectors b and c) and a vector store (for a) are needed. In fact, arithmetic operations are chained with memory accesses, thereby reducing the original number of 5 instructions per section, as in the first solution, to 3 instructions per section. Chained vector instructions may have a longer initialization delay, but they produce a result per cycle time once the pipeline is filled up.

If we process very long vectors, that is if n is large, we can roughly estimate the performance as follows: we need 3 vector instructions to perform 2 Z floating-point operations (a multiply and an add on each element of a section).

3.1.2. Scalar products

Vectorizing scalar products is more difficult than vectorizing AXPY operations, because some feedback must be inserted in the arithmetic pipeline that executes the operation. Consider the loop

```
S = 0
for i = 1 to n do
        S = S + a(i) * b(i)
```

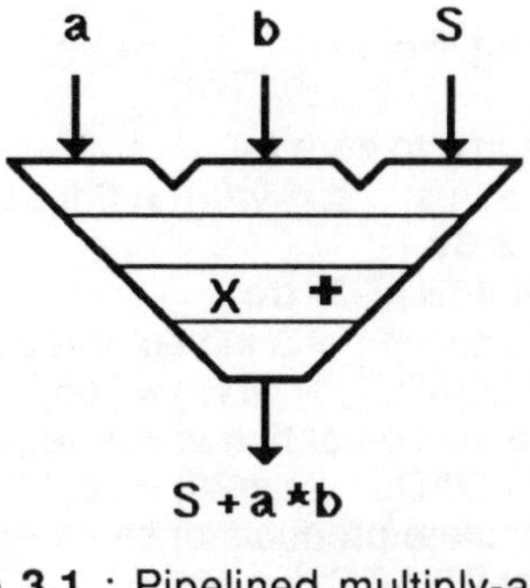

Figure 3.1 : Pipelined multiply-and-add

Assume for simplicity that we have an arithmetic pipeline of k stages which is able to perform a multiply-and-add operation (figure 3.1). If we let the elements of vectors a and b be input to the pipeline every cycle, and if we feed back the output of the pipe on its S-input (figure 3.2), we will not obtain the correct result !

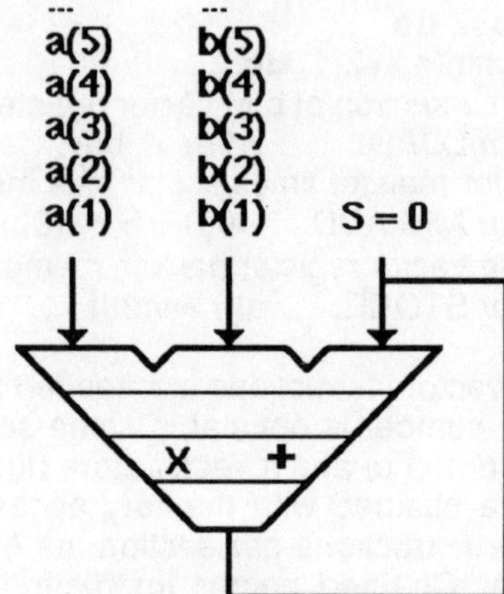

Figure 3.2 : Feedback in the multiply-and-add pipeline

At cycle time 1, the first inputs a(1), b(1) and $S_1 = 0$ are fed in the pipe. The first output is S_1 = a(1)*b(1). It is produced at cycle time k+1 and is fed back into the pipe together with the other two inputs a(k+1) and b(k+1). Then, k cycles later, the value S_1 = a(1)*b(1) + a(k+1)*b(k+1) will be produced and fed back in the pipe, and so on ... The final value produced will be

$$S_1 = a(1)*b(1) + a(k+1)*b(k+1) + a(2k+1)*b(2k+1) + ... = \sum_{i \bmod k = 1} a(i)*b(i)$$

Simultaneously, we compute $S_2, S_3, ..., S_{k-1}, S_0$, where S_j is the partial sum of the products a(i)*b(i) such that i mod k = j. During the computation, the k partial sums are held in a vector register (its first k elements) and updated each time a new section of Z elements is processed. Once computed, they are added together in order to produce the final result.

We are led to a code looking like:

```
{ initialize k partial sums to zero }
Vector Zero Partial Sums:        vr0(j) = 0 for 0≤j≤k-1
for ii = 1 to n step Z do
    for i = ii to min(n,ii+Z-1) do
        { load a section of a in vector register 1 }
        Vector LOAD:        vr1(i) =  a(i)
        { load a section of b in vector register 2 }
        Vector LOAD:        vr2(i) =  b(i)
        { accumulate products of same modulus j in vr0(j) }
        Vector MULACC:
                if i mod k = j then vr0(j) = vr0(j) + vr1(i)*vr2(i)
{ add partial sums }
Vector PARSUM :  S = vr0(0) + ... + vr0(k-1)
```

From an implementation point of view, it is important to add the k partial sums only when all sections have been processed, and not at the end of the processing of each section. The overhead associated with this final summation is not critical, because only a few vector elements are involved (e.g. k=4 on the IBM 3090).

To summarize this analysis, we conclude that scalar products can be vectorized with 3 vector instructions per 2 Z floating-point operations, as for AXPY operations, but with some extra overhead due to the reduction of the k partial sums into a scalar sum required at the end of the processing.

From a numerical point of view, it is clear that the result S produced by the vectorized computation is not equal to the result that a scalar execution would produce. This is simply due to the fact that floating-point addition is neither commutative nor associative. Finally, we note that scalar products are often called reduction operations, because they involve a statement like

$$S \leftarrow ... + S + ...$$

Other examples of reduction operations are the addition of all the elements of a vector, or the addition of the squares of the elements of a vector (Euclidean norm computation).

3.1.3. Basic Linear Algebra Subroutines

The Basic Linear Algebra Subroutines (BLAS) (Lawson et al. [1979]) are a well-known collection of elementary vector-vector operations that are the basic kernels of the LINPACK linear algebra package (Dongarra [1988]). Manufacturers of vector processors only need to replace each BLAS by a highly tuned assembly-written procedure to get an efficient implementation of the whole library.

Together with the AXPY routine and the scalar product DOT routine, we will use the MAXABS routine which returns the largest element in absolute value of a vector and/or its position. Most vector processors provide a vector instruction for returning the maximum element of a vector, hence an efficient implementation of the routine MAXABS.

3.1.4. Stride effects

In all vector-vector operations, performance is maximized when the vectors involved in the computation are accessed in contiguous memory locations. Consider the following situation: declare a matrix A of size 501 by 501 and store it by columns. First perform an AXPY operation between two columns of the matrix (stride 1):

```
for i = 1 to n do
        a(i,3) = S * a(i,1) + a(i,2)
```

and then perform an AXPY operation between two rows of the matrix (stride 501):

```
for i = 1 to n do
        a(3,i) = S * a(2,i) + a(1,i)
```

We show in table 3.1 the degradation due to the large stride 501. Data is obtained with the IBM 3090 model E (i.e.with a cycle time of 17.2 ns).

Vector length n	Stride 1	Stride 501
100	44.9	263.8
200	65.9	520.3
300	74.2	729.5
400	83.3	941.6
500	92.7	1161.9

Table 3.1 : Influence of the stride on AXPY operations (time in microseconds)

Of course, this example is a made-on-purpose one, because memory accesses completely dominate the cost of the computation. However, generally speaking, stride has a great influence on the performance of vector operations, especially for hierarchical memory machines. In a nest of loops, it is very important to vectorize the one which corresponds to contiguous accesses in memory. For example consider the initialization to zero of an n by n matrix A stored by columns. The solution

```
for j = 1 to n do
    for i = 1 to n do
        a(i,j) = 0
```

is more efficient than the solution

```
for i = 1 to n do
    for j = 1 to n do
        a(i,j) = 0
```

because a(i,j) and a(i+1,j) are stored in consecutive memory locations, whereas it is not the case for a(i,j) and a(i,j+1).

3.1.5. Performance of vector-vector operations

Consider a vector-vector operation;, such as the addition of two vectors, to be executed on a vector computer with a pipelined adder:

```
for i = 1 to n do
    c(i) = a(i) + b(i)
```

Following Schönauer [1987], the time to execute this vector operation can be expressed as

$$t(n) = [\, p + s + (n-1) \,]\, \tau$$

where τ is the cycle time and

- p = number of cycles to prepare the pipeline (we need to store the vector length n in the pipe control and to fetch the first operands for entry to the pipe)
- s = number of stages in the pipeline, or equivalently number of cycles needed to fill up the pipe until the first result appears at the "exit" (which can mean either "back in memory" or "at the entry of a vector register").

We can rewrite t(n) as $t(n) = t_0 + n\,\tau$, where $t_0 = (p+s-1)\tau$ is the start-up delay. If we define r(n) to be the performance obtained for processing a vector of length n, in terms of millions of floating-point operations per second (Mflops), we obtain

$$r(n) = \frac{n}{10^6\, t(n)} \rightarrow r_\infty = \frac{1}{10^6\, \tau} \quad \text{for large n}$$

which means that the peak Mflops rate is the inverse of the cycle time expressed in microseconds. Of course, if two arithmetic operations such as a multiply and an add can be chained, r_∞ will be doubled.[1] Clearly, this value can be approached only for very long vectors, and the value of r_∞ is not truly representative of actual performance. A very intuitive proposal has been made by Hockney [1987]: let $n_{1/2}$ denote the vector length which is necessary to obtain half the peak performance r_∞, that is $r(n_{1/2}) = r_\infty/2$. We obtain the equation $t(n_{1/2}) = 2\, n_{1/2}\, \tau$, therefore $n_{1/2} = p+s-1$. We can now rewrite t(n) as $t(n) = (n + n_{1/2})\ \tau$.

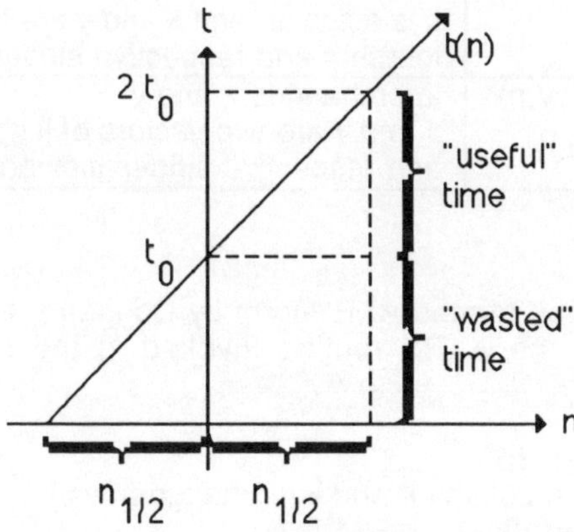

Figure 3.3 : Illustrating Hockney's parameter $n_{1/2}$

We illustrate the definition of the parameter $n_{1/2}$ in figure 3.3: $n_{1/2}$ is the number of cycles "wasted" before one result is produced, hence it can be viewed as a fictitious vector length which must be treated additionally to the n elements of the vectors. For a vector length $n = n_{1/2}$, just half the time is "wasted" and half the time is "useful" time. If $n < n_{1/2}$, more time is wasted than there is useful time, hence we should try to have $n >> n_{1/2}$ for efficient use of a vector computer. See Hockney and Jesshope [1988] for a thorough analysis of $n_{1/2}$, and its value on modern vector computers.

3.2. Gaussian elimination in terms of vector-vector kernels

Using vector-vector kernels, we can easily recast the three variants of Gaussian elimination which were described in chapter 1. Let A be a matrix of size n x n, whose elements are stored by columns, so that a(i,j) and a(i+1,j) are stored in consecutive memory locations. We also assume that the matrix A has been declared as an array of dimension n x n. For FORTRAN programmers, this means that the leading dimension of A is taken to be n. C

---

[1] This doubled value is the one advertised by the manufacturers.

programmers can think of an array of pointers to the beginning of each column of A. We discuss Gaussian elimination with partial pivoting. However, for the sake of clarity, we omit the processing to handle zero pivots. We use the following BLAS-like routines:

Routine	Description
axpy(x,incx,s,y,incy,n)	computes y ← y + s * x s is a scalar, and x and y are two vectors of length n and respective strides incx and incy
maxabs(x,incx,n,l)	returns l such that $\|x(l)\| = \max_{1 \le i \le n} \|x(i)\|$ x is a vector of length n and stride incx
scal(x,incx,s,n)	computes x ← s * x s is a scalar, and x is a vector of length n and stride incx
dot(x,incx,y,incy,n,s)	returns s = s + < x,y > s is a scalar, and x and y are two vectors of length n and respective strides incx and incy
swap(x,incx,y,incy,n)	interchanges x and y x and y are two vectors of length n and respective strides incx and incy

3.2.1. KJI-form

The KJI-form has been termed AXPY-form by Dongarra, Gustavson and Karp [1984], because of the AXPY routine invoked in the main computational kernel:

```
for k = 1 to n-1 do
        { prepare column k and interchange rows }
        maxabs(a(k,k),1,n-k+1,l)
        pivot(k) := l + k-1
        swap(a(pivot(k),k),n,a(k,k),n,n-k+1)
        scal(a(k+1,k),1,-1/a(k,k),n-k)
        { update }
        for j = k+1 to n+1 do
                axpy(a(k+1,k),1,a(k,j),a(k+1,j),1,n-k)
```

This algorithm is the one implemented in the LINPACK package, see Dongarra et al. [1979].

3.2.2. JKI-form

We obtain the following code:

```
for j = 1 to n do
        { update column j }
        for k = 1 to j-1 do
                axpy(a(k+1,k),1,a(k,j),a(k+1,j),1,n-k)
        { prepare column j and interchange rows }
        maxabs(a(j,j),1,n-j+1,l)
        pivot(j) := l + j-1
        swap(a(pivot(j),j),n,a(j,j),n,n-j+1)
        scal(a(j+1,j),1,-1/a(j,j),n-j)
```

Let c_k denote the k-th column of A. The main computational kernel is based on AXPY operations. It can be concisely expressed as

$$c_j \leftarrow c_j + \sum_{k=1}^{j-1} \alpha_k * c_k$$

Consider the first AXPY operation $c_j \leftarrow c_j + \alpha_1 * c_1$. We load c_j and c_1 in vector registers and perform the updating. But rather than storing c_j back in memory, we should proceed on the fly to the second AXPY operation $c_j \leftarrow c_j + \alpha_2 * c_2$. This would save two vector instructions: the storing of c_j after the first AXPY, and its loading for the second one. However, there is a problem that prevents the compiler from using such a technique, called vector register re-use: the lengths of the AXPY operations are decreasing by 1 with each increment of the k loop, and the (k+1)-th updating starts one position after the k-th one. Most vector computers can do vector operations starting only with the first element of vector registers. To circumvent this difficulty, we could use an assembly-written kernel where we would load into a vector register the j-th column c_j in reverse order, as suggested by Fong and Jordan [1977]. In section 3.3 we discuss further the technique of vector register re-use, and we show how to apply it to Gaussian elimination in section 3.4.

3.2.3. JIK-form

The computational kernel of the JIK version is based on scalar products:

```
for j = 1 to n do
        { update column j }
        for i = 1 to n do
                dot(a(i,1),n,a(1,j),1,min(i,j)-1,a(i,j))
        { prepare column j and interchange rows }
        maxabs(a(j,j),1,n-j+1,l)
        pivot(j) := l + j-1
        swap(a(pivot(j),j),n,a(j,j),n,n-j+1)
        scal(a(j+1,j),1,-1/a(j,j),n-j)
```

For computing a(i,j), we perform the scalar product of elements of row i with elements of column j. In each scalar product, the first vector has a stride n whereas the second one as a stride 1.

3.2.4. Performance of the three forms on the IBM 3090

We show in table 3.2 the performance in Mflops of the three forms on one processor of the IBM 3090 model E.

Matrix Size	KJI-form	JKI-form	JIK-form
128 x 128	17.9	16.8	14.9
256 x 256	19.0	18.5	18.0
512 x 512	20.4	21.0	20.2
1024 x 1024	21.6	22.5	22.7

Table 3.2 : Standard Gaussian elimination on the IBM 3090 VF

The performance of the three forms is similar. This is due to the predominance of memory references in the cost of all versions, since on average we perform one vector load and one vector store for every vector arithmetic instruction (accounting for two flops).

3.3. Vector register re-use

To describe the technique of vector register re-use and its effects on algorithm performance, we use the example of matrix-vector multiplication. Let A be an n by n matrix stored by columns, and let x and y be two vectors with n components. We want to discuss the implementation of the kernel y ← y + A x.

3.3.1. Matrix-vector multiplication

The first possible solution is based upon the usual routine, where we update the components of y one after the other, using scalar products:

```
for i = 1 to n do                       for i = 1 to n do
    for j = 1 to n do                       dot(a(i,1),n,x,1,n,y(i))
        y(i) = y(i) + a(i,j) * x(j)
```

The second possible solution is to use AXPY operations, accessing A by columns:

```
for j = 1 to n do                       for j = 1 to n do
    for i = 1 to n do                       axpy(a(1,j),1,x(j),y,1,n)
        y(i) = y(i) + x(j) * a(i,j)
```

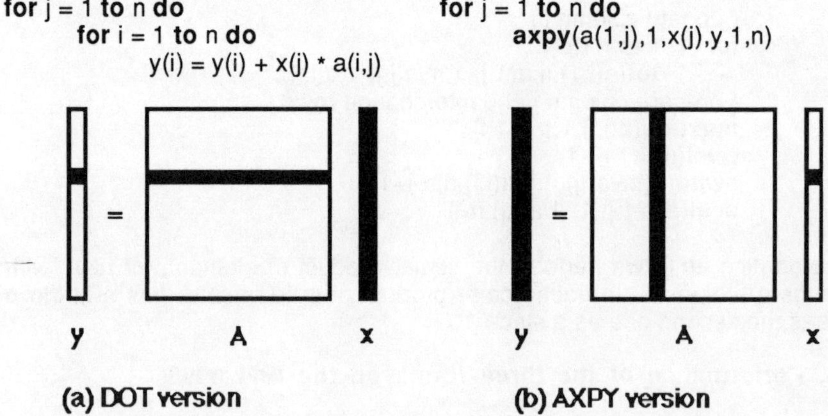

Figure 3.4 : Access patterns for matrix-vector product

The access patterns for both versions are illustrated in figure 3.4. Similar performances are obtained on the IBM 3090 for both versions, because 3 vector instructions per 2 Z floating-point operations are needed. Again, in both versions, the cost is dominated by memory references. We show how to improve the performance by modifying the AXPY-based version.

3.3.2. Loop unrolling

To improve performance, the technique of loop unrolling has been advocated by Dongarra and Hinds [1979]. It consists of rewriting the product by explicitly assigning several multiply-and-add updatings in the innermost loop. For example, with an unrolling of depth 2 we obtain

```
{ clean up odd vector }
j = n  mod 2
if j=1 then
        for i = 1 to n do
                y(i) = y(i) + x(j) * a(i,j)
{ main loop }
jmin = j + 2
for j = jmin to n step 2 do
        for i = 1 to n do
                y(i) = y(i) + x(j-1) * a(i,j-1) + x(j) * a(i,j)
```

If n is odd, we need to separately process the first column of A. In the main loop, we process columns of A by groups of 2. The pseudo-code generated when vectorizing the inner loop in the main kernel is the following:

```
{ unrolling with depth 2 }
for ii = 1 to n step Z do
        for i = ii to min(n,ii+Z-1) do
                { load a section of y in vector register 0 }
                Vector LOAD:      vr0(i) =  y(i)
                { scalar times memory plus vector register }
                Vector MULADD:  vr0(i) = vr0(i) + x(j-1) * a(i,j-1)
                { scalar times memory plus vector register }
                Vector MULADD:  vr0(i) = vr0(i) + x(j) * a(i,j)
                { store vector register back in memory }
                Vector STORE:     y(i) = vr0(i)
```

Now we clearly see the advantage of unrolling: we have re-used the vector register after the first multiply-and-add to update it with a second multiply-and-add before storing its contents in memory. On the contrary in the AXPY version, we had to load and store the contents of the vector register for each multiply-and-add, because we were processing section by section for each AXPY operation. As a consequence, instead of 3 vector instructions per 2 Z flops, we have here 4 vector instructions per 4 Z flops, an improvement of 50 %.

Of course nothing prevents us from unrolling to a greater depth (except maybe the growth of code length). For instance with an unrolling of depth 8 we obtain:

```
{ clean up odd vector }
j = n  mod 2
if j=1 then
        for i = 1 to n do
                y(i) = y(i) + x(j) * a(i,j)
{ clean up odd group of two vectors }
j = n  mod 4
if j≥2 then
        for i = 1 to n do
                y(i) = y(i) + x(j-1) * a(i,j-1) + x(j) * a(i,j)
```

```
{ clean up odd group of four vectors }
j = n  mod 8
if j≥4 then
        for i = 1 to n do
                y(i) = y(i) + x(j-3) * a(i,j-3) + x(j-2) * a(i,j-2)
                                + x(j-1) * a(i,j-1) +x(j) * a(i,j)
{ main loop }
jmin = j + 8
for j = jmin to n step 8 do
        for i = 1 to n do
                y(i) = y(i) + x(j-7) * a(i,j-7) + x(j-6) * a(i,j-6)
                                + x(j-5) * a(i,j-5) + x(j-4) * a(i,j-4)
                                + x(j-3) * a(i,j-3) + x(j-2) * a(i,j-2)
                                + x(j-1) * a(i,j-1) +x(j) * a(i,j)
```

In the main loop, we have eight multiply-and-add vector instructions for only one vector load and one vector store. More generally, unrolling to a depth of k leads to performing 2k Z flops per k+2 vector instructions (k multiply-and-adds, 1 load and 1 store): the larger k, the more efficient the vectorization. However, the overheads due to the preprocessing of the first columns may in practice limit the performance for very large k (see table 3.3).

3.3.3. Loop segmentation

Vector register re-use can be achieved without any overhead via the technique called loop segmentation, which consists in operating on strips of data of length Z, the size of the vector registers. Rather than unrolling the inner i-loop of the original AXPY version, we exchange the loops on i and j and vectorize the outer loop:

```
VECT ------- for i = 1 to n do
I                    accum = y(i)
I                    for j = 1 to n do
I                            accum = accum + x(j) * a(i,j)
__________           y(i) = accum
```

The temporary variable *accum* , used to accumulate the value of y(i), is expanded into a vector of length Z to accumulate the value of a section of y in a vector register. The corresponding pseudo-code is the following:

```
for ii = 1 to n step Z do
        for i = ii to min(n,ii+Z-1) do
                { load a section of y in vector register 0 }
                Vector LOAD:        vr0(i) =  y(i)
                { loop on j with multiply-and-adds,
                re-using the content of vector register 0 }
                for j = 1 to n do
                        Vector MULADD:   vr0(i) = vr0(i) + x(j) * a(i,j)
                { store vector register back in memory }
                Vector STORE:       y(i) = vr0(i)
```

Note that we use n+2 vector instructions for performing 2n Z flops, which is nearly a 300 % improvement over the first AXPY version. Figure 3.5 illustrates the order in which the sections of y and A are processed for both the AXPY and the loop-segmented version. In figure 3.5, we show the possibility of vector register re-use through loop segmenting.

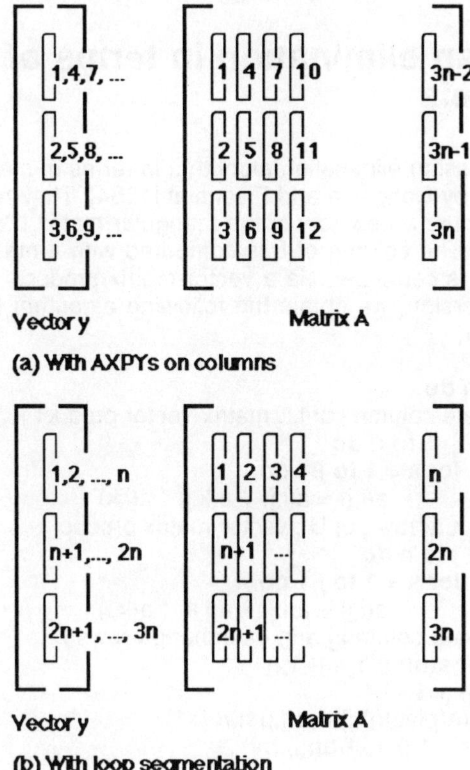

Figure 3.5 : Vector sections processing order in the matrix-vector product

Matrix Size	Depth 2	Depth 4	Depth 8
128 x 128	1.40	1.73	1.95
256 x 256	1.41	1.76	1.98
512 x 512	1.42	1.77	2.00
1024 x 1024	1.38	1.71	1.81

Matrix Size	Depth 16	Depth 32	Segmentation
128 x 128	2.07	2.09	2.09
256 x 256	2.13	2.17	2.26
512 x 512	2.01	2.11	2.20
1024 x 1024	1.92	2.18	2.25

Table 3.3 : Speedup over standard matrix-vector product on the IBM 3090

We give in table 3.3 some performance data for the matrix-vector product, based upon the AXPY version unrolled to several depths, and also for the loop-segmented version. Rather than giving the Mflops rate, we give the speedup over the standard AXPY version on columns. As demonstrated by table 3.3, the loop-segmented version is the more efficient. Note that the term GAXPY, for generalized AXPY, has been proposed in Dongarra, Gustavson and Karp [1984] for accumulating several AXPY updates on the same vector.

3.4. Gaussian elimination in terms of matrix-vector kernels

Recasting the Gaussian elimination algorithm in terms of matrix-vector kernels was first proposed by Dongarra and Eisenstat [1984]. They restructure the JIK-form so as to compute a new row of the triangular matrix L and a new column of U at each step. The column of L is computed with a matrix-vector product while the row of U is computed via a vector-matrix product. If we consider the column-oriented version, we obtain the following algorithm (see figure 3.6 for the access pattern):

```
for j = 1 to n do
        { update column j of L : matrix-vector product }
        for i = j+1 to n do
                for k = 1 to j-1 do
                        a(i,j) = a(i,j) + a(k,j) * a(i,k)
        { compute row j of U : vector-matrix product }
        for i = j to n do
                for k = 1 to j-1 do
                        a(i,j) = a(i,j) + a(j,k) * a(k,i)
        { prepare column j and interchange rows }
        maxabs(a(j,j),1,n-j+1,l)
        pivot(j) := l + j-1
        swap(a(pivot(j),j),n,a(j,j),n,n-j+1)
        scal(a(j+1,j),1,-1/a(j,j),n-j)
```

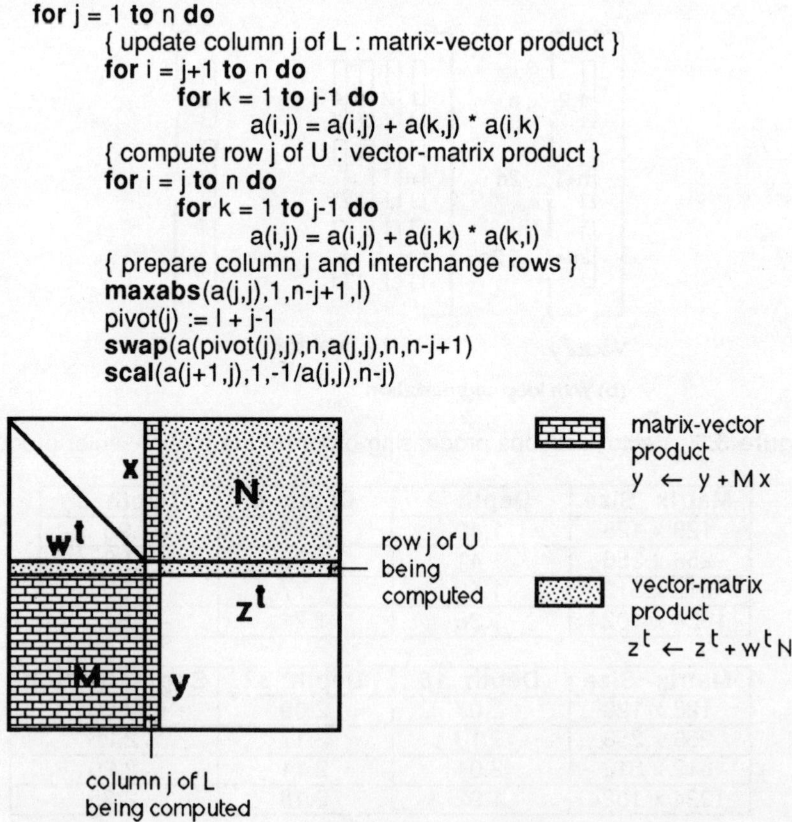

Figure 3.6: Access pattern for the Dongarra-Eisenstat algorithm

Therefore, using the following matrix-vector kernels:

matvec(y,incy,ny,x,incx,nx,m,ldm)	computes $y \leftarrow y + m * x$ y is a vector of length ny and stride incy x is a vector of length nx and stride incx m is a matrix of size ny x nx and of leading dimension ldm
vecmat(y,incy,ny,x,incx,nx,m,ldm)	computes $y^t \leftarrow y^t + x^t * m$ y is a vector of length ny and stride incy x is a vector of length nx and stride incx m is a matrix of size ny x nx and of leading dimension ldm

we obtain:

```
for j = 1 to n do
        matvec(a(j+1,j),1,n-j,a(1,j),1,j-1,a(j+1,1),n)
        vecmat(a(j,j),n,n-j+1,a(j,1),n,j-1,a(1,j),n)
        search for pivot, interchange rows and scale
```

Matrix Size	Standard	Segmentation	Speedup
128 x 128	14.9	25.4	1.70
256 x 256	18.0	27.3	1.52
512 x 512	20.2	28.1	1.39
1024 x 1024	22.7	33.4	1.47

Table 3.4 : Performance (Mflops)
of the Dongarra-Eisenstat algorithm on the IBM 3090

We report in table 3.4 the performance of this algorithm. The standard version refers to an implementation of the routine *matvec* using AXPYs on columns and of the routine *vecmat* using scalar products. The segmented version corresponds to a loop-segmented implementation of both routines. Note that *vecmat* does not perform so well as *matvec* , since it operates on vectors with a stride n. We refer to Robert and Sguazzero [1987] for detailed performance of both routines on the IBM 3090. As a conclusion, we obtain a 50 % improvement when recasting Gaussian elimination in terms of matrix-vector kernels.

3.4.1. Level 2 BLAS kernels

The need to restructure the algorithms in terms of matrix-vector kernels - so as to obtain efficient implementations through the technique of vector register re-use - has led Dongarra et al. [1986] to propose a standardized set of matrix-vector kernels, termed Level 2 BLAS kernels, to enhance the performance of the LINPACK library. See also Daly and Du Croz [1985].

3.5. Cache re-use

To illustrate the impact of cache re-use on performance, we move to a third level of granularity, namely matrix-matrix modules. Consider the matrix-matrix multiplication $C \leftarrow C + A\,B$, where A, B and C are three n by n matrices stored by columns:

```
VECT ------- for i = 1 to n do
|                 for j = 1 to n do
|                         accum = c(i,j)
|                         for k = 1 to n do
|                                 accum = accum + b(k,j) * a(i,k)
_________                 c(i,j) = accum
```

The pseudo-code generated is the following (to avoid any confusion, we take scalar registers into account):

```
for ii = 1 to n step Z do
        for i = ii to min(n,ii+Z-1) do
                for j = 1 to n do
                        { load a section of c(.,j) in vector register 0 }
                        Vector LOAD:       vr0(i) =  c(i,j)
                        { loop on k with multiply-and-adds,
                        re-using the content of vector register 0 }
                        for k = 1 to n do
                                { load b(k,j) in scalar register sr0 } sr0 = b(k,j)
                                Vector MULADD:  vr0(i) = vr0(i) + sr0 * a(i,k)
                        { store vector register back in memory }
                        Vector STORE:      c(i,j) = vr0(i)
```

Just as for the matrix-vector product, the content of vector registers is extensively re-used through loop segmentation, and we need n+2 vector instructions for 2n Z flops, that is about 1 vector instruction per 2Z flops for large n. The total number of arithmetic operations is $\eta_a = 2\ n^3$.

Let us now discuss the number of data transfers from main memory to cache. The elements of matrix C are loaded only once, since each time one new section of a column of C is loaded into a vector register, it is repeatedly updated there until its processing is complete. The elements of A are loaded n times because for each section of C being computed we need to scan a whole strip of n sections of A. If n is large, n sections of Z elements cannot fit in cache, and the last sections loaded will displace the first ones, which will have to be re-loaded for processing the next section of C. Finally, each row of B is loaded as many times as the number of sections in a column of C, that is $\frac{n}{Z}$ times. The total number of data transfers is equal to $\eta_l = n^3\ (1 + \frac{1}{Z}) + O(n^2)$, and it is dominated by the references to matrix A.

We need an alternative strategy to decrease the number of accesses to A. Assume that a block of r sections of A, that is a block of r columns of Z elements of A, can fit in cache. We will re-use the elements of such a block once loaded rather than proceeding to the next block. To this purpose, we manually section the k-loop in the preceding code. We obtain:

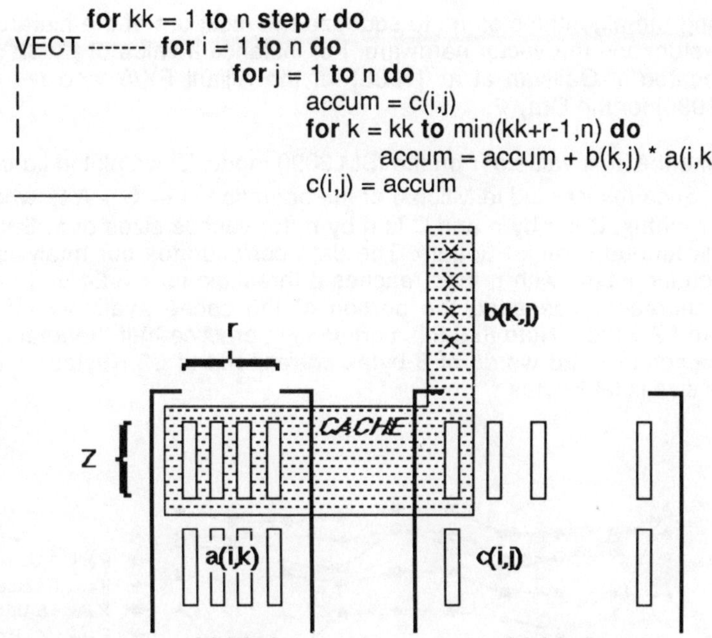

Figure 3.7 : Access pattern for partitioned matrix-matrix product

Figure 3.7 illustrates the access pattern for this implementation. The effect of sectioning the k-loop is to partition matrix A into submatrices smaller than the effective cache size, so that each submatrix needs to be loaded into cache only once. When evaluating the number of data transfers from main memory to cache, we see that the elements of C are now loaded $\frac{n}{r}$ times rather than once, due to the sectioning of the k-loop. But the elements of A are loaded only once, provided that r sections fit in cache, or equivalently $r\,Z \le CS$, where CS is the effective cache size in words. Finally, the elements of B are loaded $\frac{n}{Z}$ times as before. The total number of data transfers is thus $\eta_l = n^3\,(\frac{1}{r}+\frac{1}{Z}) + O(n^2)$.

To summarize, the ratio $\mu = \frac{\eta_l}{\eta_a}$ of data transfers over arithmetic operations is $\mu \approx \frac{1}{2}+\frac{1}{2Z}$ in the first version, whereas it is only $\mu \approx \frac{1}{2r} + \frac{1}{2Z}$ in the second version if $r\,Z \le CS$. As pointed out in Gallivan et al. [1988], the parameter μ represents the average cache-miss; ratio, which it is crucial to minimize. Therefore, one wishes to select the largest value for r that allows cache re-use.

Several researchers have experimentally determined the value of r on various machines. This value represents the best block size to be used when reformulating the algorithms so as to squeeze the most out of the hierarchical memory system and the vector hardware. For instance a value of r = 32 or r = 64 is advocated in Gallivan et al. [1988] for the Alliant FX/8, and r = 16 in Calahan [1986] for the Cray 2.

To determine the best value of r on the IBM 3090 model E, we plot in figure 3.8 the performance (expressed in Mflops) of the operation C ← C + A B, where A is an n by r matrix, B is r by n and C is n by n, for various sizes of n. Such an operation is termed a rank-r update. The data corroborates our analysis: the performance increases with r, then reaches a threshold for r = 24 and r = 32, and then decreases, because the portion of the cache available for A is smaller than r Z words. Note that this portion is in practice half the total cache size: 32 sections of 128 words of 8 bytes correspond to 32 Kbytes, and the total cache size is 64 Kbytes.

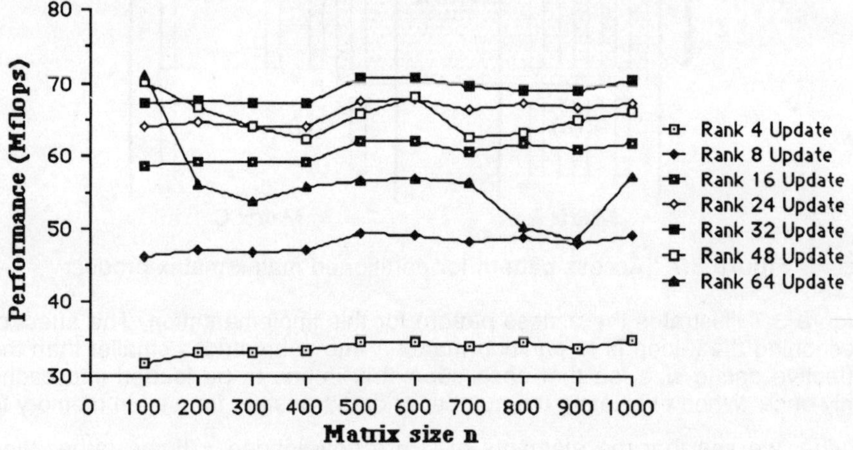

Figure 3.8 : Performance of the rank-r update kernel on the IBM 3090 model E

3.6. Gaussian elimination in terms of matrix-matrix kernels

To gain a third level of granularity in the Gaussian elimination algorithm, we have to move from processing a single column to processing blocks of columns: we need to replace the n steps of the computation (preparation of a single column followed by a rank-1 update) by n/r macro-phases which will consist of the preparation of a block of r consecutive columns followed by a rank-r update. The parameter r will be chosen so as to allow efficient cache re-use. Roughly speaking, we have the following scheme:

for k = r **to** kmax **step** r **do**
    (1) prepare the (k/r)-th macro-transformation
    using columns k-r+1 to k of A
    (2) apply this macro-transformation to columns k+1 to n

Step (2) now corresponds to O(r $(n-k)^2$) flops. Such a restructuring is possible for the three basic versions of the algorithm, and we now describe the most efficient one on the IBM 3090, namely the restructuring of the KJI-form. This description is based on Dongarra and Sorensen [1986] and Radicati, Robert and Sguazzero [1988a, 1988b]. See Calahan [1986] for a restructuring of the JIK-form, and Berry et al. [1986] or Gallivan et al. [1988] for a variation based on the Gauss-Jordan algorithm.

Each macro-phase proceeds as follows: first we perform a standard elimination on a partial rectangular matrix, made up of r columns of A. Then we apply the transformation corresponding to this elimination - a rank-r update - on the remaining columns. Consider the first phase of the algorithm: we split A as follows:

$$A = \begin{pmatrix} A_{11} & A_{12} \\ A_{21} & A_{22} \end{pmatrix}$$

where A_{11} is r x r, A_{21} is (n-r) x r, A_{21} is r x (n-r) and A_{22} is (n-r) x (n-r). First we apply Gaussian elimination with partial pivoting on the first r columns of A, that is on the rectangular matrix $R = \begin{pmatrix} A_{11} \\ A_{21} \end{pmatrix}$. We begin by searching for a pivot in the first column, then we swap elements and scale coefficients below the diagonal. But rather than applying the elimination to all the other columns of A, we only update the columns 2 to r (those of R). The idea is to postpone the updating of columns r+1 to n until the end of the processing of R, so as to apply simultaneously the eliminations generated by the first r columns. Next we prepare the second column of R, and apply the corresponding transformation to columns 3 to r only, and so on.

There is a slight technical difficulty, however. Applying a rank-r transformation to the remaining columns r+1 to n requires that all the r elements of each pivoting row should have been interchanged during the computation of the transformation. On the contrary, we would only interchange elements after the diagonal in the usual algorithm. We undo these temporary interchanges after having applied the transformation. We can now sketch the global procedure:

```
kmax = n - mod(n,r) - 32
for k = r to kmax step r do
        prep(a,n,pivot,r,k)
        klim1 = k + 1
        klim2 = n
        apply(a,n,pivot,r,k,klim1,klim2)
        undo(a,n,pivot,r,k)
gauss_standard(a,n,pivot,kmax+1)
```

In the previous code, *kmax* is chosen so as not to deal with too small matrices using rank-r transformations. Rather, we end up the computation with a standard Gaussian elimination routine, called *gauss_standard*, starting at column kmax+1. The routine *prep* processes columns k-r+1 to k as follows:

```
prep(a,n,pivot,r,k)
...
for kk = k-r+1  to k do
        maxabs(a(kk,kk),1,n-kk+1,l)
        pivot(kk) := l + kk-1
        swap(a(pivot(kk),k-r+1),n,a(kk,k-r+1),n,r)
        scal(a(kk+1,kk),1,-1/a(kk,kk),n-kk)
        for j = kk+1 to k do
                axpy(a(kk+1,kk),1,a(kk,j),a(kk+1,j),1,n-kk)
```

The main computational kernel is the routine *apply*, in which we update columns of index *klim1* to *klim2* via a rank-r transformation:

```
apply(a,n,pivot,r,k,klim1,klim2)
...
{ update rows k-r+1 to k }
for j = klim1 to klim2 do
        for kk = k-r+1  to k do
                swap(a(pivot(kk),j),n,a(kk,j),n,1)
        for kk= k-r+1 to k-1 do
                axpy(a(kk+1,kk),1,a(kk,j),a(kk+1,j),1,k-kk)
{ main kernel: rank-r update of bottom right submatrix }
for i = k+1 to n do
        for j = klim1 to klim2 do
                accum = a(i,j)
                for kk = k-r+1  to k do
                        accum = accum + a(k,j) * a(i,k)
                a(i,j) = accum
```

Note that the i loop is the one to be vectorized for an efficient implementation of the rank-r update. This may require the insertion of a directive to help the compiler make the right decision. Also, the nest of loops apparently involves dependences on A that would prevent the desired vectorization: the solution to trick the compiler is either to use a phantom copy of A, or (much better) to call a rank-r update subroutine.

Finally, the routine *undo* is responsible for undoing temporary exchanges that were needed for generating the rank-r transformation. We execute it in scalar mode:

```
undo(a,n,pivot,r,k)
...
for kk = k to k-r+2 step -1 do
        swap(a(pivot(kk),k-r+1),n,a(kk,k-r+1),n,kk-k+r-1)
```

In table 3.5, we report the performance (expressed in Mflops) obtained for five values of r ranging from 4 to 32, and for several sizes of matrices, ranging from 600 to 1000. The performance improvement over the standard implementation is 150 % for the largest values of r.

Matrix Size	Rank 4	Rank 8	Rank 16	Rank 24	Rank 32
600 x 600	33.4	40.4	49.0	52.2	52.4
800 x 800	34.3	41.9	51.6	55.0	56.0
1000 x 1000	35.0	42.9	53.0	57.1	58.1

Table 3.5: Performance of the rank-r LU update algorithm on the IBM 3090 model E

3.6.1. Level 3 BLAS

It is possible to further recast the rank-r algorithm in terms of matrix-matrix kernels. For instance the first part of the routine *apply* can be expressed as the solution of a triangular system of equations of size r, i.e. a computation of the form $B \leftarrow T^{-1} B$, where T is a lower triangular r x r matrix. Dongarra et al. [1987] identify four basic matrix-matrix kernels to build up a Level 3 BLAS collection:

• matrix-matrix products (e.g. $C \leftarrow \alpha A B + \beta C$)
• rank-r updates of a symmetric matrix (e.g. $C \leftarrow \alpha A A^t + \beta C$)
• multiplying a matrix by a triangular matrix (e.g. $B \leftarrow T B$)
• solving triangular systems of equations with multiple right-hand sides (e.g. $B \leftarrow T^{-1} B$).

See Dongarra et al. [1987] or Berry et al. [1986] for the use of Level 3 BLAS kernels in the standard procedures of numerical linear algebra.

3.6.2. Vectorization epilogue

We summarize here our discussion on efficient vectorization techniques. To obtain optimal performance, it is essential to minimize the ratio of the cost of data transfers to the cost of arithmetic operations. On modern vector processors with a hierarchical memory system, this can be achieved by:

• efficient data transfer from main memory to cache

the number of cache-misses is minimized by accessing main memory in a local manner, operating on contiguous memory locations

• re-use of data in cache

it is essential to re-use the data resident in cache as much as possible before it is displaced by a new cache-line brought from main memory. For numerical linear algebra algorithms, this requires us to split the matrix operation into blocks that fit in cache, so as to avoid scanning the entire matrix many times.

• re-use of data in vector registers

even when all the data is in cache, we have to minimize the number of loads to and stores from vector registers. This can be achieved by segmentation (operating on strips of data of length Z, where Z is the length of the vector registers), and by chaining (explicitly, or using compound vector instructions *multiply-add* and *multiply-accumulate* as with the IBM 3090).

3.7. Multiprocessor programming

In this section we survey some software tools that are currently available on shared memory multiprocessors for the parallel execution of programs. The idea is to partition programs into independent pieces of work which may be executed concurrently on parallel hardware. From the user's point of view, the use of the parallel hardware is supported by operating system primitives and multitasking library routines. The current possibilities can be classified as follows (Nagel and Szelényi [1989]):

• programming in parallel with sequential languages using a particular multitasking interface, such as library calls

• addition of compiler directives made to a sequential language. Explicit parallelism is introduced by specifying directives for parallel language constructs, with the advantage of obtaining portable source code

• addition of new language elements made to an existing sequential language. Explicit parallelism is introduced then by using this dialect of a programming language

• for a sequential programming language, the introduction of implicit parallelism is done automatically by a vectorizing compiler

• a combination of the approaches described above (e.g. implemented in a new parallel programming language) supporting implicit and explicit parallelism.

Our favourite vector-vector operations, the AXPY and the dot product, are good candidates for introducing the parallel concepts that we need in order to map Gaussian elimination onto a parallel machine.

3.7.1. Multitasking

The use of multitasking system primitives through library calls is the oldest and simplest mechanism that has been proposed. A master task can initiate several slave tasks that will execute in parallel provided there is sufficient hardware available.

Consider for instance the AXPY operation $y \leftarrow y + s * x$, where s is a scalar, and x and y are two vectors of size n stored with stride 1. The AXPY can be easily split into p independent computations. Assume for the sake of simplicity that p divides n. We divide x and y into p segments of length n/p. For $1 \le i \le n/p$, let $init(i) = 1 + (i-1)\frac{n}{p}$ be the index of the first component of the i-th segment:

```
   segment 1    segment 2    segment 3              ...              segment p
|---------------|---------------|---------------|-----      ...      -------|---------------|
1 = init(1)     init(2)         init(3)          ...                 init(p)              n
```

Rather than executing a single procedure

axpy(x,1,s,y,1,n)

we can schedule p concurrent tasks:

```
for q =1 to p do
        fork ( axpy(x(init(q)),1,s,y(init(q)),1,n/p) )
join
```

The *join* procedure is used to synchronize the completion of the parallel parts when it is necessary to ensure the completion of prior work before the program can continue. For instance here we need to synchronize before making further use of the vector y, so as to be sure to process the correct values. What is the effect of the *fork* ? p tasks will be created and scheduled by the operating system. If p processors are available, a single task will be allocated to each processor. But if there are less processors than tasks, the tasks will be queued and dispatched to the processors by the operating system. Scheduling more tasks than there are processors available is not recommended, because it usually increases the system overhead.

There is a price to pay for multitasking, and the associated overhead is usually rather important. To give numbers, the cost for the basic *fork-join* primitive is around 60 μs on the Cray XMP/416 under COS, and around 170 μs on the IBM 3090 under MVS/XA. To give a rough estimation, assume that the uniprocessor speed for an AXPY operation is M = 40 Mflops. How large should n be to compute faster with 4 processors than with 1 ? The uniprocessor time is $T_1 = \frac{2n}{M}$ (in μs), the time with p processors is $T_p = \frac{T_1}{p} + T_{multi}$, where T_{multi} is the fork-join overhead. We obtain the condition

$$n \geq \frac{M}{2} \frac{p-1}{p} T_{multi}$$

With p = 4, we obtain $n \geq 900$ for the Cray and $n \geq 1550$ for the IBM.

This explains that multitasking is essentially intended for coarse-grain applications, where the computational granularity of the tasks is high enough: in this case, the system overhead will not significantly affect the performance.

Now, to compute the dot product of x and y:

```
s = 0
dot(x,1,y,1,n,s )
```

we can also concurrently compute the dot products of the p segments, and then make a final summation. However, we need to take care that the p partial dot products are written in distinct memory locations. The simplest way to ensure this is to declare an auxiliary array *ps* of p components, where we will store the p partial sums. We are led to the following code:

```
s = 0
for q =1 to p do ps(q) = 0 { initialize partial sums to zero }
for q =1 to p do
        fork ( dot(x(init(q)),1,y(init(q)),1,n/p,ps(q)) )
join
for q =1 to p do s = s + ps(q)  { perform final summation }
```

In other words, concurrent writing is not authorized (because the results would be unpredictable). In addition to the multitasking overhead, we have here an overhead due to the fact that one portion of the code, namely the final summation, is inherently sequential.

3.7.2. Fine-grain parallelism

Multitasking features designed for fine-grain parallelism perform the parallel execution of small segments of code, such as chunks of loops. Assume that parallel extensions have been written for our high level language. Consider the previous AXPY operation. Using the concept of parallel loop we can write

```
parallel for i = 1 to n do
        y(i) = y(i) + s * x(i)
endfor
```

A parallel FORTRAN compiler, for instance, such as the one available on the ALLIANT FX/Series (Alliant [1987]) or on the IBM (Toomey et al. [1988]) will automatically parallelize such a loop, even without the *parallel* construct (implicit parallelism). If we do not want to rely on the compiler, we can either use the parallel loop construct, or make use of compiler directives, e.g. write before the loop some manufacturer-dependent magic sentence (something like C$PAR PREFER PARALLEL on the IBM).

In the parallel loops above, several processors (their number is determined at run time) will share the execution of the iterations. Rather than dispatching the work iteration by iteration, we usually dispatch chunks of iterations to processors, in order to minimize the overhead associated to the distributions. The parallel loop construct is much cheaper than multitasking: the cost is 0.313 * ch + 6.2 μs on the Cray and 0.758 * ch + 9.0 μs on the IBM. Assigning the work in large chunks minimizes the overhead. On the other hand, it makes it more difficult to equally spread the workload among processors.

By default, in a parallel loop all variables are shared. It is sometimes useful to declare private variables, as in the dot product example (Toomey et al. [1988]):

```
s = 0
parallel for i = 1 to n do
        private ps
        do first ps = 0
        do every ps = ps + x(i) * y(i)
        do final lock  s = s + ps
endfor
```

Each processor needs its private copy of ps, hence the *private* statement. Further, we need to initialize this private variable before executing any iteration of the loop, hence the *do first* statement. At the end, each processor will reference the final value of its private variable ps and add it to the global sum s, hence the *do final* statement. To prevent concurrent writing, only one processor at a time is to be permitted to execute an addition to s, hence the *lock* statement which is equivalent to the declaration of a critical section: a piece of code that all processors will eventually enter, but one at a time.

Various language extensions and parallel constructs are available. We refer to Nagel and Szelényi [1989], Toomey et al. [1988] for more details.

A last note: while concurrent writing is forbidden, concurrent reading is always possible. For instance the p AXPY computations y(.,j) ← y(.,j) + s(j) * x, where p different multiples of x are added to p distinct vectors y(.,j), are independent and can be parallelized as follows:

```
PARAL ----- for j = 1 to p do
I           VECT ------- for i = 1 to n do
________    I_________            y(i,j) = y(i,j) + s(j) * x(i)
```

Several processors can concurrently access the same data location (the components of x), at the possible expense of some overhead due to read conflicts. In some cases, it might save time to make copies of the commonly referenced data so that each processor works on its personal copy.

This last example illustrates a desirable situation in a nest of loops: the outermost loop is parallelized, the next one is vectorized, the innermost ones (if any) are scalar. Efficient large-grain distribution of work is achieved through the parallelization of the outermost loop, while efficient vectorization takes place inside each processor by vectorizing at the higher level.

3.8. Parallel Gaussian elimination

In this section we describe parallel implementation of the Gaussian elimination algorithm. The parallelization process turns out to be much easier than the vectorization one, due to the facilities available for the concurrent execution of subroutines on shared memory vector multiprocessors.

3.8.1. Simple parallel implementation of the rank-r LU update algorithm

As we have previously discussed, the main body of the rank-r LU update algorithm can be concisely expressed as follows:

for k = r **to** kmax **step** r **do**
- (1) prepare the (k/r)-th macro-transformation using columns k-r+1 to k of matrix A:
  prep(k,...)
- (2) update: apply this macro-transformation to columns k+1 to n:
  apply(k,...,klim1,klim2), where klim1 = k+1 and klim2 = n

We include in the routine *prep* the undoing of the temporary exchanges that were performed for the previous transformation; *prep* now begins with the additional statement:

undo(a,n,pivot,r,k-r)

In other words, we let prep(k,...) denote the task of preparing the (k/r)-th macro-transformation (processing of columns k-r+1 to k, plus if needed the undoing of exchanges in columns k-r to k-1). Similarly, apply(k,...,klim1,klim2) denotes the task of updating columns klim1 to klim2 for the (k/r)-th macro-transformation. Given k, the tasks

apply(k,...,klim1,klim2) and **apply**(k,...,klim3,klim4)

are independent and can be executed in parallel provided that the intervals [klim1,klim2] and [klim3,klim4] do not intersect: the update phase is easily parallelized. On the other hand, the preparation phase is not. So the simplest parallelization of the algorithm is as follows: within the iteration loop, we let the preparation phase be processed by a single processor, then we set up a parallel fork to decompose the updating of the columns equally among the processors, and we synchronize before moving to the next iteration. Assuming that we have p processors, we are led to the following kernel for parallel execution:

```
for k = r to kmax step r do
  (1)   serial part: on processor 1 :
        - prepare rank-r transformation: prep(k,...)
        - compute bounds for the p copies of routine apply
          to be executed in parallel:
              processor q will update columns klim1(q) to klim2(q)
  (2)   in parallel, update one p-th fraction of remaining columns
        on each processor:
              for q = 1 to p do
                        fork( apply(k,...,klim1(q),klim2(q)) )
  (3)   synchronize:
              join
```

We determine the bounds klim1(q) and klim2(q) as follows: at step k, there remains n-k columns to update, so that each processor will update approximately $col = \frac{n-k}{p}$ columns. More precisely, processor q updates columns klim1(q) to klim2(q), where

- klim1(1) = k + 1
- klim1(q) = klim2(q-1) + 1 for $q \geq 2$
- klim2(q) = klim1(q) + col for $q \leq p-1$
- klim2(p) = n

This kernel should give a good insight of the procedure. Rather than using multitasking primitives, we could use parallel loops. But consider for instance the main kernel of the routine *apply* :

```
for i = k+1 to n do
      for j = klim1 to klim2 do
            accum = a(i,j)
            for kk = k-r+1  to k do
                  accum = accum + a(kk,j) * a(i,kk)
            a(i,j) = accum
```

It is not easy to get the desired processing. Since we want the j loop on columns to be parallelized, we can interchange the i and j loops to obtain:

```
PARA ------- for j = klim1 to klim2 do
|            VECT ------- for i = k+1 to n do
|            |                accum = a(i,j)
|            |                for kk = k-r+1  to k do
|            |                    accum = accum + a(kk,j) * a(i,kk)
________     |________        a(i,j) = accum
```

But even though we are still able to re-use vector registers, we have lost the locality of cache references. What is needed here is really a restructuring of the code with an outermost fourth loop to dispatch the work ... which of course is equivalent to manually multitasking several copies of the routine *apply*.

3.8.2. Tuned parallel implementation of the rank-r LU update algorithm

In the previous decomposition, each instance of the subroutine *prep* is executed sequentially on processor 1, and only the computations relating to the routine *apply* have been parallelized. Some performance improvement can be achieved by a better balancing of the work among the processors: rather than splitting the updating of the remaining columns of matrix A into p equal blocks, we could assign to processor 1 fewer columns than to the others. In turn, processor 1 would prepare the next phase of the algorithm (the next instance of routine *prep*) once it has finished its own (smaller) amount of updating. Assuming that preparing a column in *prep* costs the same as updating one in *apply* , we want the first processor to update r fewer columns than the other ones (see figure 3.9).

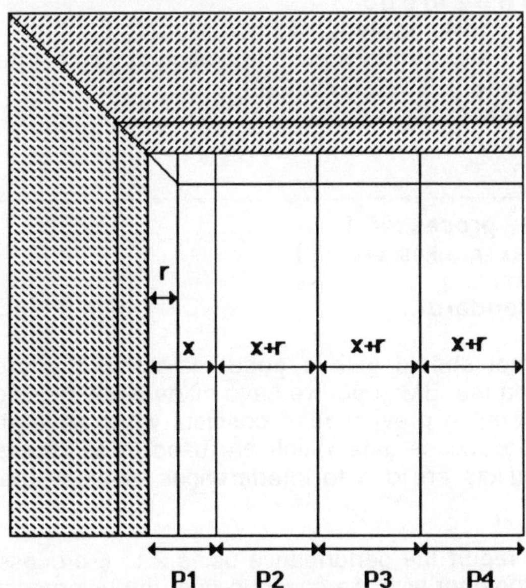

Figure 3.9 : Load balancing for the rank-r LU update algorithm (p=4)

If there are n-k columns to update at step k, we let processor 1 update x columns, while the other processors update r more, that is x+r columns. We have the equation x + (p-1)(x+r) = n-k, hence $x = \frac{n-k}{p} - r + \frac{r}{p}$. This strategy is valid only if x ≥ r, that is n-k ≥ (2p-1) r. Since this condition cannot be satisfied at the end of the computation, we will have to come back to the previous simple algorithm after reaching some point in the elimination.

There will be almost no sequential part in this implementation: processor 1 updates r fewer columns than the other ones, hence it has enough time to prepare the next transformation while the other processors are still updating columns for the current transformation. The work is then well balanced among all processors. The only serial computing is the first instance of the routine *prep* , i.e. the processing of the first r columns of the matrix. We obtain the following algorithm:

initialization : on processor 1, prepare the first r columns: **prep**(r,...)

---

parallel body : **for** k = r **to** kmax **step** r **do**

(1) on processor 1, compute bounds for the p copies of routine apply to be executed in parallel: let col = (n-k)/p.
Processor q will update columns klim1(q) to klim2(q), where

- klim1(1) = k + 1
- klim2(1) = klim1(1) + col - r + r/p
- klim1(q) = klim2(q-1) + 1 for q ≥ 2
- klim2(q) = klim1(q) + col + r/p for 2 ≤ q ≤ p-1
- klim2(p) = n

(2) in parallel, update remaining columns and prepare next step:

for q = 2 **to** p **do**
fork(**apply**(k,...,klim1(i),klim2(i))

Processor 1 also performs the preparation of the next macro-step:

apply(k,...,klim1(1),klim2(i))
prep(k+r,...)

(3) synchronize:

join

---

termination on processor 1:

apply(kmax+r,...,kmax+r+1,n)
undo(kmax+r,...)
gauss_standard(...)

Again, this kernel should give a good insight of the procedure. When implementing it on the IBM 3090, we have made a few modifications (such as duplicating vectors) to prevent read conflicts when several processors try simultaneously to access data which are used in all copies of the routine *apply* (such conflicts are due to interferences between the caches of the processors).

In table 3.6, we report the performance using 2 to 6 processors on the IBM 3090 model E, together with the speedup over the uniprocessor version. We report data for r=24, the value experimentally found to lead to the best performance.

(a) Mflops rate

Matrix Size	2 processors	4 processors	6 processors
600 x 600	98.1	171.3	217.4
800 x 800	105.0	188.8	248.5
1000 x 1000	109.4	199.4	269.3

(b) Speedup

Matrix Size	2 processors	4 processors	6 processors
600 x 600	1.88	3.28	4.16
800 x 800	1.91	3.43	4.51
1000 x 1000	1.92	3.49	4.72

Table 3.6 : Performance of the parallel rank-24 LU update algorithm (IBM 3090 model E)

In figure 3.10 we plot the efficiency of the rank-24 LU algorithm for 600 x 600 and 1000 x 1000 matrices, for 2 to 6 processors. The good efficiencies that we obtain demonstrate the suitability of the rank-r algorithm to a parallel execution. Indeed, two nice features of our parallel implementation are the following:

- the algorithms are composed of high-granularity tasks
- few synchronization points are required (less than $\frac{n}{r}$, compared to n for a pointwise algorithm)

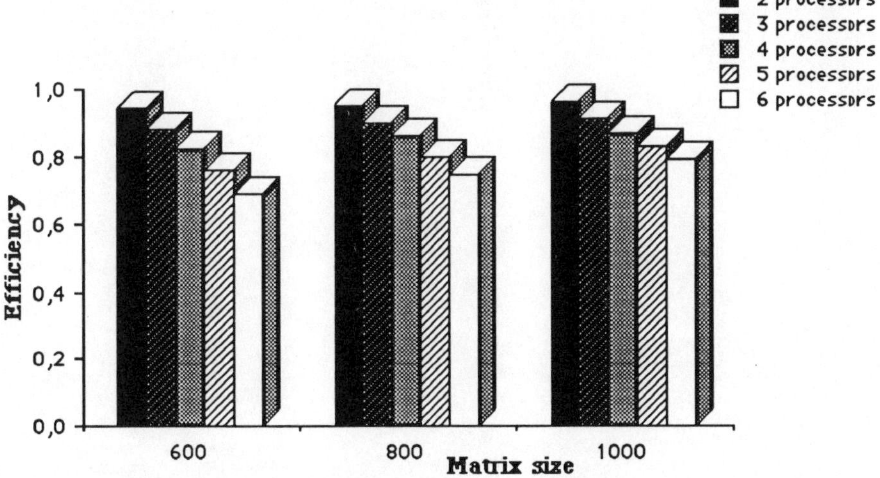

Figure 3.10 : Efficiency of the parallel LU rank-24 update algorithm

3.9. Bibliographic notes

Recasting numerical linear algebra algorithms in terms of Level 3 BLAS kernels has motivated a great deal of work in recent years. In addition to the references concerning Gaussian elimination that have been quoted in the text, see Jalby and Meier [1986], Liu and Strother [1988], and Samukawa [1988].

Our treatment of multiprocessor programming is very short. See Gajski and Peir [1985], chapter 7 of Stone [1987] and chapter 5 of Almasi and Gottlieb [1989] for further information. See also Chen, Dongarra and Hsiung [1984].

CHAPTER
FOUR

HYPERCUBE COMPUTING

In this chapter we deal with hypercube computing. We first review some topological properties of hypercubes (section 4.1). We discuss broadcasting kernels (the movement of the same data from a given node to all other nodes) in section 4.2. Then we present centralized implementations of the Gaussian elimination algorithm, both pointwise and block variants (section 4.3). In section 4.4 we move to local algorithms, using only neighbour-to-neighbour communications. In section 4.5 we briefly discuss speedup evaluation criteria for distributed memory machines. In section 4.6, we present very efficient algorithms for matrices over finite fields.

4.1. Topological properties of hypercubes

In this section we adopt a graph-theoretic point of view and review the topological properties of hypercubes that make them attractive. The basic reference for this section is Saad and Schultz [1988].

4.1.1. Node labelling and paths

In chapter 2 we said that hypercubes grow by replication. Given two identical m-cubes (that is, with 2^m nodes), we obtain an (m+1)-cube by linking their corresponding nodes in a one-to-one fashion. Adding that a 0-cube consists of one node, we have a recursive definition of hypercubes.

Another definition is the following: an m-cube consists of 2^m nodes numbered by m-bit binary numbers, from 0 to 2^m-1, and interconnected so that there is a link between two processors if and only if their binary labels differ by exactly one bit. With the recursive construction it is easy to label the processors likewise. Indeed, given two m-cubes, it suffices to renumber the nodes of the first one as $0 \wedge a_i$ and those of the second one by $1 \wedge a_i$, where a_i is a binary number representing two similar nodes of the n-cubes and where $\wedge$ denotes the concatenation of binary numbers.

Given this labelling of the nodes of an m-cube, it is easy to construct a communication path between any two processors. Let A and B by any two nodes of the m-cube, and consider the problem of sending data from node A to node B. Since A and B are not necessarily connected, we must construct a path along which the data will be sent. To reach B from A, it suffices to cross successively the nodes whose labels are those obtained by modifying the bits of A one by one in order to transform A into B.

Let H(A,B) denote the Hamming distance between A and B, defined as the number of bits that differ between A and B.[1] Assume that H(A,B) = i. Since the Hamming distance of two neighbouring processors in the m-cube is exactly one, the length of a path from A to B will be greater than or equal to i. It is easy to construct a path of length exactly i between A and B. Let $A = a_{n-1}...a_1a_0$ and $B = b_{n-1}...b_1b_0$ be the labels of A and B where a_i and b_i are the bits zero or one. For convenience assume without loss of generality that A and B differ in their i least significant bits:

$A = x_{n-1}\ x_{n-2} \ldots x_{i+1}\ x_i\ a_{i-1}\ a_{i-2} \ldots a_1\ a_0$

$B = x_{n-1}\ x_{n-2} \ldots x_{i+1}\ x_i\ b_{i-1}\ b_{i-2} \ldots b_1\ b_0$, with $b_q \neq a_q$ for $0 \leq q \leq i-1$.

Then one path from A to B is the following:

A =	node 0 =	$x_{n-1}\ x_{n-2} \ldots x_{i+1}\ x_i\ a_{i-1}\ a_{i-2} \ldots a_2\ a_1\ a_0$;
	node 1 =	$x_{n-1}\ x_{n-2} \ldots x_{i+1}\ x_i\ a_{i-1}\ a_{i-2} \ldots a_2\ a_1\ b_0$;
	node 2 =	$x_{n-1}\ x_{n-2} \ldots x_{i+1}\ x_i\ a_{i-1}\ a_{i-2} \ldots a_2\ b_1\ b_0$;
	node 3 =	$x_{n-1}\ x_{n-2} \ldots x_{i+1}\ x_i\ a_{i-1}\ a_{i-2} \ldots b_2\ b_1\ b_0$;
	...	...
B =	node i =	$x_{n-1}\ x_{n-2} \ldots x_{i+1}\ x_i\ b_{i-1}\ b_{i-2} \ldots b_2\ b_1\ b_0$;

An important question is the following: how many parallel paths of minimum length exist from A to B ? By definition, two parallel paths have no common nodes except A and B. Using parallel paths, it is possible to simultaneously transfer data from A to B by using different communication links, and therefore to speed up communications.

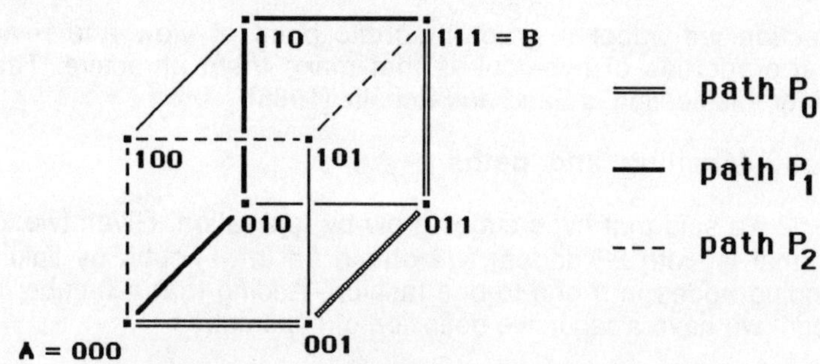

Figure 4.1: Parallel paths from A to B (i=3)

Clearly, there exist i! paths of length i from A to B, obtained by correcting the leading i bits in any order. How many parallel paths? First we can easily construct i parallel paths between A and B, with a similar construction to that above. Consider the path P_j obtained by changing first the bit in position j, then the bit in position j+1, ..., and so forth until the bit in position i-1 is reached, after which we correct, in turn, bits in positions 0, 1, ..., j-1 (see figure 4.1). To show that these i paths are parallel, let h be the label of the node X_h of any path $X_0=A, X_1, ..., X_h, ..., X_i = B$ in the i paths. By construction, any two different paths starting the corrections in positions j_0 and j_1 respectively,

---

[1] To see that H is indeed a distance, note that $H = \sum_{q=0}^{m-1} h_q$, where $h_q(A,B) = 1$ if the q-th bits of A and B are distinct, and 0 otherwise. It is easy to see that h_q is a distance, hence the result.

cannot reach the same node X_h in the same number of steps. Also, they cannot reach this same node in two different numbers of steps, otherwise one path would correct A into X_h in changing l_1 bits while the other one would achieve the same result in changing l_2 bits with $l_1 \neq l_2$, a contradiction. Finally, we cannot add an (i+1)-th path parallel to the collection, because its second node X_1, obtained by correcting one bit in A, say bit j, would be in common with P_j. As a result, we can construct exactly i parallel paths of length i from A to B, but the construction is by no means unique. Note that in our construction we only visit i(i-1)+2 distinct nodes of the hypercube, and we make use of the full communication bandwidth only when i=m, where we can use m distinct paths in parallel.

4.1.2. Mapping rings and grids into hypercubes

Perhaps the most important advantage of the hypercubes is that many of the classical topologies such as rings, 2D-torus and 3D-torus can be embedded preserving proximity in them. By preserving proximity, we mean that any two adjacent vertices in the original graph are mapped to neighbouring nodes in the hypercube.

Gray codes are the tool we need to embed a ring in an m-cube. A Gray code of dimension m is a finite sequence $G_m = \{g_0^{(m)}, g_1^{(m)}, ..., g_{2^m-1}^{(m)}\}$ of 2^m binary numbers which represent all m-bit binary numbers and so that $H(g_i^{(m)}, g_{i+1}^{(m)}) = 1$ for all i. Indices should be considered modulo 2^m, so that the Hamming distance between the last and first numbers is also 1. Thus, a Gray code defines a sequence of all the nodes of a hypercube so that any two successive nodes in the sequence are neighbours. In other words, a Gray code of dimension m enables us to embed a ring of 2^m nodes into an m-cube: we map the node i in the ring, $0 \leq i \leq 2^m-1$, into the node of the m-cube whose binary label is $g_i^{(m)}$, the i-th element of G_m.

There are many different ways in which Gray codes can be generated. The best known method is the construction of the binary reflected Gray code. We start with the sequence of two 1-bit numbers $G_1 = \{0, 1\}$. This is a Gray code of dimension 1. To build a Gray code of dimension 2, we take the same sequence and insert a 0 in front of each number. Then we take the same sequence in reverse order, and insert a 1 in front of each number. We obtain $G_2 = \{00, 01, 11, 10\}$ which is a Gray code of dimension 2. Repeating the process, we take the sequence G_2, insert a 0 in front, then take the reverse of G_2 and insert a 1 in front. We obtain $G_3 = \{000, 001, 011, 010, 110, 111, 101, 100\}$, a Gray code of dimension 3. Repeating the process again, we obtain $G_4 = \{0000, 0001, 0011, 0010, 0110, 0111, 0101, 0100, 1100, 1101, 1111, 1110, 1010, 1011, 1001, 1000\}$. G_4 is the Gray code of dimension 4 which we have used to label the nodes of the 4-cube reproduced in figure 4.2, where we outline in bold the ring embedded in the cube. Formally, given G_i, denote by $G_i^{(R)}$ the sequence obtained by reversing its order, and by $0G_i$ (resp., $1G_i$) the sequence obtained from G_i by prefixing a 0 (resp., a 1) to each element of the sequence: G_{i+1} is generated as $G_{i+1} = \{0G_i, 1G_i^{(R)}\}$.

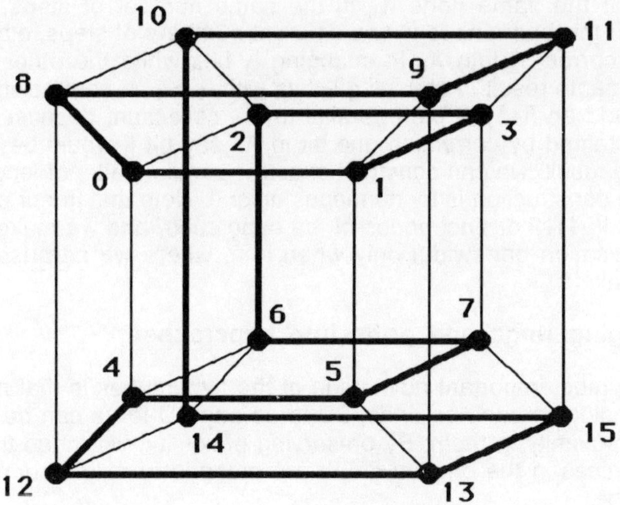

Figure 4.2 : Gray code numbering of a 4-cube

The technique described here permits us to embed rings whose length is a power of 2. However, rings of arbitrary length l can be embedded in an m-cube provided that l is even and $4 \le l \le 2^m$ (see Saad and Schultz [1988] for a proof).

To embed a 2D-torus of size $2^u \times 2^v$ in an m-cube, where u+v=m, we simply map the node (i,j) of the grid, $0 \le i \le 2^u-1$, $0 \le j \le 2^v-1$, into the node of the hypercube whose binary label is $g_i^{(u)} \wedge g_j^{(v)}$, where $\wedge$ denotes concatenation. Observe that the set of nodes obtained by fixing one coordinate and letting the other vary, forms a subcube. In other words, the mapping of every row or column of processors in the grid forms a subcube of the cube.

4.2. Broadcasting

In a distributed memory system, processors communicate by message passing. Two neighbouring processors can exchange data directly, but two remote processors can only exchange data by routing a message through intermediate processors. A very frequently encountered communication kernel is the broadcasting of a message, i.e. the distribution of the same data from one node to all the other nodes. For instance, when implementing Gaussian elimination, the processor holding the pivot column at a given step will have to distribute the information to all the other processors. We discuss in this section several implementations of the broadcast procedure on a hypercube.

4.2.1. Standard broadcast

Let processor 0 originate a broadcast in the m-cube. We cannot simply say that it sends the message to all its neighbours, which in turn will forward it to their own neighbours, and so on; such a process would be very difficult to control, and a lot of redundant information would be propagated. A simple way to perform a broadcast in the m-cube is to generate a spanning tree of height m for the routing: see figure 4.3.

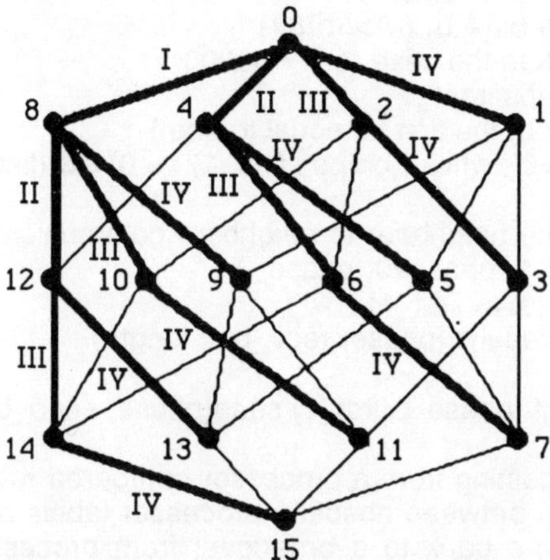

Figure 4.3 : A spanning tree embedded in a 4-cube
(Roman numbers represent broadcast steps)

Processors are numbered according to the standard binary reflected Gray code (denoted *abs*). The critical path in the spanning tree is of length m. Suppose that the syntax for sending and receiving a message between two neighbours is the following:

{ receiving } **receive**(hypercube_link,receive_buffer,length) ;
{ sending } **send**(hypercube_link,send_buffer,length) ;

where *hypercube_link* is the dimension along which the message is passed, i.e. the index of the bit which differs in the Gray code numbering of the two neighbours.

The idea is that the processors receive on the link corresponding to their first bit equal to one, and they send on the links corresponding to the preceding zeros. There are m phases in the algorithm, numbered from m-1 to 0 in decreasing order. Time steps are numbered from 1 to m (step = m - phase). At phase i, those processors whose first bit equal to one is in a position greater than i send on link dimension i. See figure 4.3 where m=4 and the broadcast is initiated from processor 0, which is supposed to have a fictitious 1 in position m=4:

- at step 1, P_0 sends on link dimension m-1 =3, that is to P_8
- at step 2, P_0 and P_8 send on link dimension m-2 =2, that is to P_4 and P_{12} respectively
- and so on until step m where each even-numbered processor P_{2q} sends to P_{2q+1}.

We have the following broadcast procedure (written in C):

Broadcast procedure from processor *root*

```
{ bit(A,b) is the b-th bit of A }
        #define bit(A,b) ((A>>b)&1)
{ coming back to the case root = 0000 }
        pos = abs^root ;
{ first_1 index of the first bit equal to one }
        first_1=0 ; while ((bit(pos,first_1) == 0) && (first_1<m)) first_1++ ;

{ beginning the neighbour to neighbour communication process }
for (phase=m-1; phase≥0; phase--)
        if (phase == first_1)
                receive(phase, recv_buf, length) ;
        else
                if (phase < first_1) send(phase, send_buf, length) ;
```

Note that for broadcasting from a processor numbered *root* , we perform a bit-wise XOR operation between absolute processor labels *abs* and the value of *root* . Thus we come back to a broadcast from processor 0 using relative labels *pos* .

The time to transfer L words between two adjacent processors is modelled by $\beta + L\,\tau_c$, where β is the communication start-up and τ_c the elemental transfer time. The time to broadcast L words using the above procedure is then equal to $m\,(\beta + L\,\tau_c)$.

4.2.2. Parallel broadcast

The standard broadcast does not make full use of the hypercube connectivity: we are using only 2^m-1 links while there are $m.2^{m-1}$ (bidirectional) links available in the m-cube.[1] In fact each node uses only one of its links for sending and receiving. For most commercial hypercubes, however, all the communication links of a node can be activated in parallel. We can improve our first broadcast algorithm by simultaneously generating m different spanning trees in the m-cube, so as to make full use of the hypercube connectivity. As depicted in figure 4.4 for m = 4, we rotate the Gray code numbering of the nodes to generate m spanning trees which can be used to schedule m distinct broadcasts in parallel. Note that at a given step, we always communicate on different links for different broadcasts. Note also that at step m all the links of the m-cube are used. We split the data into m pieces and transmit them in parallel using the m broadcasts, as stated below:

Rotating broadcast procedure from processor *root*

```
{ bit(A,b) is the b-th bit of A }
        #define bit(A,b) ((A>>b)&1)
{ rotation of A of b bits leftwards }
        #define rot(A,b) (((A>>(m-b))|(A<<b))&(2^m-1))
{ coming back to the case root = 0000 }
        pos = abs^root ;
```

[1] There are 2^m processors each with m neighbours, hence $m2^m$ links, but each link is counted twice.

```
{ index of the first bit equal to one and bookkeeping }
        length_m = length / m ;
        send_buffer[0]=send_buffer ;  recv_buffer[0]=receive_buffer ;
        for (tree=0 ;tree<m; tree++) {
                first_1[tree]=0 ;
                while((bit(rot(pos,tree),first_1[tree])==0)&&(first_1[tree]<m))
                        first_1[tree]++ ;
                send_buffer[tree+1]=send_buffer[tree]+length_m ;
                recv_buffer[tree+1]=recv_buffer[tree]+length_m ; }
{ beginning the neighbour to neighbour communication process }
{ loop on phases and inside loop on spanning trees }
        for (phase=m-1; phase≥0; phase--)
                for (tree=0;tree<m;tree++) {
                        link=(phase-tree+m)%m;
                        if (phase == first_1[tree])
                                receive(link, recv_buffer[tree], length_m);
                        else if (phase < first_1[tree])
                                send(link, send_buffer[tree], length_m); }
```

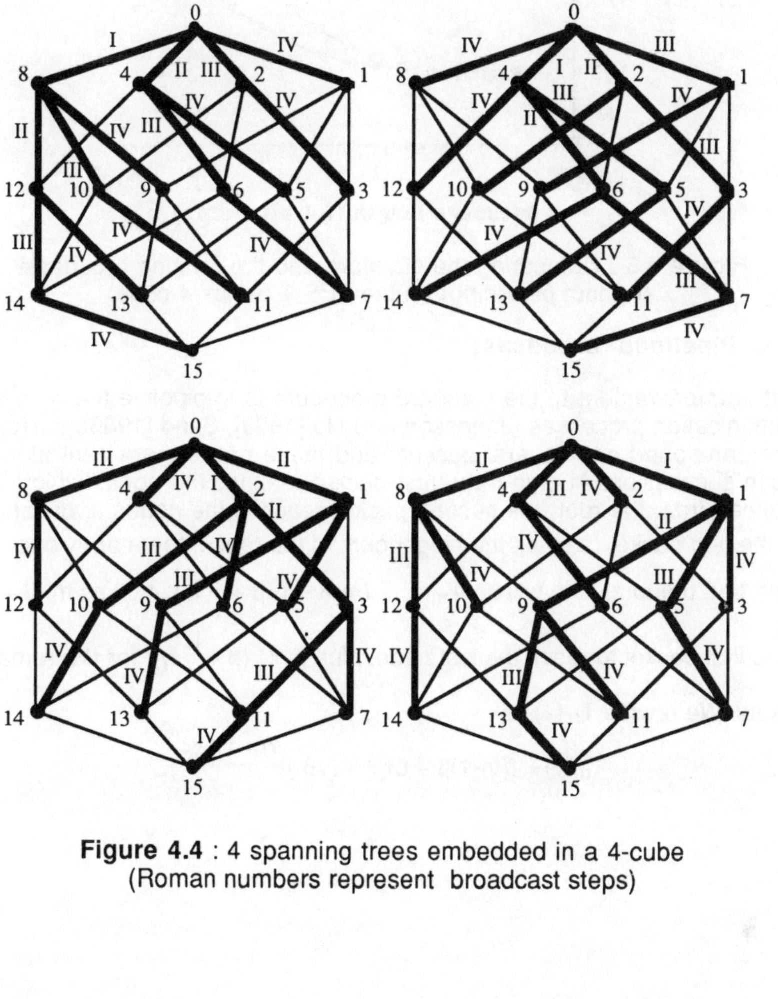

Figure 4.4 : 4 spanning trees embedded in a 4-cube
(Roman numbers represent broadcast steps)

The time to broadcast L words using the new procedure is simply the time to broadcast L/m words using the first procedure, because the initial message has been split into m packets of the same length. We obtain the value $m\ (\beta + \frac{L}{m}\tau_c) = m\beta + L\tau_c$. In figure 4.5, we report the performance of the two broadcast procedures on an FPS T Series hypercube using 16 processors. Each node has a Transputer T414 whose 4 links can be activated in parallel. We obtain experimentally β = 750 µs and τ_c = 1.44 µs per byte (or equivalently τ_c = 11.5 µs per 64-bit word). We see that the rotating broadcast is about four times as fast as the standard broadcast, as soon as the length of the message reaches 8K words, which nicely corroborates the timing formulae.

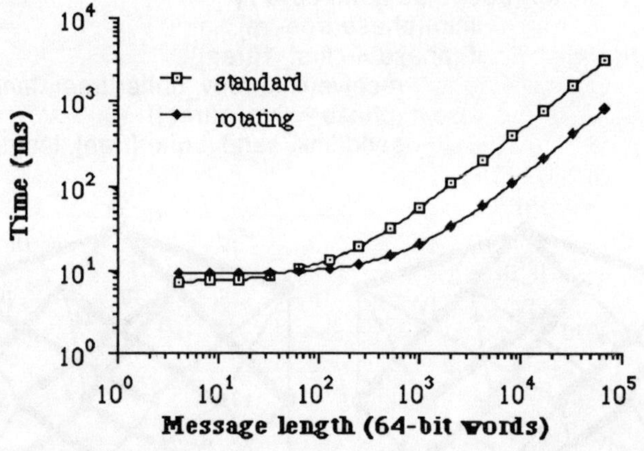

Figure 4.5 : Comparing the standard and the rotating broadcast (without pipelining) on the FPS T Series 4-cube

4.2.3. Pipelined broadcast

Another improvement to the standard procedure is to pipeline the data in the communication processes (Johnsson and Ho [1989], Saad [1986b]). The data set is partitioned into several packets and these packets are sent along the links in succession. At step j, the first packet reaches the nodes which are at distance j from the root, the second packet reaches the nodes at distance j-1 and the j-th packet reaches the neighbours of the root. If there are ν packets of length L/ν, the total time will be $T_m(\nu) = (m+\nu-1)\ (\beta + \frac{L}{\nu}\tau_c)$: it takes $m\ (\beta + \frac{L}{\nu}\tau_c)$ for the first packet to reach the last node, plus $(\nu-1)\ (\beta + \frac{L}{\nu}\tau_c)$ for the remaining packets. We rewrite $T_m(\nu)$ as

$$T_m(\nu) = ((m-1)\beta + L\tau_c) + (\nu\beta + \frac{(m-1)L\tau_c}{\nu}),$$

so that the optimal number of packets ν_{opt} satisfies $\nu\beta = \frac{(m-1)L\tau_c}{\nu}$, hence

$\nu_{opt} = \sqrt{\frac{(m-1)L\tau_c}{\beta}}$, leading to a time $T_m(\nu_{opt}) = \left(\sqrt{L\tau_c} + \sqrt{(m-1)\beta}\right)^2$.

Note that we assume here that each processor can activate all its communication links in parallel. However, communication is unidirectional, from low-numbered nodes to high-numbered nodes, so that half of the full connectivity is used if we assume that links are bidirectional (simultaneous sending and receiving on the same link).

It is tempting to include pipelining in the rotating broadcast procedure. However, this is not possible, because the m generated spanning trees are not edge-independent. We have to resort to a more complex construction termed the m-Edges disjoint Spanning Binomial Tree (m-ESBT) in the literature, Johnsson and Ho [1989]. The construction of the m-ESBT is illustrated in figure 4.6:
• first take a standard Spanning Binomial Tree rooted at node 0, SBT_0 in figure 4.6 (a)
• rotate it just as before to build m-1 other spanning trees using the left rotation operator: formally, if $s=(s_{m-1},\ldots,s_0)$ is any node of the m-cube, the left rotation (of the bits) of s is $R(s)=(s_{m-2},\ldots,s_0,s_{m-1})$. The d-th left rotation of s, $2 \le d \le m-1$, is defined by $R^d(s)=R(R^{d-1}(s))$. Let us call the SBT obtained with the d-th left rotation the d-th spanning tree.
• as we said above, these m spanning trees are not edge-disjoint. Thus translate the d-th spanning tree by negating the (d-1)-th bit of each node, $1 \le d \le m-1$, and translate the original spanning tree SBT_0 by negating the most significant bit: see figure 4.6 (a).
• now node 0 is a leaf in each of the m resulting spanning trees. Merge the m trees into a single one, of height m+1, rooted in 0: figure 4.6 (b). This last tree is the m-ESBT.

Note that we use here bidirectional links: for instance 100 sends to 110 in the leftmost subtree of figure 4.6, while 110 sends to 100 in the rightmost subtree. To compute the communication time, we come back to the expression

$$T_m(\nu_{opt}) = \left(\sqrt{L\tau_c} + \sqrt{(m-1)\beta}\right)^2$$

We simply replace the length L of the message by L/m, and the longest path m by m+1 in this expression; we obtain the value

$$T_m(\nu_{opt}) = \left(\sqrt{\frac{L\tau_c}{m}} + \sqrt{m\beta}\right)^2$$

$T_m(\nu_{opt})$ is within a factor 2 of the universal lower bound $m\beta + (\frac{L}{m}+m-1)\tau_c$ for broadcasting L words in an m-cube: it necessarily takes m $(\beta+\tau_c)$ for the first word to reach the last node. At that time the last node can have received at most m words, one per link. We need to add at least (L-m)/m transmission units for receiving the L-m remaining words on the m channels.

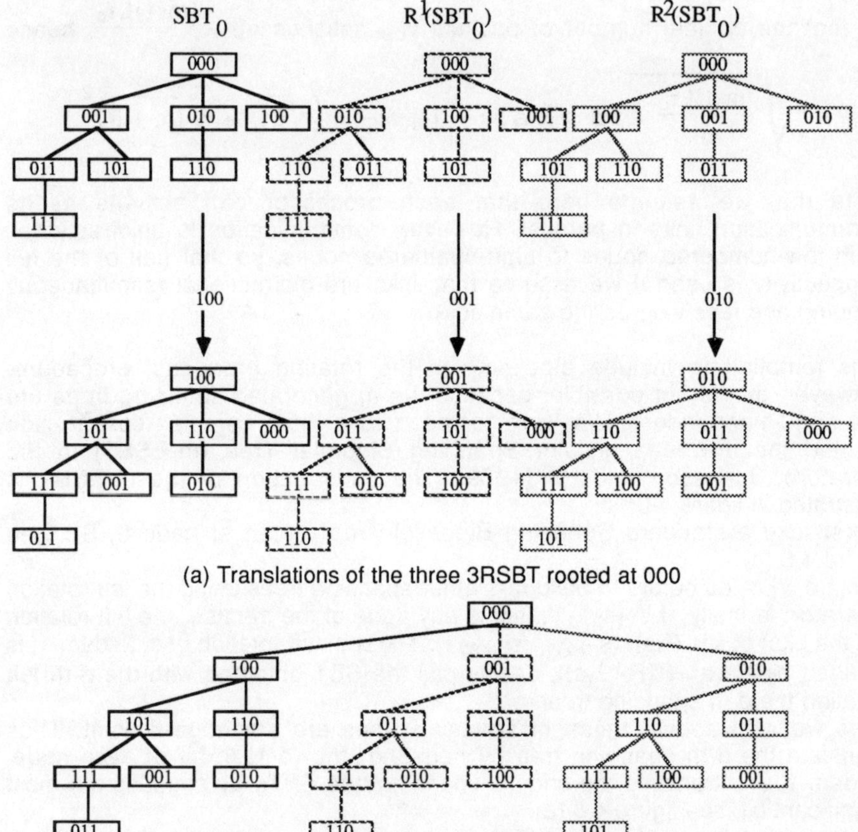

(a) Translations of the three 3RSBT rooted at 000

(b) Merge at 000 of the three translated 3RSBT

Figure 4.6 : Construction of the m-EBST (m=3)

4.3. Centralized Gaussian elimination

The first solution for implementing Gaussian elimination on a distributed memory machine is to emulate a shared-memory machine. In this section we deal with a centralized implementation where data needed by all processors will be broadcast through the hypercube.

Column-oriented algorithm

First of all we have to allocate the coefficients of the matrix to the processors. Two possible strategies come to mind: we can distribute either the rows or the columns of the matrix to the processors. But recall the generic elimination algorithm with partial pivoting, where A is an n x n matrix (we do not consider the right-hand side):

```
for k := 1 to n-1 do
    execute T_kk { preparation of k-th transformation - routine prep(k) }
        < find p such that |a_pk| = max { a_kk, ..., a_nk } ; pivot(k) := p ;
        interchange a_pivot(k),k and a_kk ; c := 1 / a_kk ;
        for i := k+1 to n do
            a_ik := a_ik * c >
    for j := k+1 to n do { update trailing columns - routine apply(k,j) }
        execute T_kj
            < interchange a_pivot(k),j and a_kj ;
            for i := k+1 to n do
                a_ij = a_ij - a_ik * a_kj >
```

Following Geist and Heath [1986], Moler [1986] and Saad [1986b], we consider column-oriented algorithms. If a processor holds a whole column of the matrix, it can generate transformation T_{kk} (search for the pivot and scaling of the column) without any communication. On the other hand, if rows of the matrix were distributed among the processors, the execution of T_{kk} would require communication between all the processors.

There are several strategies for distributing the columns of the matrix A among the processors. Assume that the size n of the problem is divisible by the number of processors p, and number the processors from 0 to p-1. The first strategy is to assign consecutive columns to a given processor (full block allocation). For instance, with n=16 and p=4:

	P_0	P_1	P_2	P_3
columns:	1,2,3,4	5,6,7,8	9,10,11,12	13,14,15,16

As the elimination progresses, some processors become idle: in the example, at step 5 processor 0 has finished its work. In the general case, at step $\frac{qn}{p} + 1$, q processors will be definitely idle, resulting in a decrease of efficiency.

The second strategy is to assign the columns with the same number modulo p to a given processor (wrap allocation). With the same example:

	P_0	P_1	P_2	P_3
columns:	1,5,9,13	2,6,10,14	3,7,11,15	4,8,12,16

This strategy is more attractive, since all processors are kept active until the very end of the computation.

Let *alloc* denote the allocation function: alloc(j) = k if column j is assigned to processor k; for instance we obtain

- alloc(j) = $\lceil \frac{j\,p}{n} - 1 \rceil$ mod p $\quad 1 \le j \le n$, for the full block strategy
- alloc(j) = (j - 1) mod p $\quad 1 \le j \le n$, for the wrap strategy.

Once the allocation strategy is chosen, we can design a very simple centralized implementation. At each step, the processor which holds the pivot column in its local memory broadcasts it to all the other processors, so that they can use it to update their own internal columns. Hence each step k will consist of two phases:

• a communication phase: a broadcast originated by the processor which holds column k in its local memory, that is the processor i such that alloc(k) = i
• a computation phase: each processor independently updates its internal columns.
We have the following algorithm:

```
Broadcast Gaussian Elimination Algorithm :
{ program of processor P_i }
for k=1 to n-1 do
      if alloc(k) = i { P_i holds the pivot column } then
            execute T_kk ;
            broadcast column k and pivot(k) to the other processors
      else
            receive column k and pivot(k)
      endif
      { perform the eliminations }
      execute T_kj for all columns j≥k+1 such that alloc(j) = i
endfor
```

It is worth explaining the procedure in more detail, because of the distribution of the matrix among the processors. Consider for instance the wrap strategy, and assume that the problem size n is a multiple of the number of processors p, i.e. n = pq. Each processor stores in its private memory a matrix A of size n x q, and a pivot vector of size q. Note that element a(1,1) for P_0 is the coefficient a(1,p+1) of the original matrix, while a(1,1) for P_1 is the coefficient a(1,p+2) of the original matrix. In the procedure below, we have a pointer which keeps track of the local column indices within each processor.

```
program of processor P_abs

{ call to a system routine which returns
- the dimension m of the hypercube
- the number of processors p = 2^m
- the Gray code labelling abs of the processor }
config_hyp(m, p, abs)

l = 1 { point to first column }
for k=1 to n-1 do
      piv_proc = k-1 mod p { wrap strategy; could use allocation function }
      if (abs = piv_proc) then
            begin { I hold the pivot column }
                  maxabs(a(k,l),1,n-k+1,ipiv)
                  pivot(l) = ipiv + k - 1
                  buf(n-k+1) = pivot(l)
                  swap(a(k,l),1,a(pivot(l),l),1,1)
                  scal(a(k+1,l),1,-1/a(k,l),n-k)
                  copy(a(k+1,l),1,buf,1,n-k) { buf is used for broadcasting }
                  l = l+1 { increment local column index }
            end
      broadcast(broad,piv_proc,buf,buf,n-k+1)
      wait(broad)
```

```
        { update columns of absolute index greater than k }
        ipiv = buf(n-k+1) { pivot index }
        for j=l to q do
            t = a(ipiv,j)
            swap(a(k,j),1,a(ipiv,j),1,1)
            axpy(buf,1,t,a(k+1,j),1,n-k)
        endfor
    endfor
```

We have used the elementary vector routines from section 3.2, plus a new one:

copy(x,incx,y,incy,n)	copy x into y: $y \leftarrow x$ x and y are two vectors of length n and respective strides incx and incy

Our syntax for the broadcast procedure is the following:

broadcast(broad, pos,send_buf, recv_buf, message_length)

where *broad* is a communication descriptor, *pos* is the sender labelling, *send_buf* is the starting address in P_{pos}' s memory of the message to be sent, and *recv_buf* is the starting address of where to write the message. The communication descriptor is used for reference at the synchronization point.

The only trick in the procedure is the following: rather than performing two broadcasts, one for the scaled pivot column and the other for the pivot index, we have concatenated the two messages: we store the pivot index in the last component of vector *buf*. At step k, the broadcast message contains n-k+1 words, n-k for column coefficients and an additional one for the pivot index.

4.3.1. Performance data

We plot in figure 4.7 the performance (expressed in Mflops) of the centralized algorithm, using each of the three available levels for programming the VPU.[1] This is mainly to show that good performance can be obtained with a very simple code: hypercube programming can be rewarding !

---

[1] As mentioned in section 2.4, generic and parameter block routines should always operate on vectors aligned on a tap of the memory, to avoid the memory moves required before loading into the VPU registers. This is not the case in the previous implementation: whenever n-k is not a multiple of 128, vectors must be copied on tap 0 of a memory scratch location before being loaded into the registers. If we choose to represent each column of A backwards, from the last element to the first one, we can meet this requirement. We locate the matrix A on tap 0 of a memory slice and we let its leading dimension be a multiple of 128. Hence every column will start on tap 0. Since we have reversed the order of the elements, we will operate on the first (n-k) memory locations for updating each column at step k, thereby avoiding any memory move. We just have to remember that the i-th element of column j is in position a(n-i+1,j).

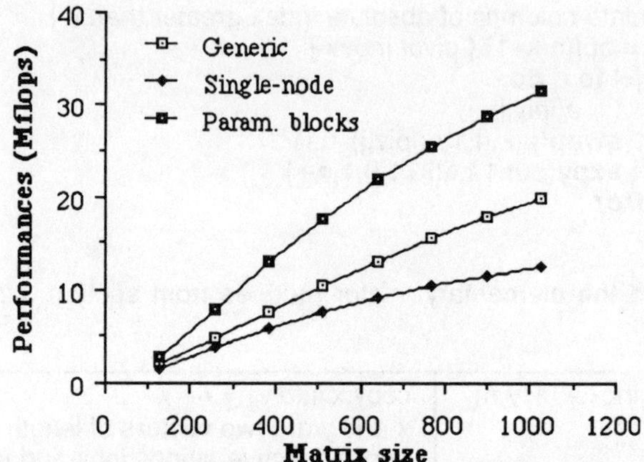

Figure 4.7 : Gaussian elimination (broadcast algorithm, 16 processors)

To give an insight of the performance that can be obtained on larger hypercube configurations, we report in figure 4.8 the performance obtained with 16 to 64 processors.

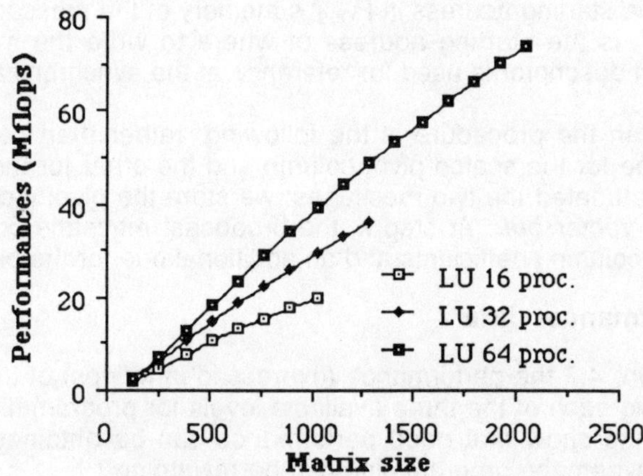

Figure 4.8 : LU factorization (generic routines, broadcast algorithm)

4.3.2. Block version

Moving to a block version of the algorithm has two main advantages. First the block scheme squeezes the most out of the VPU, because it allows us to re-use data stored in vector registers before unloading them back to memory. This is exactly the same argument as for shared memory machines (see chapter 3). Moreover the block scheme allows internode communication of larger packets of data, thereby reducing the start-up time overhead in the communication protocols (a critical parameter for many commercial hypercubes, as already mentioned).

To design a block-r variant, we have to modify the allocation strategy. Rather than distributing columns of processors in a wraparound fashion, we distribute *blocks* of r consecutive columns in a wraparound fashion. For instance with n = 24, p =4 and r = 3:

	P_0	P_1	P_2	P_3
columns:	1,2,3	4,5,6	7,8 9	10,11,12
	13,14,15	16,17,18	19,20,21	22,23,24

The allocation function by blocks of size r, $1 \le r \le \frac{n}{p}$, is defined by

$$\text{alloc}(j) = \lceil \frac{j}{r} - 1 \rceil \bmod p \qquad 1 \le j \le n$$

Of course if r = 1 we retrieve the wrap allocation and if $r = \frac{n}{p}$ the full block one.

The block-r algorithm is very similar to the rank-r LU update algorithm described in section 3.6. It can be concisely expressed as the following kernel:

```
program of processor P_abs

config_hyp(m, p, abs)
l = 1 { point to first column }
for k=1 to n-1 step r do
    piv_proc = (k-1)/r mod p { block-r allocation }
    if (abs = piv_proc) then
        begin { I hold the r pivot columns }
            prepare k-th macro-transformation
            copy r scaled columns and corresponding pivot indices
                into buffer buf
            l = l+r { increment local column index }
        end
    broadcast(broad,piv_proc,buf,buf,(n-k+1)r)
    wait(broad)
    { update columns of absolute index greater than k }
    apply k-th macro-transformation to columns l to q
endfor
```

The communication kernel is the broadcast of a packet of r vectors. With large values of r, messages will be longer, and the overhead due to the start-up will diminish. See Robert and Tourancheau [1989] for more implementation details. Experimentally, the best value is r = 4 (figure 4.9). It represents the best compromise between the efficiency of the implementation and the balancing of the workload among the processors. On one hand, the larger r, the better the use of the VPU and the more efficient the broadcasting of the buffers. On the other hand, the larger r, the longer the processors remain waiting during the scaling part and the sooner they become idle at the end of the computation.

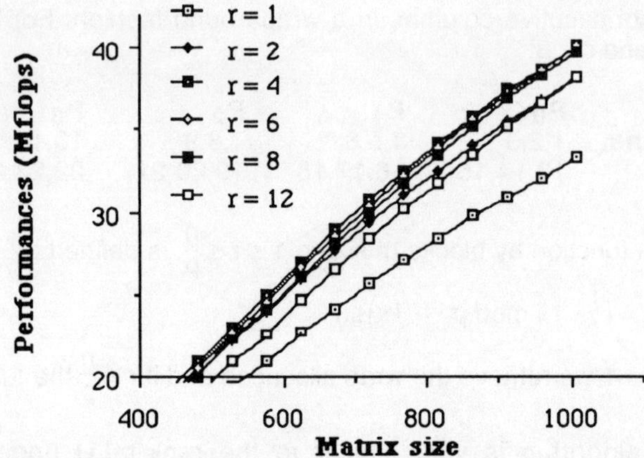

Figure 4.9 : Performance of the block-r algorithm (16 processors)

Several authors have reported on the superiority of a Level 3 BLAS approach, based on high level matrix-matrix modules, for shared memory vector multiprocessors with a hierarchical memory system. We conclude from our experiments that such an approach also has a high performance on a hypercube vector multiprocessor.

Finally, we can summarize our results on block algorithms as follows:

• **shared memory vector multiprocessor**

large block-size	⇒	re-use of vector registers
	but	cache capacity exceeded

• **distributed memory vector multiprocessor**

large block-size	⇒	re-use of vector registers
		+ less communication start-ups
	but	workload less balanced

4.4. Local pipelined algorithms

In this section, we use two subtopologies of the cube, namely the ring and the grid, to derive pipeline algorithms that use only neighbour-to-neighbour communications.

4.4.1. Pipelined ring algorithm

We first configure the hypercube as an oriented ring of p processors numbered from 0 to p-1. Processor P_i receives messages from its predecessor P_{i-1} and sends messages to its successor P_{i+1} (the subscripts are taken modulo p): see figure 4.10.

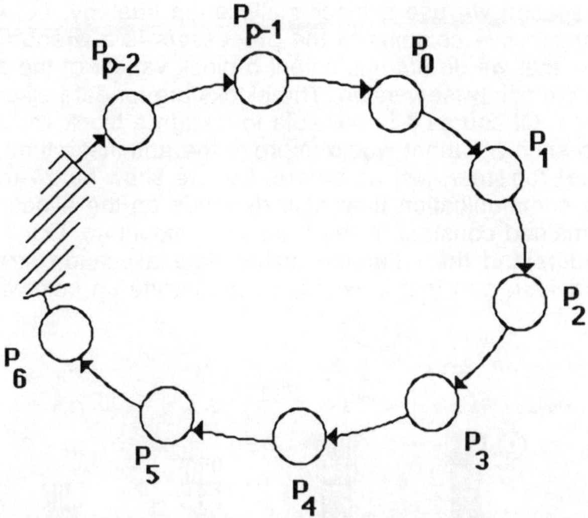

Figure 4.10 : Oriented ring of p processors

At step k, the processor holding the pivot column, say P_i, sends it to its right neighbour P_{i+1}, which in turn sends it to P_{i+2}, and so on until the pivot column reaches the left neighbour of P_{i-1}. The main advantage of this asynchronous strategy is that communication and computation can be overlapped. A processor can start updating its internal columns as soon as it has received the pivot column and transmitted it to its neighbour. Their is no need to wait for all the processors to receive the information before starting the computation. The pipeline ring algorithm is as follows (processor indices are taken modulo p) :

Pipelined Ring (PR) Algorithm :
{ program of processor P_i }
for k=1 **to** n-1 **do**
    if alloc(k) = i **then**
        execute T_{kk}
        send column k to P_{i+1}
    else
        receive column k from P_{i-1}
        if (i+1 mod p) ≠alloc(k) **then send** column k to P_{i+1}
    endif
    { perform the eliminations }
    execute T_{kj} for all columns j≥k+1 such that alloc(j) = i
endfor

It might seem more natural at first to perform the eliminations as soon as the pivot column is available, and propagate the pivot column to the next processor after the arithmetic is completed, but this is not as efficient since the next processor will be idle waiting for the column to arrive while the processor P_i is computing.

Again in this section we use a block-r allocation strategy, i.e. we distribute blocks of r consecutive columns to the processors in a wraparound fashion. Note, however, that we do not implement a block variant of the algorithm: we only deal with the pointwise version. The blocks are for data allocation, not for the computation. Of course it is possible to design a block variant of the PR algorithm, and such a variant would improve the arithmetic time, through the re-use of vector registers, just as before. But we show below that in the PR algorithm, the communication time also depends on the allocation strategy, whereas it remained constant in the broadcast algorithm. Our main concern here is to understand the influence of the data allocation strategy on the algorithm behaviour, and that is why we concentrate on pointwise Gaussian elimination.

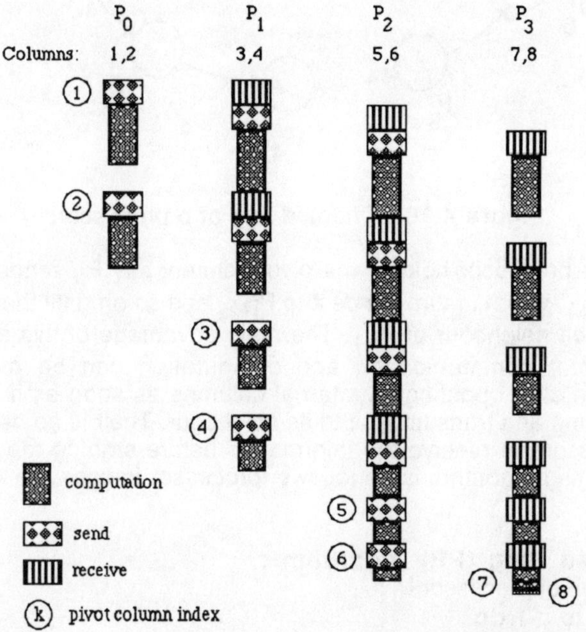

Figure 4.11 : Pipelined ring algorithm, full block allocation

First consider the PR algorithm with the full block allocation, that is $r = \frac{n}{p}$. We depict its execution in figure 4.11. We see in the figure that communication and arithmetic do overlap. Now we use the same representation in figure 4.12 for the wrap allocation (r =1). We see that the communication time T_c is less for the full block allocation than for the wrap one, because of the idle time introduced every time that the pivot columns at two consecutive steps are not held by the same processor. This is a general result: the larger r, the smaller T_c. On the other hand, the arithmetic obeys the same rules as in the centralized case: the larger r, the greater the arithmetic time T_a. In other words, T_a is minimum for the wrap allocation (r=1), while T_c is minimum for the block allocation (r=n/p). The smaller r, the more balanced the computations, but the more expensive the communications. As the total time takes into account these two opposite laws, we must be prepared to find a compromise for the choice of the best block size r. As evidenced by figure 4.13, the best value is found to be r=4 for a matrix of order 1024 on the FPS T Series. We return in chapter 7 to the influence of data allocation strategies on algorithm performance, and we analytically determine the best allocation as a function of p, n and some machine-dependent parameters.

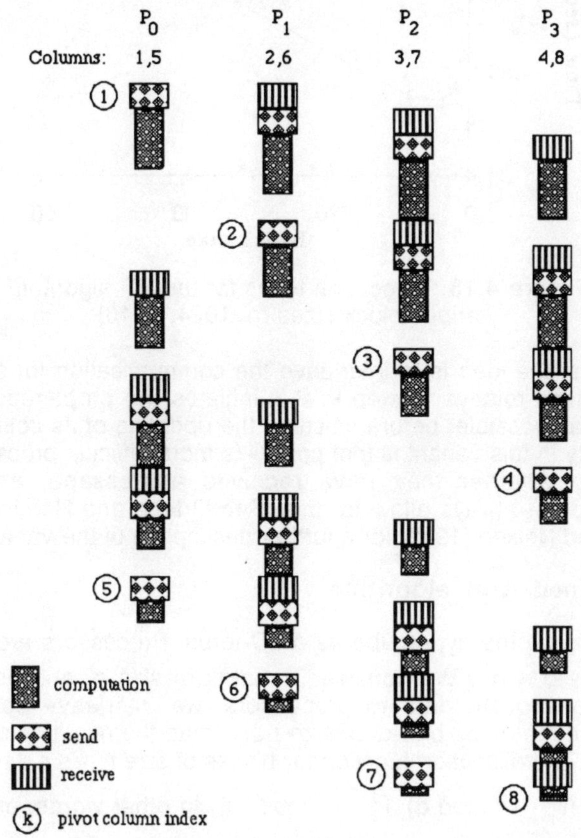

Figure 4.12 : Pipelined ring algorithm, wrap allocation

An interesting variant of our implementation of the pipelined ring algorithm is the compute-and-send-ahead strategy. Consider the wrap allocation. At step k, the processor P_i which holds the pivot column (alloc(k)=i) sends it to P_{i+1}, which holds column k+1. The action of P_{i+1} is the following:

- propagate column k to its successor P_{i+1}
- execute task $T_{k,k+1}$
- send column k+1 to P_{i+2}
- terminate updating for step k: execute tasks T_{kj} with j>k+1 and alloc(j)=i+1

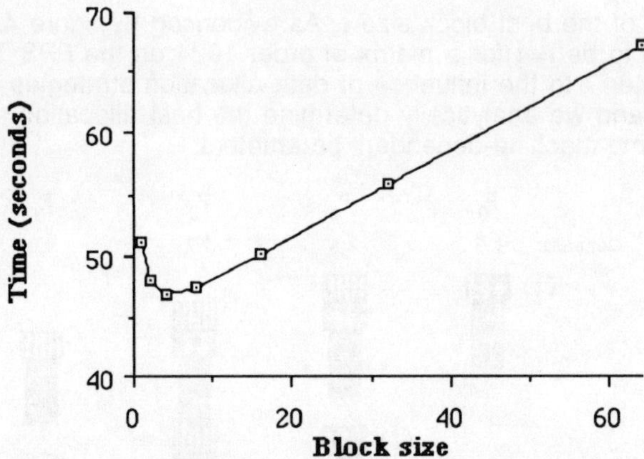

Figure 4.13 : Execution times for the PR algorithm, various block sizes (n=1024, p=16)

In other words, the idea is to interleave the communication for step k+1 with the computations relative to step k: P_{i+1} initiates the propagation of column k+1 as soon as possible, before finishing the updating of its columns for step k. The difficulty in this variant is that control is more difficult: processors should keep probing whether they have received a message, and hardware constraints do not always allow for this. See Ortega and Romine [1988] and Gerasoulis and Nelken [1988] for a further description of the variant.

4.4.2. Pipelined grid algorithm

Now we configure the hypercube as a 2D-torus. Processors are labelled P_{ij}, $0 \le i,j < q$, where $p = q^2$. We consider a matrix of size n, and assume that q divides n. To allocate data to processors, we interleave both rows and columns of the matrix by blocks of size r and map the resulting square blocks onto the grid. The allocation function for blocks of size r, $1 \le r \le n/q$, is defined by $\mathrm{alloc}(i,j) = (\lceil \frac{i}{r} - 1 \rceil \bmod q), \lceil \frac{j}{r} - 1 \rceil \bmod q)$. In other words, processor P_{uv} holds the i-th element of column j if alloc(i,j) = (u,v): see figure 4.14, where a label (u,v) in a block means that this block is mapped into the processor which lies in row u and column v of the processor grid. The full wrap (r=1) and the full block (r=n/q) allocation strategies have been discussed in Saad [1986b].

First of all we deal with an implementation without pivoting. We implement the KJI-inside version of Gaussian elimination on the grid:

```
for k = 1 to n do { step k : column k is the pivot column }
    for j = k+1 to n do { update column j }
        task T_kj : < a_kj ← a_kj / a_kk
                      for i = k+1 to n do a_ij ← a_ij - a_ik * a_kj >
```

We derive a pipelined grid algorithm in a similar way to that for the ring. At step k, let l = alloc(.,k) be the index of the column of processors in the grid which holds the pivot column.

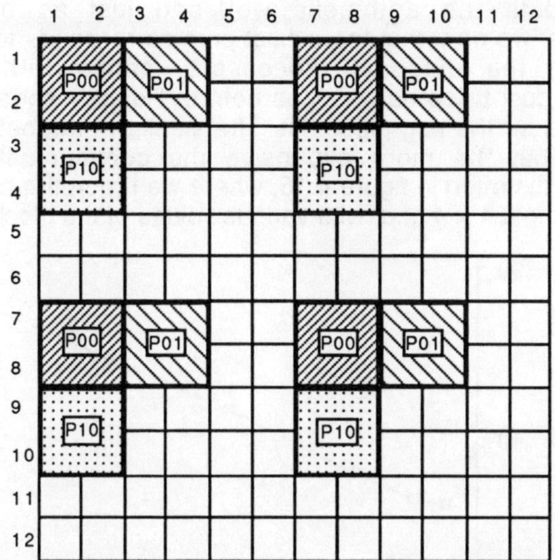

Figure 4.14: Data allocation of a 12 x 12 matrix with q=3 and r=2

First, each processor P_{ul}, $0 \le u < q$, transmits its segment of the pivot column horizontally along the u-th row of the grid, in a pipeline fashion. Then, each processor P_{lv}, $0 \le v < q$, transmits its segment of the pivot row vertically along the v-th column of the grid, again in a pipeline fashion. In the following algorithm, processor indices are taken modulo q:

Pipelined Grid Algorithm :

```
{ program of processor P_uv }
for k=1 to n-1 do
    { horizontal communications }
    if alloc(.,k)=v then
        { the v-th column of processors holds the pivot column k }
        send_horizontally segment of column k to P_u,v+1
    else
        receive_horizontally segment of column k from P_u,v-1
        if (v+1 mod q) ≠ alloc(.,k) then
            send_horizontally segment of column k to to P_u,v+1
    endif
    { vertical communications }
    if alloc(k,.) = u then { the u-th row of processors holds the pivot row k }
        send_vertically segment of row k to to P_u+1,v
    else
        receive_vertically segment of row k from P_u-1,v
        if (u+1 mod q) ≠ alloc(k,.) then
            send_vertically segment of row k to P_u+1,v
    endif
    { perform the eliminations }
    execute T_kj for all elements a_ij such that j≥k+1 and alloc(i,j) = (u,v)
endfor
```

We can compute the arithmetic workload just as before. For the communications, we note that the critical path corresponds to a virtual ring of size q linking the diagonal processors, hence with an elemental communication cost twice as much as before. Roughly speaking, the results are the same as for the ring algorithm. The smaller r, the better balanced the computations, but the more expensive the communications. The best compromise is illustrated in figure 4.15, where we report the performance for a 1024 matrix, using a 4 x 4 grid, with various values of the block size r.

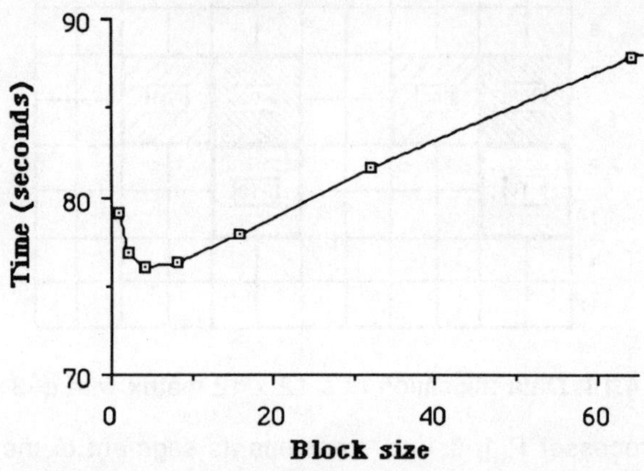

Figure 4.15 : Execution times for Gauss on the grid, various block sizes (n=1024, p=16)

The main difference between the ring and the grid concerns pivoting issues. If partial pivoting is to be introduced, vertical all-to-all communication must occur between the processors which hold the pivot column. At step k, each processor P_{uv}, $0 \le u < q$, where alloc(.,k) = v, will:
(i) compute its local maximum in the segment of the pivot column that it holds
(ii) send the value of this maximum, together with its row index, to all the other processors in the same grid column (all-to-all exchange)
Now every processor in grid column v knows the value of the pivot, and which processor holds it. Hence each P_{uv}, $0 \le u < q$, will:
(iii) scale its segment of the pivot column
(iv) perform the horizontal communication as before, in order to transmit the scaled pivot column. Additional information on the pivot index is added for the vertical communication that follows for the transmission of the pivot row.
Steps (i) and (iii) can be executed in parallel for all processors of column v.

We see that the pipelined ring algorithm is faster than the pipelined grid algorithm on the FPS T Series; there are two main reasons for this:
• the overhead due to communications when pivoting
• the shorter length of the vectors operated upon in the grid

4.5. A word on speedup evaluation

Our aim in this section is to compare two different ways of evaluating the speedup of parallel algorithms on a distributed memory machine. We set the problem and report experimental data, but we defer performance modelling until chapter 7.

The usual way for computing speedups is to consider a fixed-size problem and to evaluate the ratio of the time spent by a single processor over the time spent with several processors. According to Amdahl's law (see section 1.3), this ratio is bounded by the inverse of the sequential fraction of the program, thereby prohibiting massive parallelism.

However, solving a fixed-size problem, independent of the number of processors, has little sense using a distributed memory machine. Gustafson [1988] has recently proposed another way to compute speedups. For each number of processors, we consider the largest instance of the problem that can be solved and compute the time it would have taken on a single processor. The ratio between these times is Gustafson's speedup.

Consider again the pipeline ring algorithm with a wrap distribution. We report in figure 4.16 experimental data using from 1 up to 16 processors.

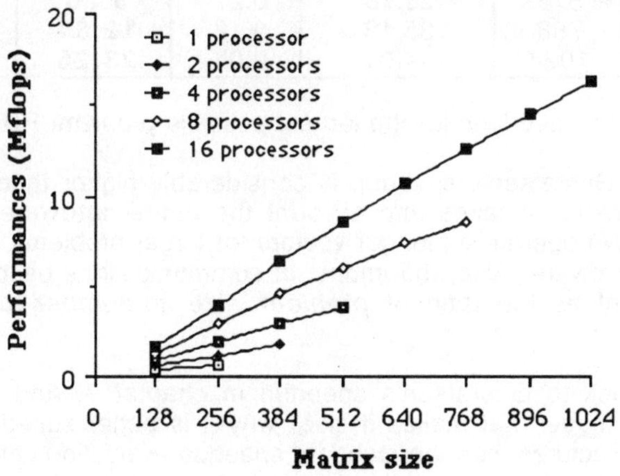

Figure 4.16 : Performance of the PR algorithm for various ring sizes

If we compute speedups in the usual way, we take the largest problem that can be solved with one processor and we find n = 256. The corresponding speedups for the PR algorithm are given in table 4.1.

Processors	Pb Size	Time (seconds)	Speedup	Efficiency
1	256	15.98	**1**	1
2	256	9.35	**1.71**	0.85
4	256	5.69	**2.80**	0.70
8	256	3.75	**4.26**	0.53
16	256	2.80	**5.71**	0.36

Table 4.1 : Speedups for a fixed-size problem (n=256), PR algorithm

We obtain very low values for p=16. This is mainly due to the communication overhead on such a small problem size. Note that the serial part is negligible: the communications are actually predominant. But with 16 processors available, we would like to evaluate somehow the performance obtained for factoring a large 1024 x 1024 matrix. For each number of processors p, we consider the largest problem size that can be solved using the available memory. We compute $\tau_{max}(p)$, the average time needed for one arithmetic operation, as the inverse of the Mflops performance for this largest problem size. This is a renormalization of the problem. The ratio between the values of $\tau_{max}(p)$ for different p gives Gustafson's speedup (see table 4.2).

# Proc.	Pb Size	Time (sec.)	$\tau_{max}(p)$	Speedup	Efficiency
1	256	15.98	1.43	**1**	1
2	384	21.75	0.58	**2.47**	1.23
4	512	23.78	0.27	**5.26**	1.31
8	768	35.13	0.12	**12.31**	1.53
16	1024	44.01	0.06	**23.26**	1.45

Table 4.2 : Speedups for the largest possible problem, PR algorithm

We see that Gustafson's speedup is considerably higher than the standard speedup, because it takes into account the entire hardware and memory capabilities. We operate on longer vectors for larger problems, making better use of the hardware. Also, the impact of communications becomes less and less important as the ratio of *problem size* to *number of processors* increases.

We come back to Gustafson's speedup in chapter 7, and we present a performance model that makes it clear why it is better suited to distributed memory architectures than the standard speedup evaluation criterion.

4.6. Matrices over finite fields

We deal in this section with the implementation of Gaussian elimination for matrices over finite fields GF(p), and we let p=2 for the sake of simplicity. We refer to Parkinson and Wunderlich [1984] for a survey of application domains of modular arithmetic triangularization algorithms. We only mention two representative applications:

• the large integer factoring routines, where the final stage necessitates performing the triangularization (e.g. via Gaussian elimination with partial pivoting) on a large dense matrix over GF(2)

• the factorization of polynomials over GF(p), where p is a prime number, via Berlekamp's algorithm.

We can implement the centralized algorithm just as before. However, we have the possibility of storing larger matrices, by compressing several 0-1 row coefficients into one integer word. We report some performance data in figure 4.17. Note that we use random test matrices, because the timings are data dependent.

Partial pivoting is a *sine qua non* over GF(2), because in average every second coefficient is zero. But when scanning a column, we do not need any global information: the first non-zero element that we find below the diagonal will be chosen as pivot. The basic remark that no global information is needed for the choice of a pivot can be exploited further: we can use several distinct pivots to zero out the elements of a given column simultaneously. To this purpose, we move to a row-oriented version where we distribute the rows of the matrix rather than the columns. We first describe a row-oriented pipeline algorithm, and then a modification of it called the local pivot algorithm.

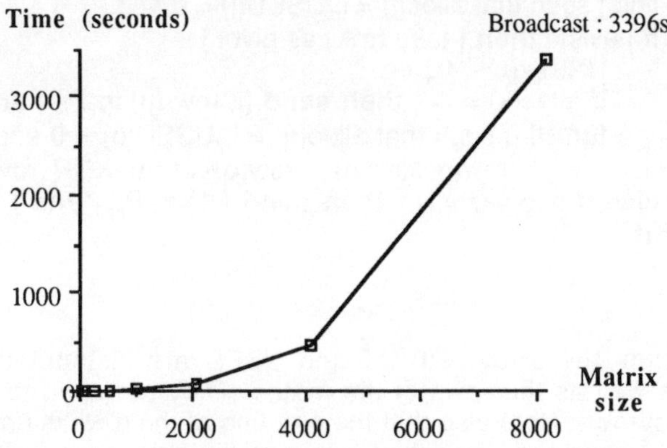

Figure 4.17 : Broadcast algorithm over GF(2), with 16 processors

Let us informally describe step k of the row-oriented pipeline algorithm, where alloc(k)=l and processor indices are taken modulo p:

• P_l searches among its rows for a pivot row, i.e. a row j which has not been previously used as pivot and such that $a_{jk}=1$. Then P_l sends the pivot row or a failure message (if such a row does not exist) to its right-hand neighbour. If P_l has found a pivot row, it performs the elimination step, updates the array containing the pivot indices, and then goes to step k+1.

• P_i, $i \neq l$, receives the message from its left neighbour. If the message contains a pivot row, P_i forwards it to the right neighbour, performs the elimination step and then goes to step k+1. If the message does not contain a pivot row, P_i searches among its rows for a pivot row, sends the pivot row or a failure message (if such a row does not exist) to its right neighbour, performs (if necessary) the elimination step, updates the array containing the pivot indices, and then goes to step k+1. We obtain the following algorithm:

```
Row oriented pipelined ring algorithm over GF(2)
{ program of processor P_i }
for k =1 to n do
    if alloc(k) = i then { pivot processor }
        find j such that alloc(j) = i, USED(j) = 0 and a_jk = 1
        if j exists then { found a pivot }
            PIVOT(k) = j and USED(j) = 1
            send (j, row (j)) to P_i+1
            for all q such that alloc(q) = i, USED (q) = 0 and a_qk = 1 do
                row (q, k+1::n) = row (q,k +1::n) XOR row (j, k+1:: n)
        else send (-1) to P_i+1 { failure message } endif
    else {non pivot }
        receive (PIV, row (PIV)) from P_i-1
        if PIV ≠ -1 then {receiving a pivot }
            if alloc(k) ≠ i+1 then send (PIV, row (PIV)) to P_i+1 endif
            for all q such that alloc(q) = i, USED (q) = 0 and a_ik = 1 do
                row (q, k+1::n) = row (q,k +1::n) XOR row (PIV, k+1:: n)
        else { no pivot found previously }
            find j such that alloc(j) = i, USED(j) = 0 and a_jk = 1
            if j exists then { take row j as pivot }
                USED(j) := 1 ;
                if alloc(k) ≠ i+1 then send (j, row (j)) to P_i+1 endif
                for all q such that alloc(q) = i, USED(q) = 0 and a_qk = 1 do
                    row(q, k+1::n) = row(q,k+1::n) XOR row(j, k+1:: n)
            else if alloc(k) ≠ i+1 then send (-1) to P_i+1 endif
        endif
    endif
endfor
```

In this algorithm, the arrays PIVOT and USED are distributed among the processors as well as the rows of the matrix. They are used to avoid costly interchanges of rows. Note also that the ordering of the rows is unimportant for the algorithm. Hence the distinction between the processor which holds the pivot row and the others is purely artificial. We could choose any processor to initiate the computation, for instance the first one. With this modification, it is not necessary to use a ring: a linear array of processors is sufficient.

The major factor in the communication time arises from the pipelining of the pivot row. The last processor p-1 must wait until it receives the information coming from the first processor. Indeed, the basic operation of each processor is to combine two rows with the same number of non-zero elements in order to introduce a new zero. So the pivot row can be any row of the matrix A with a good configuration (i.e. the right number of zeros before the first non-zero element). Hence instead of waiting to receive the information from its left neighbour each processor could begin the search for a pivot candidate and could use it to eliminate its own rows. Such a candidate, if it exists, will be called a local pivot. However, such a local pivot must be updated using the information coming from the left neighbour. As a consequence, when a processor finds a local pivot, it immediately sends it to its right neighbour so that it can eliminate its own pivot. If the processor does not find a local pivot, it simply transmits the information coming from the left. We obtain the following algorithm:

Local pivot ring algorithm over GF(2)

```
{ program of processor P_i }

if i = 1 { program of first processor } then
    for k =1 to n do
        find j such that alloc(j) = i, USED(j) = 0 and a_jk = 1
        if j exists then { found a pivot }
            PIVOT(k) = j and USED(j) = 1
            send (j, row (j)) to P_i+1
            for all q such that alloc(q) = i, USED (q) = 0 and a_qk = 1 do
                row (q, k+1::n) = row (q,k +1::n) XOR row (j, k+1:: n)
        else send (-1) to P_i+1 { failure message }
        endif
    endfor

else { program of processor P_i, i≠1 }
    for k =1 to n do
        find j such that alloc(j) = i, USED(j) = 0 and a_jk = 1
        if j exists then { found a local pivot }
            PIVOT(k) := j
            if i≠p then send (j, row (j)) to P_i+1 endif
            for all q such that alloc(q) = i, USED (q) = 0 and a_qk = 1 do
                row (q, k+1::n) = row (q,k +1::n) XOR row (j, k+1:: n)
            receive (PIV, row (PIV)) from P_i-1
            if PIV=-1 then { local pivot is final pivot } USED(j) = 1
            else row (j, k+1::n) = row (j,k +1::n) XOR row (PIV, k+1:: n)
            endif
        else
            receive (PIV, row (PIV)) from P_i-1
            if PIV = -1 and i≠p then send (-1) to P_i+1
            if PIV ≠ -1 and i≠p then send (PIV, row (PIV)) to P_i+1
        endif
    endfor
endif
```

Evaluating the execution time of this algorithm is very difficult since it is very data sensitive. See figure 4.18, where we report some experiments for random test matrices. Note that we do not use the VPU, but only the Transputers T414. The (standard) speedup with 16 processors ranges from 12 (matrix size 128) to 19 (matrix size 1024). Such a superlinear speedup is due to the fact that the strategy of local pivoting can be much better than the single pivot strategy, even for a sequential algorithm. More experiments are reported in Cosnard and Robert [1987]. Finally, we note that a systolic counterpart of the local pivot algorithm has been developed: see section 5.4.

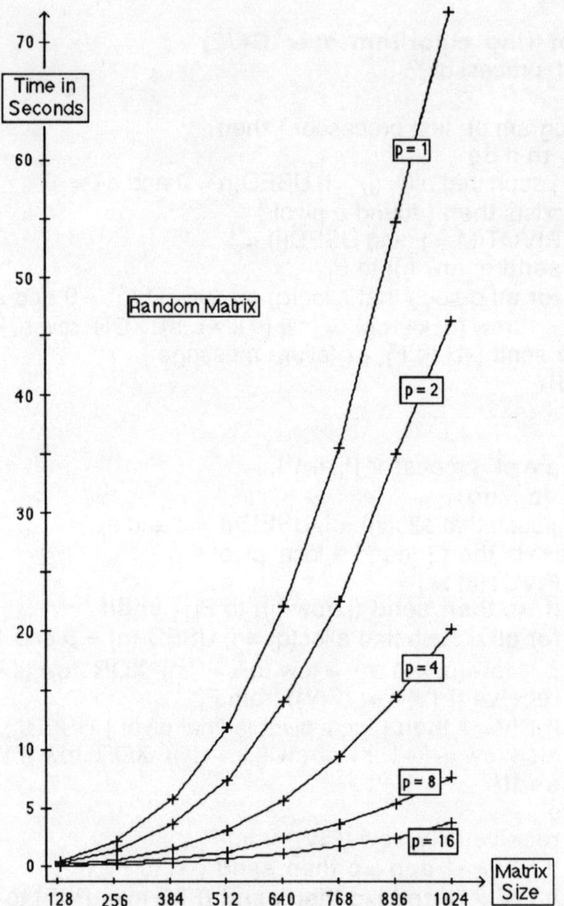

Figure 4.18 : Computation times for a random matrix over CG(2) of order 128 to 1024, with 1 to 16 Transputers

4.7. Bibliographic notes

Data communications in distributed memory machines are surveyed in Saad and Schultz [1989] and chapter 1 of Bertsekas and Tsitsiklis [1989]. See Johnsson and Ho [1989] for a very thorough analysis specialized to hypercubes. The pipelined ring algorithm is introduced in Geist and Heath [1986], Saad [1986b], and Cosnard, Tourancheau and Villard [1988]. See also Ortega and Romine [1988]. Section 4.6 is based on Cosnard and Robert [1987].

CHAPTER

FIVE

SYSTOLIC COMPUTING

In this chapter we present some systolic arrays for Gaussian elimination. We start (section 5.1) with implementations on two-dimensional (2D) arrays, and we include the on-the-fly solution of the triangular system that remains to be solved after triangularization (section 5.2). In section 5.3 we move to 1D linear arrays, and we present a unidirectional modular design parametrized by the storage capacity of the cells. We conclude the chapter (section 5.4) by discussing the systolic counterparts of the algorithms presented in section 4.6 for matrices over finite fields.

5.1. 2D arrays

We first deal in this section with the implementation of Gaussian elimination on two-dimensional (2D) systolic arrays *without pivoting* . See below for a discussion on pivoting issues. Let A x = b (1) be a linear system of equations, where A is a dense square matrix of order n, and b a vector with n components. We consider the matrix A augmented with the right-hand side b, that is, we let A := (A,b) be an n by (n+1) matrix. We recall the basic generic versions presented in section 1.2:

{ column-oriented version: KJI-outside }
for k = 1 **to** n-1 **do**
    execute task T_{kk} : < **for** i = k+1 **to** n **do** $a_{ik} := - a_{ik} / a_{kk}$ >
    for j = k+1 **to** n+1 **do**
        execute task T_{kj} : < **for** i = k+1 **to** n **do** $a_{ij} := a_{ij} + a_{ik} * a_{kj}$ >

{ row-oriented version:[1] KIJ-inside }
for k = 1 **to** n-1 **do**
    for i = k+1 **to** n **do**
        execute task T_{ki} : < $a_{ik} := - a_{ik} / a_{kk}$
                for j = k+1 **to** n+1 **do** $a_{ij} := a_{ij} + a_{ik} * a_{kj}$ >

We use each version as a starting point to retrieve two well-known 2D systolic solutions, those of Ahmed, Delosme and Morf [1982] and Gentleman and Kung [1981].

---

[1] This version is row-oriented rather than column-oriented because we do not want to scale the k-th row at step k, as for the column-oriented KJI-inside version.

5.1.1. A first solution

Assume that a task can be processed within a time unit. We can implement the first version on a linear array of n general-purpose processors, as illustrated in figure 5.1. Column j is input to the top processor at step j. Tasks are assigned to processors as shown by table 5.1.

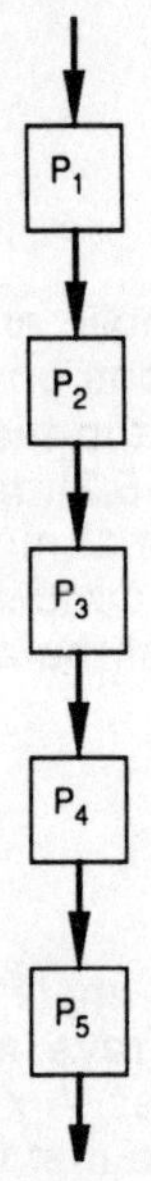

Figure 5.1 : The linear array of macroscopic processors (n=5)

Step	P_1	P_2	P_3	P_4	P_5
1	T_{11}				
2	T_{12}				
3	T_{13}	T_{22}			
4	T_{14}	T_{23}			
5	T_{15}	T_{24}	T_{33}		
6	T_{16}	T_{25}	T_{34}		
7		T_{26}	T_{35}	T_{44}	
8			T_{36}	T_{45}	
9				T_{46}	T_{55}
10					T_{56}

Table 5.1 : Task assignment for the column-oriented version (n=5)

The program of the processors can be detailed as follows:

```
Processor Pi
if step = 2i-1 then
    begin
        receive column i from Pi-1
        execute task Tii
    end
for step := 2i to i+n do
    begin
        receive column j = step - i + 1 from Pi-1
        execute task Tij
        send column j to Pi+1
    end
```

For simplicity, we have assumed that the top processor P_1 receives messages from its predecessor (i.e. the host) and that the bottom processor P_{n-1} sends messages to its successor.

To move to a systolic design, we need to replace each general-purpose processor, capable of operating on column vectors whose length is problem-size dependent, by more simple cells, capable of processing a single coefficient at a time. In other words, we move from a macroscopic time scale, where a unit is a vector-vector operation, to a microscopic time scale, where a unit is an elementary arithmetic operation such as a multiply-add.

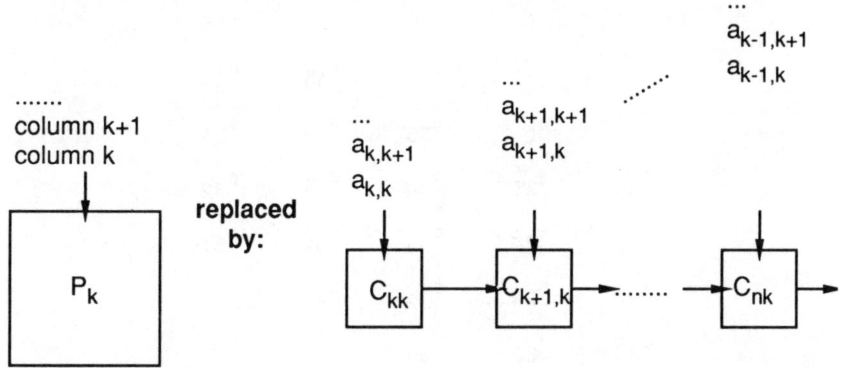

Figure 5.2 : Replacing each processor by an array of elementary cells

We see that P_k operates on vectors of length n-k+1. Thus, we can replace P_k by an array of n-k+1 elementary cells C_{kk}, $C_{k+1,k}$, ..., C_{nk} (see figure 5.2), and pipeline the execution of each task: rather than executing each task serially, we pipeline its execution on the array of cells. For instance with task T_{11}:

for i = 2 **to** n **do** $a_{i1} := a_{i1} / a_{11}$

we obtain the following linear array of n elementary cells:

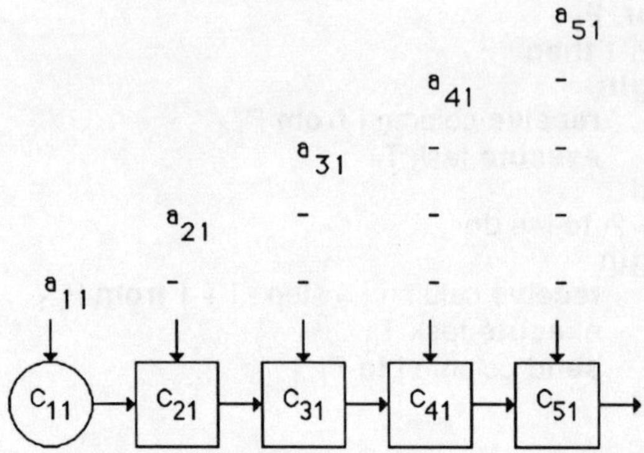

Figure 5.3 : First row of the 2D systolic array (n=5)

Cell C_{11} simply transmits its input a_{11} rightwards at step 1, while cell C_{i1}, $2 \le i \le n$, stores in its internal register the coefficient $a_{ik} \leftarrow a_{ik} / a_{kk}$ at step i.

After task T_{11}, we process tasks T_{1j}, $2 \le j \le n+1$, in a pipeline fashion. Figure 5.4 shows the input format for our linear array of n elementary cells, and table 5.2 summarizes the operation of each cell C_{i1}, $1 \le i \le n$.

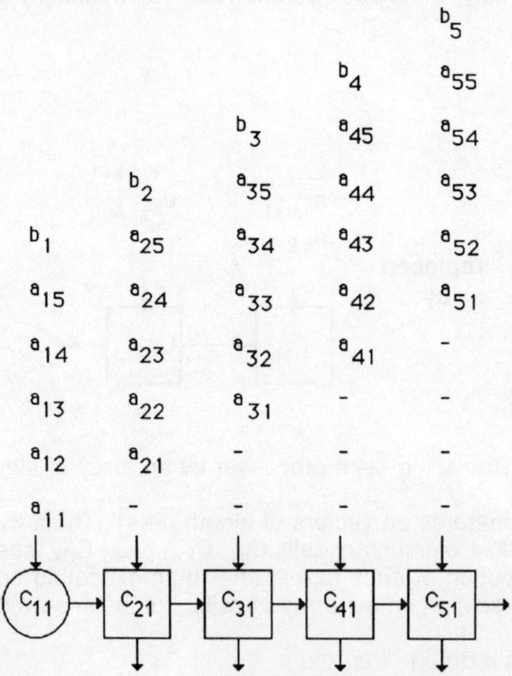

Figure 5.4 : Input to the first row of the 2D systolic array (n=5)

Step	C_{11}	C_{21}	C_{31}	C_{41}	C_{51}
1	transmit a_{11}				
2	transmit a_{12}	$r \leftarrow -\frac{a_{21}}{a_{11}}$			
3	transmit a_{13}	$a_{22} \leftarrow a_{22} + r * a_{12}$	$r \leftarrow -\frac{a_{31}}{a_{11}}$		
4	transmit a_{14}	$a_{23} \leftarrow a_{23} + r * a_{13}$	$a_{32} \leftarrow a_{32} + r * a_{12}$	$r \leftarrow -\frac{a_{41}}{a_{11}}$	
5	transmit a_{15}	$a_{24} \leftarrow a_{24} + r * a_{14}$	$a_{33} \leftarrow a_{33} + r * a_{13}$	$a_{42} \leftarrow a_{42} + r * a_{12}$	$r \leftarrow -\frac{a_{51}}{a_{11}}$
6	transmit $a_{16} = b_1$	$a_{25} \leftarrow a_{25} + r * a_{15}$	$a_{34} \leftarrow a_{34} + r * a_{14}$	$a_{43} \leftarrow a_{43} + r * a_{13}$	$a_{52} \leftarrow a_{52} + r * a_{12}$
7	-	$b_2 \leftarrow b_2 + r * b_1$	$a_{35} \leftarrow a_{35} + r * a_{15}$	$a_{44} \leftarrow a_{44} + r * a_{14}$	$a_{53} \leftarrow a_{53} + r * a_{13}$

Table 5.2 : Operation of the first row (n=5, steps 1 to 7)

Next we pipeline the operation of the macro-processors, i.e. we input to the second row of cells the outputs of the first row of cells as soon as they become available. The whole array is depicted in figure 5.5. It is due to Ahmed, Delosme and Morf [1982].

We make explicit the operation of the cells in figure 5.6. The operation of a given cell depends on whether this is the first time that it operates. In the description of figure 5.6, we assume for simplicity that there is a boolean called *init* (for "initialization") stored in every processor which is set to "true" at the beginning of the computation. This boolean controls the operation of the processors. In an actual implementation, the instruction to start the computation would be input to the leftmost circular processor together with the first coefficient a_{11} and systolically propagated through the whole array (we explain such a control in the next section).

5.1.2. A second solution

We can re-do the same construction starting from the second version, KIJ inside. Assume first that a task can be processed within a time unit. We can implement this version on a linear array of n general-purpose processors, similar to that of figure 5.1. Row j is input to the top processor at step j. Tasks are assigned to processors as shown by table 5.3. Note that the tasks are now combinations of rows rather than columns.

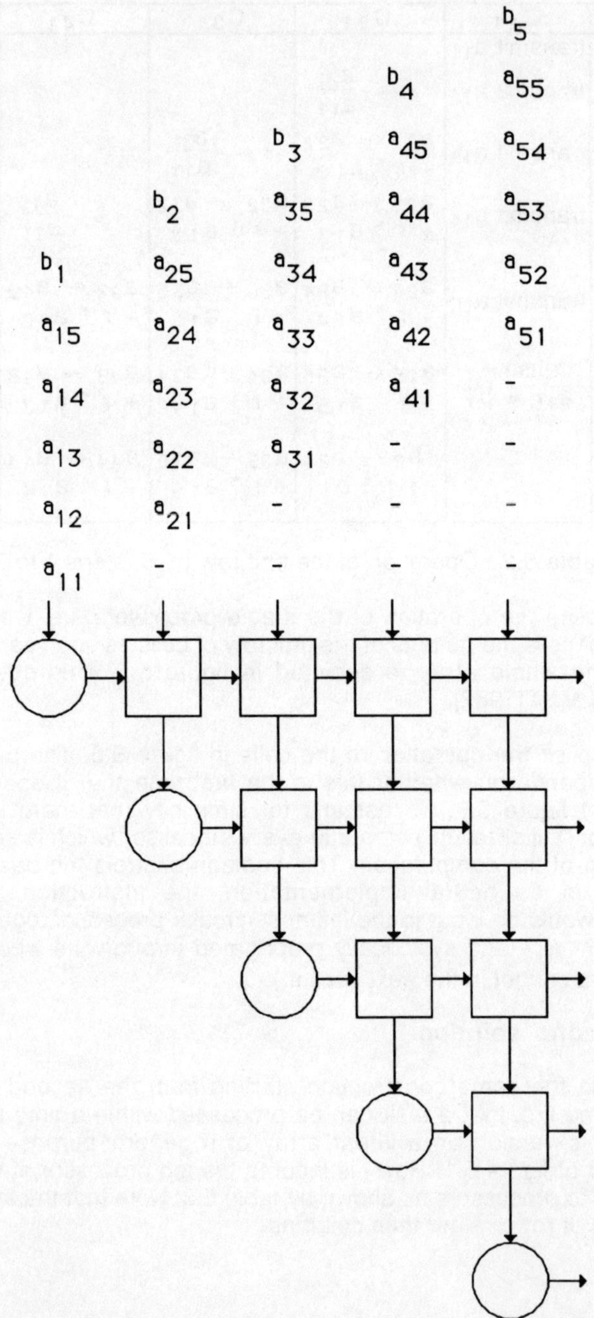

Figure 5.5 : The Ahmed-Delosme-Morf array (n=5)

a_{in} a_{out}

Step t Step t+1

{ transfer data }
$a_{out} := a_{in}$;

a_{in} b_{in} b_{out} a_{out}

Step t Step t+1

if init **then** { initialize internal register }
begin $r := - a_{in} / b_{in}$; init := false ; $b_{out} := b_{in}$; **end**
else { update a_{in} }
begin $a_{out} := a_{in} + r * b_{in}$; $b_{out} := b_{in}$; **end**

Figure 5.6. : Program of the cells

Step	P_1	P_2	P_3	P_4
1	row 1			
2	T_{12}			
3	T_{13}	row 2		
4	T_{14}	T_{23}		
5	T_{15}	T_{24}	row 3	
6		T_{25}	T_{34}	
7			T_{35}	row 4
8				T_{45}

Table 5.3 : Task assignment for the row-oriented version (n=5)

Next, we replace each general-purpose processor P_k, which operates on row vectors of length n-k+2, by an array of n-k+2 elementary cells $C_{kk}, C_{k,k+1}, ..., C_{kn}, C_{k,n+1}$, and we pipeline the execution of each task. For instance with task T_{12}:

$a_{21} := - a_{21} / a_{11}$
for j = 2 **to** n+1 **do** $a_{2j} := a_{2j} + a_{21} * a_{1j}$

we obtain the following linear array of n+1 elementary cells:

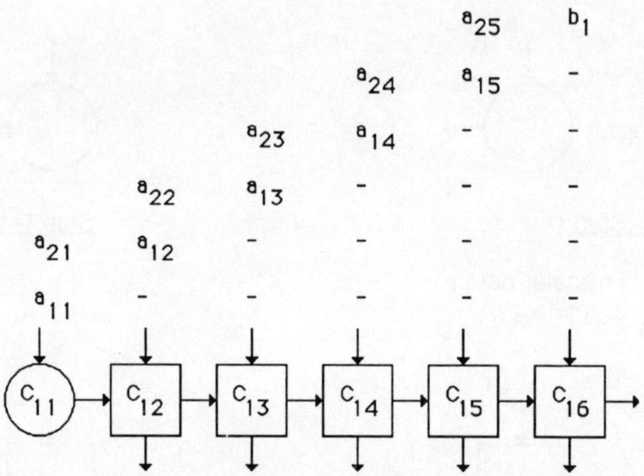

Figure 5.7 : First row of the second 2D systolic array (n=5)

Cell C_{11} stores its first input a_{11} in its internal register r, and propagates rightwards $a_{21} \leftarrow - a_{21} / a_{11}$ at step 2. Cell C_{1j}, $2 \le j \le n+1$, stores its first input a_{1j} in its internal register at step j, and updates $a_{2j} \leftarrow a_{2j} + a_{21} * r$ at step j+1.

After task T_{12}, we process tasks T_{1i}, $2 \le i \le n$, in a pipeline fashion. Next we pipeline the operation of the linear arrays of cells. The whole systolic array is depicted in figure 5.8. It is due to Gentleman and Kung [1981]. Table 5.4 summarizes the operation of the first row of the array. We explain the operation of the cells in figure 5.9.

Step	C_{11}	C_{12}	C_{13}	C_{14}	C_{15}	C_{16}
1	$r \leftarrow a_{11}$					
2	$a_{21} \leftarrow -\frac{a_{21}}{a_{11}}$	$r \leftarrow a_{12}$				
3	$a_{31} \leftarrow -\frac{a_{31}}{a_{11}}$	$a_{22} \leftarrow a_{22} + a_{21} * r$	$r \leftarrow a_{13}$			
4	$a_{41} \leftarrow -\frac{a_{41}}{a_{11}}$	$a_{32} \leftarrow a_{32} + a_{31} * r$	$a_{23} \leftarrow a_{23} + a_{21} * r$	$r \leftarrow a_{14}$		
5	$a_{51} \leftarrow -\frac{a_{51}}{a_{11}}$	$a_{42} \leftarrow a_{42} + a_{41} * r$	$a_{33} \leftarrow a_{33} + a_{31} * r$	$a_{24} \leftarrow a_{24} + a_{21} * r$	$r \leftarrow a_{15}$	
6	-	$a_{52} \leftarrow a_{52} + a_{51} * r$	$a_{43} \leftarrow a_{43} + a_{41} * r$	$a_{34} \leftarrow a_{34} + a_{31} * r$	$a_{25} \leftarrow a_{25} + a_{21} * r$	$r \leftarrow b_1$
7	-	-	$a_{53} \leftarrow a_{53} + a_{51} * r$	$a_{44} \leftarrow a_{44} + a_{41} * r$	$a_{35} \leftarrow a_{35} + a_{31} * r$	$b_2 \leftarrow b_2 + a_{21} * r$

Table 5.4 : Operation of the first row (second solution, n=5, steps 1 to 7)

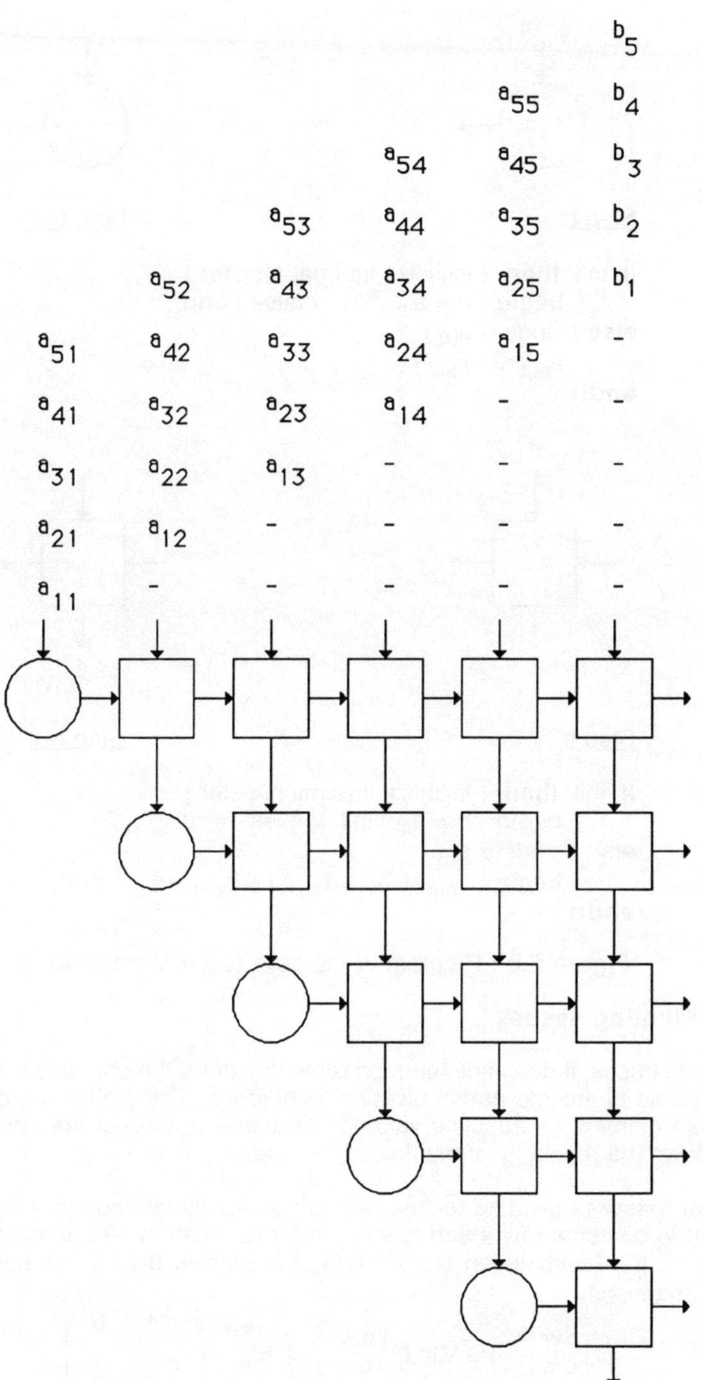

Figure 5.8 : The Gentleman-Kung array (n=5)

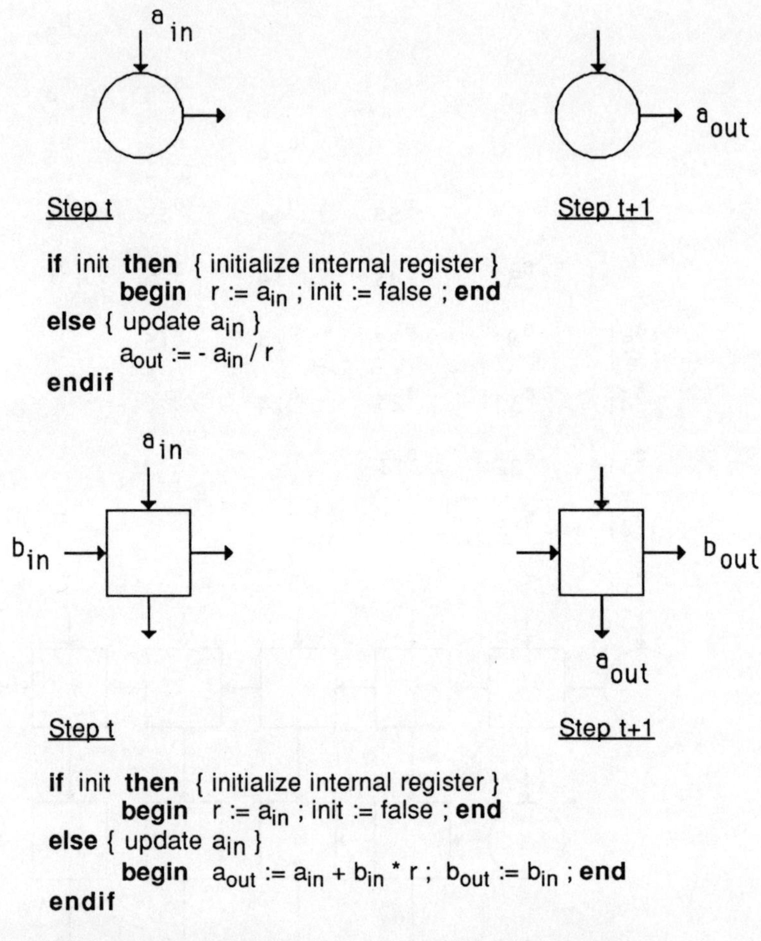

Figure 5.9 : Program of the cells (second solution)

5.1.3. Pivoting issues

For real matrices, it does not seem possible to extend the previous two systolic arrays so as to include partial pivoting techniques. The global search for the maximum element (in absolute value) in an entire column of the matrix would break down the regularity of the flow in the array.

However, pairwise pivoting techniques can be easily introduced: assume that we want to combine row k and row i in order to create a zero in position (k,i), $k+1 \leq i \leq n$. If the combination factor $|a_{ik}/a_{kk}|$ is smaller than 1, we perform the usual combination:

$$\begin{pmatrix} \text{row } k \\ \text{row } i \end{pmatrix} := M_{ik} \cdot \begin{pmatrix} \text{row } k \\ \text{row } i \end{pmatrix}, \quad M_{ik} := \begin{pmatrix} 1 & 0 \\ -\dfrac{a_{ik}}{a_{kk}} & 1 \end{pmatrix}$$

Otherwise we exchange row k and row i before performing the combination, which amounts to the following:

$$\begin{pmatrix} \text{row } k \\ \text{row } i \end{pmatrix} := M_{ik} \cdot \begin{pmatrix} \text{row } k \\ \text{row } i \end{pmatrix},\ M_{ik} := \begin{pmatrix} 1 & -\frac{a_{kk}}{a_{ik}} \\ 1 & 0 \end{pmatrix}$$

a_{in} (Step t) → a_{out} (Step t+1)

{ transfer data }
$a_{out} := a_{in}$;

a_{in}, b_{in} (Step t) → b_{out}, a_{out} (Step t+1)

```
if init then { generate combination and initialize internal register }
    begin
        if |a_in| ≤ |b_in| then { no permutation}
                begin no_perm := true ; r := - a_in / b_in ; b_out := b_in ; end
        else { permute rows }
                begin no_perm := false ; r := - b_in / a_in ; b_out := a_in ; end
        init := false
    end
else { apply combination ; update a_in or b_in according to no_perm}
    begin
        if no_perm then { no permutation}
                begin a_out := a_in + r * b_in ; b_out := b_in ; end
        else
                begin a_out := b_in + r * a_in ; b_out := a_in ; end
    end
```

Figure 5.10. : Program of the cells with pairwise pivoting

In this way, we generate a combination factor whose module is always smaller than 1. Sorensen [1984] has shown that this method is numerically stable for a wide class of matrices. We show in figure 5.10 how to modify the program of the cells of the Ahmed-Delosme-Morf array in order to include pairwise pivoting techniques. The first time they operate, rectangular cells determine which combination is to be generated according to the values of their inputs, that is, whether the corresponding two rows should be interchanged or not. After initialization, they apply the transformation (whose encoding is) stored in their internal register. The additional information costs only one bit (boolean *no_perm*). Of course a similar modification can be made for the Gentleman-Kung array.

5.1.4. Performance comparison

At first sight, the two 2D systolic arrays look very similar. Both are triangular arrays composed of two kinds of cells, with a special cell at the beginning of each row and the other cells of the row performing multiply-add operations. To triangularize a matrix of size n x (n+1) we need the same number of time steps and approximately the same number of cells:

Array	Time steps	Cells
Ahmed-Delosme-Morf	3n-1	$\frac{n\,(n+1)}{2}$
Gentleman-Kung	3n-1	$\frac{n\,(n+3)}{2}$

There is an important difference, however, between the two arrays, which makes them *dual* in some sense. In the Ahmed-Delosme-Morf array, the coefficients a_{ij} of the matrix A move through the array, while the (encoding of the) combination matrices M_{ik} stay in place in the rectangular cells. On the contrary in the Gentleman-Kung array, the coefficients a_{ij} of the matrix A are stored in the cells while the (encoding of the) combination matrices M_{ik} move through the array once computed by a given circular cell. This difference is very important if we want to solve the resulting triangular system at the end of the computation: see next section.

5.2. Solving the triangular system on the fly

Contrarily to the preceding two chapters, we devote a section to the solution of the upper triangular system that remains to be solved after triangularization. Even though the triangular system solution process costs only $O(n^2)$ arithmetic operations, as opposed to the $O(n^3)$ operations for the Gaussian elimination process, we implement both processes in linear time with systolic arrays. Also, communication costs have such a tremendous importance in a massively parallel environment that we could lose the benefits of the separate parallelization of each process without a careful chaining between them.

5.2.1. Unloading the array

First we concentrate on the Gentleman-Kung array. The triangularization phase transforms the system A x = b (1) into the upper triangular system U x = c (2). After execution of the algorithm, the matrix (U,c) is stored in the array as follows (assuming n=5):

u_{11}	u_{12}	u_{13}	u_{14}	u_{15}	c_1
	u_{22}	u_{23}	u_{24}	u_{25}	c_2
		u_{33}	u_{34}	u_{35}	c_3
			u_{44}	u_{45}	c_4
				u_{55}	c_5

According to the general philosophy of the systolic model, unloading the array must be done systolically, by propagating special boolean control instructions, because only boundary cells can communicate with the host. Moreover, we would like to pipeline the unloading of the array with the computation phase, so that n additional steps are not necessary. Various schemes are possible. We outline a scheme where each processor sends the content of its internal register to the right when it has finished operating. Let $u_{i,n+1} = c_i$, $1 \le i \le n$, for convenience.

At time t=5 in our example, C_{11} operates for the last time. At time t=6, it sends u_{11} rightwards. C_{12} finishes to work at time t=6. It transmits u_{11} to the right at t=7, and then sends u_{12} at time t=8. The process goes on, and u_{1i} is output by C_{16} at time t=10+i , for $1 \le i \le n+1$. Similarly, we start unloading the second row at time t=8. We see that the first rows of the array are unloaded, while the last rows still operate, thus achieving the pipelining that is sought. Indeed, in the general case, the last computation occurs in $C_{n,n+1}$ at time 3n-1, and u_{ki} ($1 \le k \le n$, $k \le i \le n+1$) is output from the array at time 2n+i. The total computation time is 3n+1.

There remains the triangular system U x = c (2) to be solved. We can use another systolic array, the triangular system solver of Kung and Leiserson [1980], which requires 2n time steps to solve a triangular system of size n. However, this would require the triangular matrix to be stored in the host and reordered by diagonals before being fed in the Kung and Leiserson array. Rather, it is more efficient to use the Jordan elimination scheme: this scheme can be implemented on the same array, and requires only n additional steps to provide the solution x, leading to a very efficient scheme of only n(n+3)/2 cells and 4n-1 time steps to completely solve the system A x = b.

5.2.2. The Jordan elimination scheme

The idea is to directly transform the system U x = c (2) into a diagonal one. At the end of the triangularization phase, rather than unloading the array, we start another computational phase, which we term the resolution phase. The sequential algorithm is as follows:

```
for k = 1 to n do
   { normalize row k }
   for j = k+1 to n+1 do ukj := ukj / ukk
   for i = k+1 to n do
       begin
          { add a multiple of row i to row k to create a 0 in position (k,i) }
          uki := - uki / uii
          for j = i+1 to n+1 do ukj := ukj + uki * uij
       end
   { now row k = (0, ..., 0, 1, 0,..., 0, ck) }
endfor
```

When a diagonal cell C_{kk} receives the input control *norm* (for "normalize"), it sends its internal register u_{kk} rightwards with the same control. As $C_{k,k+1}$, ..., $C_{k,n+1}$ receive u_{kk}, they divide their internal register by u_{kk}, before sending the normalized value of their register downwards, for the elimination process. Note that the Jordan elimination process is exactly the same as the triangularization operation, so that the cells have the same program for the two phases.

The extended array is depicted in figure 5.11. Data coefficients and control instructions are input to the array and move systolically, until the solution vector is output by cell $C_{n,n+1}$. The triangularization phase is pipelined with the resolution phase, and the last component of the solution vector x is delivered after 4n-1 time steps. The operation of the processors is described in figure 5.12.

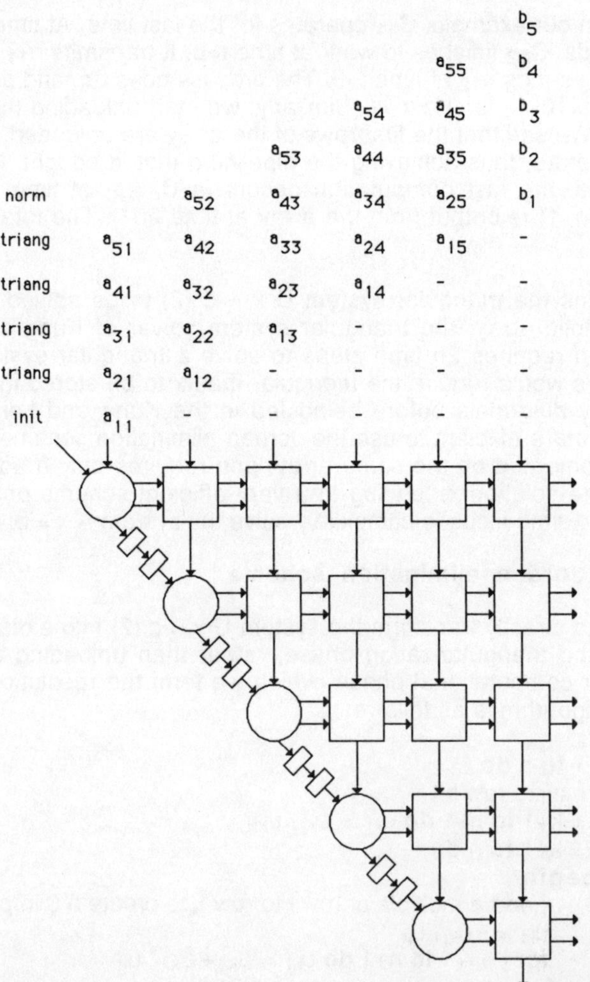

Figure 5.11 : Direct solution of the system A x = b (n = 5)

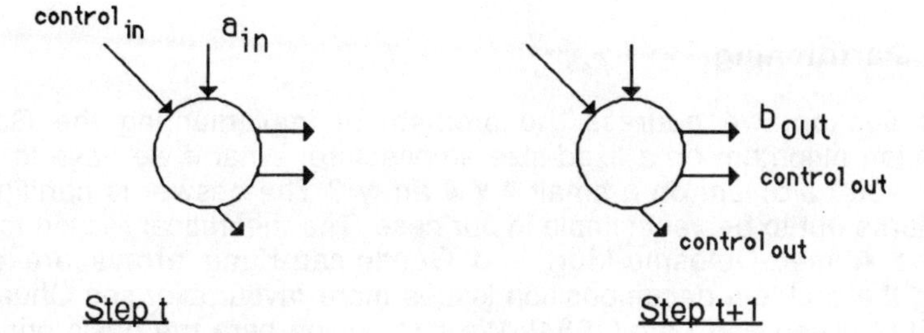

$control_{in}$ a_{in}

b_{out} $control_{out}$

$control_{out}$

Step t Step t+1

case $control_{in}$ **of**
init : { store a_{in} } $r := a_{in}$;
triang : { scale a_{in} } $a_{out} := - a_{in} / r$;
norm : { transmit register } $a_{out} := r$;
endcase
$control_{out} := control_{in}$;

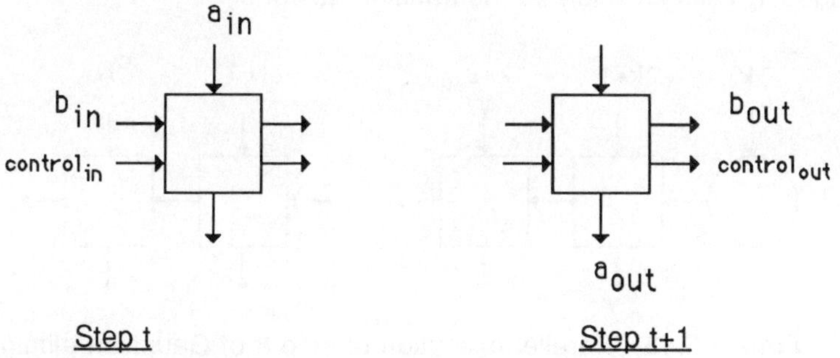

a_{in}

b_{in} $control_{in}$

b_{out} $control_{out}$

a_{out}

Step t Step t+1

case $control_{in}$ **of**
init : { store a_{in} } $r := a_{in}$;
triang : { update a_{in} } **begin** $a_{out} := a_{in} + b_{in} * r$; $b_{out} := b_{in}$; **end**
norm : { normalize } **begin** $a_{out} := r / b_{in}$; $b_{out} := b_{in}$; **end**
endcase
$control_{out} := control_{in}$;

Figure 5.12 : Solving A x = b - operation of the processors

Note that the array can be straightforwardly extended to the case where there are q systems $A x_i = b_i$ to solve, $1 \le i \le q$: this will require n(n+1)/2+qn cells and 4n+q-2 time steps. However, for large values of q, it is more efficient to use an extension of the Ahmed-Delosme-Morf array, which implements the Gauss-Jordan diagonalization algorithm: see Robert and Tchuente [1985], Comon and Robert [1987]. This array has n(n+1) cells and requires the same number of time steps, which makes it more interesting if q > (n+1)/2 (and in particular if q = n, the case of matrix inversion). On the other hand, it does not seem possible to re-use the Ahmed-Delosme-Morf array as such (i.e. without adding cells) for solving the linear system on the fly: this is because the combination matrices are stored in the cells, and we would need to generate n(n-1) such matrices, thereby requiring as many cells.

5.2.3. Partitioning

In this section, we address the problem of implementing the Gaussian elimination algorithm on a fixed-size architecture. What if we have to solve a 1000 x 1000 problem on a small 4 x 4 array ? The answer is partitioning ... and it turns out to be very simple in our case. The theoretical reason for this is that the Ahmed-Delosme-Morf and Gentleman-Kung arrays are acyclic, making the problem decomposition issues more favourable: see Chuang and He [1984], Kung and Lam [1984]. We just outline here the basic principle of the approach.

Let A be an N x N matrix, and let c_1, c_2, ..., c_i, ..., c_N be its columns. At step k of the Gaussian elimination process, we only consider the last N-k+1 columns of A. First we scale column k for generating the combination factors, then we update the trailing columns. For a fully parallel processing of step k, we need

- one (circular cell) for generating the combination factors
- n-k (square) cells for applying the transformation:

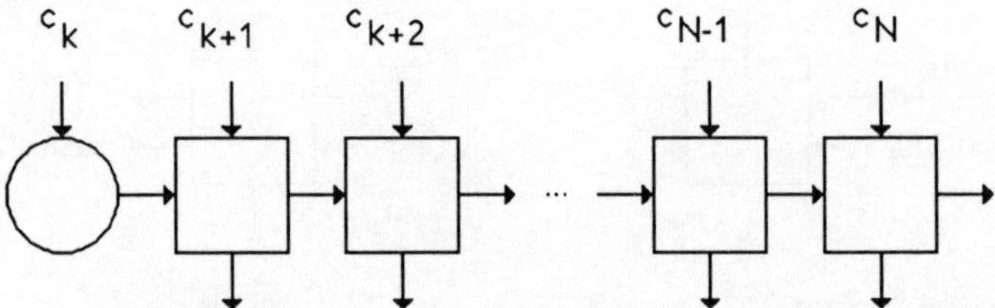

Figure 5.13 : Parallel execution of step k of Gaussian elimination

This is exactly the k-th row of the Gentleman-Kung array ! On the other hand, if we can only afford two cells, a circular and a square one, we need to process the trailing columns sequentially. Hence we need to store in temporary buffers the instructions generated by the circular cell in order to input them as many times as necessary to the square cell:

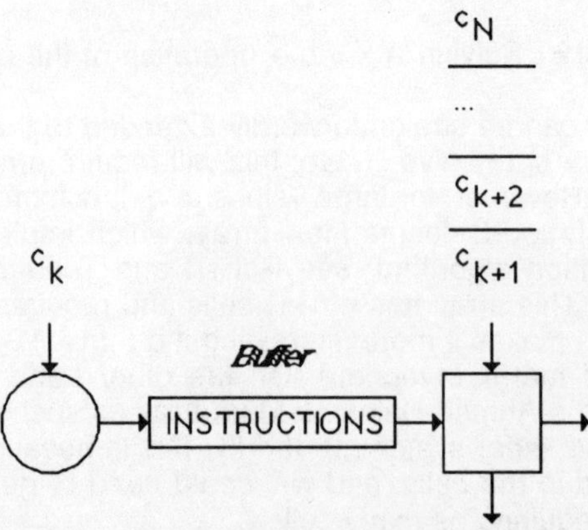

Figure 5.14 : Sequential execution of step k of Gaussian elimination

After the end of step k, the two cells can be re-used for step k+1. Of course such a processing is not very efficient, but the key idea is there: if we replace the two cells by two r x r systolic arrays, we gain a factor r^2 on the sequential execution time. Assume that N is divisible by r without loss of generality: N = r n. We partition A into n blocks C_1, C_2, ..., C_n of r consecutive columns : C_k is composed of columns (k-1)r+1 to kr. The first (triangular) r x r systolic array T plays the part of the circular processor: it generates the instructions relative to the processing of block C_k. These instructions, stored in a buffer, are sent to the second (square) systolic array for the processing of the next blocks.

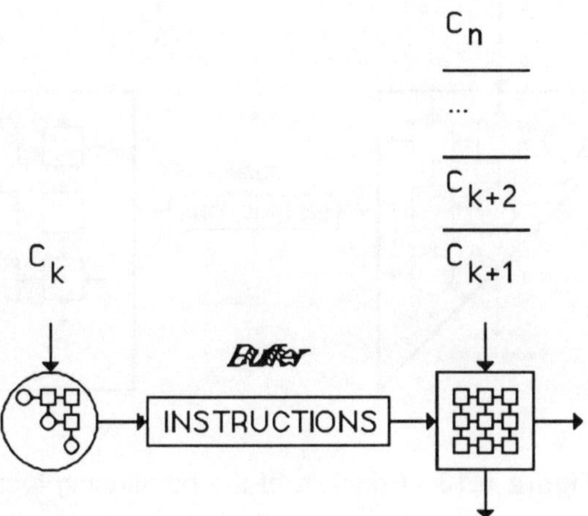

Figure 5.15 : The two r x r systolic arrays for step k

For the sake of completeness, we outline the interface between the host and the two systolic arrays in figure 5.16.

5.3. 1D arrays

In this section we present a unidimensional systolic array for LU decomposition (we do not deal with the right-hand side). Linear configurations have several advantages for a hardware realization (see Annaratone et al. [1987] concerning the Warp design):

• they are easy to implement
• it is easy to extend the number of cells in the array (modularity)
• a linear array has modest I/O requirements since only the two end-cells communicate with the outside world.

In this section, we show that we can efficiently map the Gaussian elimination algorithm onto a linear array of cells. As required by the systolic design principles, each cell must have a fixed storage capacity, making the array completely modular, and problem-size independent.

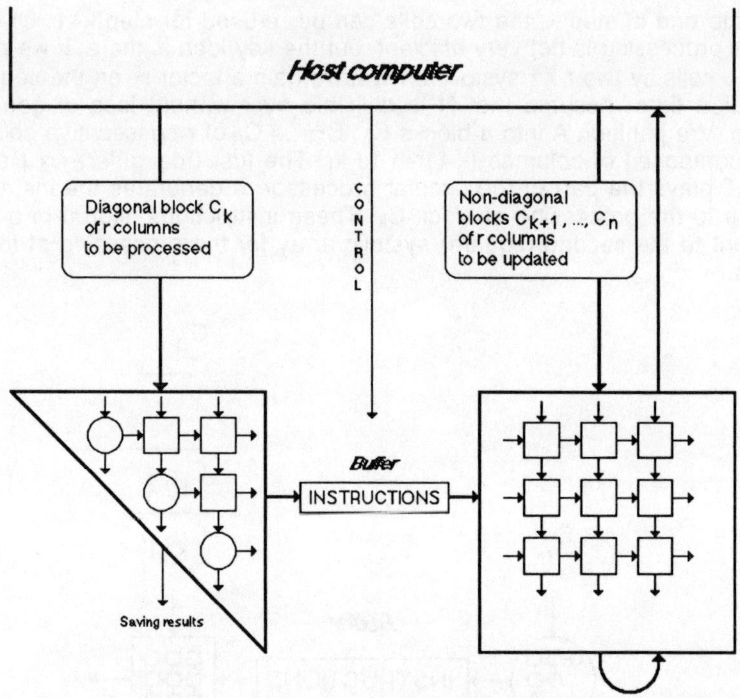

Figure 5.16 : Principle of the partitioning technique

We design a linear array composed of identical cells. All the input coefficients of the matrix A to be triangularized are read on the same input channel. All the data in the array flows in the same direction, say from left to right. Each cell has an addressable memory, and its operation is controlled by boolean signals which are systolically propagated from cell to cell. In the following, we assume that each cell is capable of storing x words, where x is a parameter of the design. The modularity of the array permits us to solve larger problems only by using more cells, without any modification in the design and/or in the programming of the cells.

For any integer x, $1 \le x \le n-1$, we design a linear array of S cells which solves a problem of size n within T time steps, where

$$S = \frac{n^2}{2x} + O(n) \qquad \text{and} \qquad T = n^2\left(1+\frac{1}{2x}\right) + O(n)$$

5.3.1. Overall description of the array

As shown in figure 5.17, the linear array is decomposed into n-1 slices. Slice k is devoted to the execution of step k of the Gaussian elimination algorithm. The matrix A is fed column by column into the leftmost cell of the array.

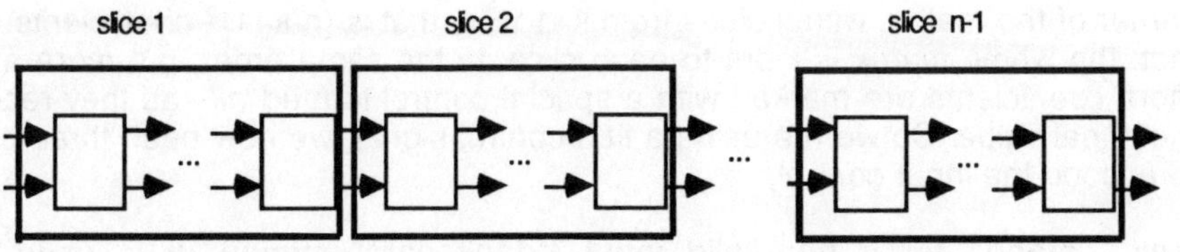

Figure 5.17 : Overall organization of the linear array

The input format is illustrated in figure 5.18. More precisely, we represent in figure 5.18 the input data for slice k of the array. We see that each coefficient is input together with a control signal, which will be used to determine the operation that the cells of slice k will perform.

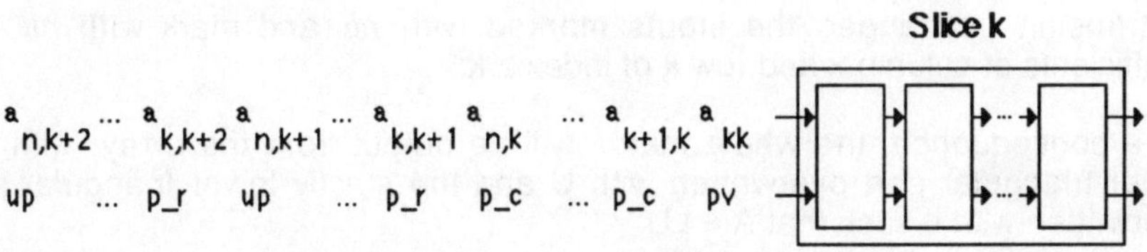

Figure 5.18 : Input data for slice k

There are four control signals:

- *pv* stands for "pivot", and is used to identify the pivot element at step k, i.e. the coefficient a_{kk}
- *p_c* stands for "pivot column", and is used to identify the pivot column at step k, i.e. the coefficients $a_{k+1,k}, a_{k+2,k}, \ldots, a_{n,k}$
- *p_r* stands for "pivot row", and is used to identify the pivot row at step k, i.e. the coefficients $a_{k,k+1}, a_{k,k+2}, \ldots, a_{k,n}$
- *up* stands for "to be updated", and is used to identify the elements of the lower right corner of the matrix that will be updated at step k, i.e. the elements whose row and column indices range from k+1 to n

Since the matrix is input column by column, the input control sequence for slice 1 is *pv* followed by n-k *p_c* , and then n-k times the sequence (*p_r* followed by n-k *up*).

The operation of slice k of the array will be the following:
a) receive the input data together with its control (row k and column k are marked according to the previous description)
b) compute the elimination factors:

for i := k+1 to n **do** $a_{ik} := - a_{ik} / a_{kk}$

c) update the lower right corner of the matrix:

for j := k+1 to n **do**

  for i := k+1 to n **do** $a_{ij} := a_{ij} + a_{ik} * a_{kj}$

d) output updated coefficients a_{ij}, $k+1 \leq i,j \leq n$, and generate new control signals: row k+1 and column k+1 should be marked for the next step.

The first slice of the array receives the whole matrix, with the corresponding controls. According to figure 5.18, slice k would only receive the lower right corner of the matrix, with indices from k+1 to n, that is $(n-k+1)^2$ coefficients. In fact, the whole matrix is input to each slice, in the same order, but more and more coefficients are marked with a special control termed *nil* , as they reach their final value. So we are using a fifth control signal (we now need three bits to encode the input control):

- *nil* stands for a non-valid input ("don't care" signal). It is used to propagate coefficients which are no longer modified through the array

More precisely, all the coefficients a_{ij}, $1 \leq i,j \leq k-1$, are input to slice k with the control *nil* . In turn, when output from slice k, the coefficients of the pivot column a_{ik}, $k+1 \leq i \leq n$ and of the pivot row a_{kj}, $k+2 \leq j \leq n$ should also have been marked to the control *nil*. So we add the following specification for the operation of slice k:
e) transmit unchanged the inputs marked with *nil*, and mark with *nil* the coefficients of column k and row k of index $\geq$ k.

As a consequence, the whole matrix will be output from the array, with the upper triangular part overwritten with U and the strictly lower triangular part overwritten with L such that A = LU.

5.3.2. A simple but non-modular solution: the case x=n-1

For the sake of the exposition, we first present a non-modular solution, where we assume that the memory inside the elementary cells is not bounded and can depend upon the problem size. For a problem of size n, this amounts to assuming that $x \geq n-1$. In this case, each slice is reduced to a single cell, so that the array is composed of n-1 identical cells. Cell k is devoted to step k of the Gaussian elimination algorithm.

The operation of a cell, say cell k, is given in figure 5.19. It is controlled by the input control signals *pv* , *p_c* , *p_r, up* and *nil* which are received together with the input coefficients. There are also two internal control signals, named *count* and *next* , which are used to generate the output control signals. The operation is as follows:
(i) the first valid input of cell k is the pivot a_{kk} (control *pv*). The pivot is stored in the internal register *R* and we reset the pointer to the addressable register (*adr := 1* in the program)
(ii) then cell k receives n-k coefficients of the pivot column (control *p_c*). Each time such a coefficient a_{ik} is input, we store the value $-a_{ik}/a_{kk} = -a_{ik}/R$ in the addressable register, and we increment the address pointer. At the end, register[adr] contains the value $-a_{ik}/a_{kk}$, where i = k + adr, for adr=1 to n-k
(iii) now cell k successively receives the next columns of the matrix, whose first element is a coefficient of the pivot row (control *p_r*), and the n-k following ones are to be updated (control *up*). For the processing of column k+1, when cell k receives $a_{k,k+1}$, it stores it in the register *R* , and resets the pointer to 1. Then, it updates the coefficients $a_{i,k+1}$, $i \geq k+1$, into

$$a_{i,k+1} + (-a_{ik}/a_{kk}) * a_{k,k+1} = a_{i,k+1} + \text{register[adr]} * R$$

We check that *adr* has the right value, because it is incremented exactly as in step (ii). The processing is the same for the next columns.

The lower right corner of the matrix is thus updated according to step k of the elimination algorithm. We still need to generate the control signals for cell k+1.

First of all, if we have $control_{in} \in \{pv, p\_r, p\_c\}$, the corresponding coefficient must be output with the control *nil* , because column k and row k are no longer used in the array. Next we have to mark the elements of column k+1 and row k+1 with the right controls. This is done using the two internal control signals *count* and *next* :
- to identify the new pivot column, we see that it is composed of the elements between the first and second inputs marked *p_r* (elements $a_{k,k+1}$ and $a_{k,k+2}$). The action of the internal control *count* is as follows: *count* is set to 0 by the pivot element. The first and second inputs marked *p_r* increment it by one. So *count* $\in$ *{0, 1, 2}*, and it can be encoded using only two bits.
- to identify the new pivot row, we see that it is composed of the elements immediately following an element marked *p_r* . The internal boolean *next* is reset to true by every input marked *p_r* , and its value is changed by the next input.

We can summarize the control generation as follows:

- if $control_{in} \in$ {pv, p_r or p_c} , coefficients are output with $control_{out}$ set to nil
- if $control_{in}$ = update, then
  - $control_{out}$ is set to pivot if count = 1 and next = true,
  - $control_{out}$ is set to piv_col if count = 1 and next = false,
  - $control_{out}$ is set to piv_row if count = 2 and next = true,
  - $control_{out}$ is set to update if count = 2 and next = false.

We are now ready to understand the program of figure 5.19.

We can prove by induction on n that the array performs the elimination. For example, assume that a_{11} is input to the first cell at time t=0. The output data of the first cell is the following:

<u>invalid outputs for cell 2</u>

$a_{out}(t) = a_{i1}$, $control_{out}(t)$ = nil,	at time $t = i$, $1 \le i \le n$
$a_{out}(t) = a_{1j}$, $control_{out}(t)$ = nil,	at time $t = (j-1)n+1$, $2 \le j \le n$

<u>valid outputs for cell 2</u>

$a_{out}(t) = a_{22}$, $control_{out}(t)$ = pivot,	at time $t = n+2$,
$a_{out}(t) = a_{i2}$, $control_{out}(t)$ = piv_col,	at time $t = n+i$, $3 \le i \le n$
$a_{out}(t) = a_{2j}$, $control_{out}(t)$ = piv_row,	at time $t = (j-1)n + 2$,
$a_{out}(t) = a_{ij}$, $control_{out}(t)$ = update,	at time $t = (j-1)n + i$, $3 \le i,j \le n$

The input data of cell 2 is identical to the input of cell 1 but corresponds to a matrix of size n-1. Valid inputs for cell 2 are interleaved with invalid inputs (for which $control_{in}$ = *nil*), but invalid inputs have no influence on the operation of the cells. As a result, this shows the correctness of the algorithm.

The performance of the array is very easy to derive: we have n-1 cells and n^2 input coefficients, so that we output the LU decomposition within $T = n^2 + n - 1$ steps.

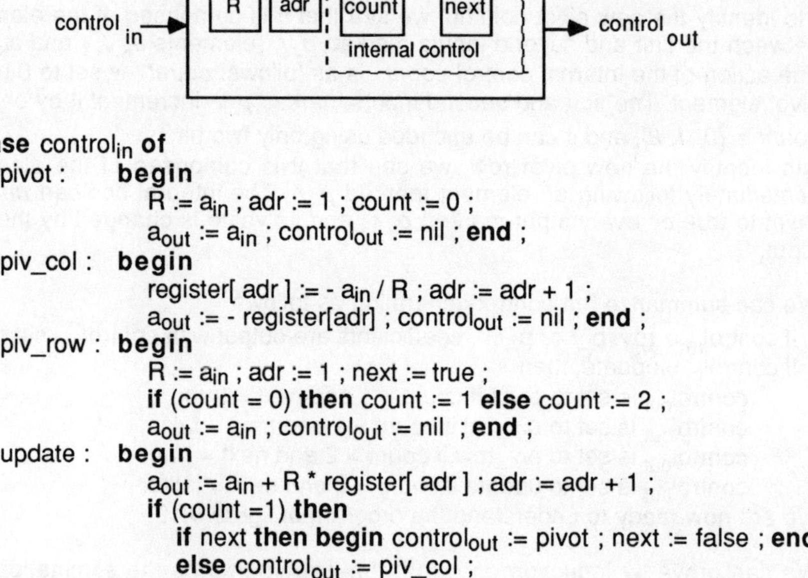


```
case control_in of
   pivot :    begin
                 R := a_in ; adr := 1 ; count := 0 ;
                 a_out := a_in ; control_out := nil ; end ;
   piv_col :  begin
                 register[ adr ] := - a_in / R ; adr := adr + 1 ;
                 a_out := - register[adr] ; control_out := nil ; end ;
   piv_row :  begin
                 R := a_in ; adr := 1 ; next := true ;
                 if (count = 0) then count := 1 else count := 2 ;
                 a_out := a_in ; control_out := nil  ; end ;
   update :   begin
                 a_out := a_in + R * register[ adr ] ; adr := adr + 1 ;
                 if (count =1) then
                    if next then begin control_out := pivot ; next := false ; end
                    else control_out := piv_col ;
                 if (count =2) then
                    if next then
                       begin control_out := piv_row; next := false; end
                    else control_out := update ; end
   nil :      begin
                  a_out := a_in ; control_out := nil ; end ;
endcase
```

Figure 5.19 : Operation of the cells (non-modular solution, $x \geq n-1$)

5.3.3. A modular solution

We move to a modular solution. Now each cell has a fixed amount of memory, whose value is a design parameter x, independent of the problem size n. The idea is to emulate the k-th cell of the previous array, which requires n-k storage words, by a slice of $s(k) = \lceil \frac{n-k}{x} \rceil$ cells of memory x. These s(k) cells will compose the k-th slice of the array mentioned in figure 5.17, and will be responsible for the execution of the k-th step of the algorithm.

The modular array operates very similarly to the non-modular one. But because of the modularity constraint, we cannot simply replace each cell k of the previous solution by the right number s(k) of bounded memory cells. On the contrary, we have to determine on the fly, during the execution, the number of cells in each slice. There is no knowledge *a priori* of the first and last cell in each slice, since this depends on the problem size n, and we aim at designing a solution independent of the problem size.

Let us first describe the implementation informally. When the first cell C_{k1} of slice k receives the pivot a_{kk}, it stores it in its R-register as before. When it receives the first x coefficients of the pivot column, marked *p_c* , it stores the corresponding elimination factors in its x-register. But once the register is full (this happens if n-k > x), coefficients marked *p_c* should move on to the next cell C_{k2}. They will have to be divided by the pivot in C_{k2}, which implies that a_{kk} should have been previously stored in the R-register of C_{k2}. We deduce the rule that the pivot must be propagated unchanged while travelling through slice k, and stored in the R-register of all the cells of the slice.

We can introduce a boolean flag that tells us whether the x register of the cell is full. Let *full_cell* denote such a flag, which we set to *true* as soon as the x-register is full. Clearly, once the pivot column has been fed into slice k, we have determined the last cell of the slice: it is the only one whose boolean flag remains equal to *false* . This is the key information that we need to generate the output control for slice k+1: this control will be generated in the last cell of the slice.

Before discussing the generation of the new control, we briefly discuss the updating of the coefficients. We have already said that a coefficient of the pivot column is stored in the first free location in any x-register that it can find while moving rightwards. Each time a new column is fed in, the address pointer to the x-register is reset, and coefficients move unchanged until they find a cell where they are updated: the address pointer should be less than or equal to x. We just need to take care that they are not updated several times. We introduce a sixth value for the control, termed *done*, which means that the corresponding coefficient has already been updated and that it should be transmitted unchanged until the last cell of the slice, which will generate a new control.

Now for the control generation: only the last cell generates the new control for slice k+1. There are two cases for the pivot column:

• the pivot a_{kk} is propagated unchanged. When a_{kk} arrives in a given cell, this cell does not yet know whether it will be the last cell of the slice or not. As a consequence, the pivot is output from slice k with the control *pv* . This contradicts our general rule that coefficients of column k and row k should be marked with the *nil* control when exiting slice k. This is the only exception to the rule, and we shall see later that it has no influence on the operation of the following slices.

• elements of the pivot column: when a coefficient marked *p_c* is stored (after division by the pivot) in an x-register, it is marked to *nil* as before and moves rightwards unchanged.

After processing the pivot column, we know where the last cell is. It is the responsibility of this cell to

• mark to *nil* the coefficients of the pivot row that were marked *p_r*

• generate the new control for coefficients marked *update* or *done* when entering the cell. This new control is generated exactly as before, using the internal control signals *count* and *next.*

To summarize, the only change compared to the non-modular solution is that the pivot coefficient is output from a given slice with the control *pv* rather than with the control *nil* . We show below that this does not affect the operation of the array. The operation of the modular cell is detailed in figure 5.20.

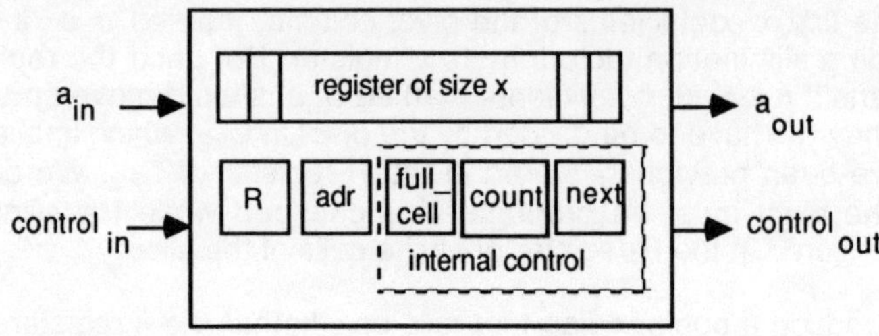


```
case controlin of

  pivot :   begin
              R := ain ; adr := 1 ; count := 0 ; full_cell := false ;
              aout := ain ; controlout := pivot ; end ;

  piv_col : begin
              if (adr≤x)  then begin
                register[ adr ] := - ain / R ; adr := adr + 1 ;
                aout := - register[adr] ; controlout := nil ; end
              else begin
                full_cell := true ; aout := ain ; controlout := piv_col ; end ;
            end ;

  piv_row : begin
              R := ain ; adr := 1 ; next := true ;
              if (count = 0) then count := 1 else  count := 2 ;
              aout := ain ;
              if full_cell then controlout := piv_row
              else controlout := nil ; end ;

  update :  begin
              if (adr≤x)  then begin
                aout := ain + R * register[ adr ] ; adr := adr + 1 ;
                if full_cell then controlout:= done else begin
                  if (count =1) then
                    if next then begin
                      controlout := pivot ; next := false; end
                    else controlout := piv_col ;
                  if (count =2) then
                    if next then begin
                      controlout := piv_row ; next := false; end
                    else controlout := update ; end ; end
              else begin
                aout := ain ; controlout := update ; end ; end ;
```

```
done :    begin
              a_out := a_in ;
              if full_cell then control_out := done else begin
                 if (count =1) then
                    if next then begin
                       control_out := pivot ; next := false; end
                    else control_out := piv_col ;
                 if (count =2) then
                    if next then begin
                       control_out := piv_row ; next := false; end
                    else control_out := update ; end ; end ;

nil :     begin
              a_out := a_in ; control_out := nil ; end ;

endcase
```

Figure 5.20 : Operation of the cells (modular solution, register of size x)

5.3.4. An example with n=6 and x=2

We describe the operation of the first slice of the array in the case n=6 and x=2. In this case, slice 1 is composed of cells 1, 2 and 3. The input data is shown in figure 5.21, together with the first 17 time steps of the execution of the algorithm (we let *dn* denote the control *done*).

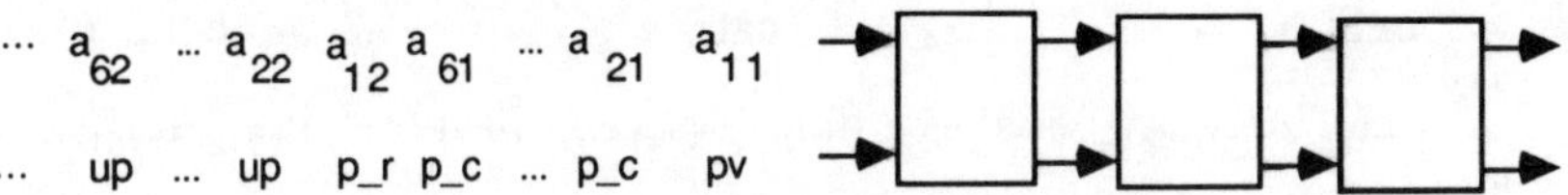

Input data to the array, n=6, x=2

CELL 1	CELL 2	CELL 3
a_{11} → **CELL 1** → pv R=?, x=?, adr=? fc=?, co=?, ne=?	→ **CELL 2** → R=?, x=?, adr=? fc=?, co=?, ne=?	→ **CELL 3** → R=?, x=?, adr=? fc=?, co=?, ne=?
a_{21} → **CELL 1** → R=a_{11}, x=?, adr=1 fc=0, co=0, ne=?	a_{11} → **CELL 2** → pv R=?, x=?, adr=? fc=?, co=?, ne=?	→ **CELL 3** → R=?, x=?, adr=? fc=?, co=?, ne=?
a_{31} → **CELL 1** → R=a_{11}, x=a_{21}, adr=2 fc=0, co=0, ne=?	a_{21} → **CELL 2** → nil R=a_{11}, x=?, adr=1 fc=0, co=0, ne=?	a_{11} → **CELL 3** → pv R=?, x=?, adr=? fc=?, co=?, ne=?
a_{41} → **CELL 1** → a_{11} R=a_{11}, x=[a_{21},a_{31}], adr=3 pv fc=0, co=0, ne=?	a_{31} → **CELL 2** → nil R=a_{11}, x=?, adr=1 fc=0, co=0, ne=?	a_{21} → **CELL 3** → nil R=a_{11}, x=?, adr=1 fc=0, co=0, ne=?
a_{51} → **CELL 1** → a_{21} R=a_{11}, x=[a_{21},a_{31}], adr=3 nil fc=1, co=0, ne=?	a_{41} → **CELL 2** → p_c R=a_{11}, x=?, adr=1 fc=0, co=0, ne=?	a_{31} → **CELL 3** → nil R=a_{11}, x=?, adr=1 fc=0, co=0, ne=?

a_{61} → **CELL 1** →	a_{51} → **CELL 2** →	a_{41} → **CELL 3** →
a_{31}		
$R=a_{11}$, $x=[a_{21},a_{31}]$, adr=3	p_c $R=a_{11}$, $x=a_{41}$, adr=2	nil $R=a_{11}$, x=?, adr=1
nil		
fc=1, co=0, ne=?	fc=0, co=0, ne=?	fc=0, co=0, ne=?
a_{12} → **CELL 1** →	a_{61} → **CELL 2** →	a_{51} → **CELL 3** →
a_{41}		
$R=a_{11}$, $x=[a_{21},a_{31}]$, adr=3	p_c $R=a_{11}$, $x=[a_{41},a_{51}]$, adr=3	nil $R=a_{11}$, x=?, adr=1
nil		
fc=1, co=0, ne=?	fc=0, co=0, ne=?	fc=0, co=0, ne=?
a_{22} → **CELL 1** →	a_{12} → **CELL 2** →	a_{61} → **CELL 3** →
a_{51}		
up $R=a_{12}$, $x=[a_{21},a_{31}]$, adr=1	p_r $R=a_{11}$, $x=[a_{41},a_{51}]$, adr=3	p_c $R=a_{11}$, x=?, adr=1
nil		
fc=1, co=1, ne=1	fc=1, co=0, ne=?	fc=0, co=0, ne=?
a_{32} → **CELL 1** →	a_{22} → **CELL 2** →	a_{12} → **CELL 3** →
a_{61}		
up $R=a_{12}$, $x=[a_{21},a_{31}]$, adr=2	dn $R=a_{12}$, $x=[a_{41},a_{51}]$, adr=1	p_r $R=a_{11}$, $x=a_{61}$, adr=2
nil		
fc=1, co=1, ne=0	fc=1, co=1, ne=1	fc=0, co=0, ne=?
a_{42} → **CELL 1** →	a_{32} → **CELL 2** →	a_{22} → **CELL 3** →
a_{12}		
up $R=a_{12}$, $x=[a_{21},a_{31}]$, adr=3	dn $R=a_{12}$, $x=[a_{41},a_{51}]$, adr=1	dn $R=a_{12}$, $x=a_{61}$, adr=1
nil		
fc=1, co=1, ne=0	fc=1, co=1, ne=0	fc=0, co=1, ne=1
a_{52} → **CELL 1** →	a_{42} → **CELL 2** →	a_{32} → **CELL 3** →
a_{22}		
up $R=a_{12}$, $x=[a_{21},a_{31}]$, adr=3	up $R=a_{12}$, $x=[a_{41},a_{51}]$, adr=1	dn $R=a_{12}$, $x=a_{61}$, adr=1
pv		
fc=1, co=1, ne=0	fc=1, co=1, ne=0	fc=0, co=1, ne=0
a_{62} → **CELL 1** →	a_{52} → **CELL 2** →	a_{42} → **CELL 3** →
a_{32}		
up $R=a_{12}$, $x=[a_{21},a_{31}]$, adr=3	up $R=a_{12}$, $x=[a_{41},a_{51}]$, adr=2	dn $R=a_{12}$, $x=a_{61}$, adr=1
p_c		
fc=1, co=1, ne=0	fc=1, co=1, ne=0	fc=0, co=1, ne=0
a_{13} → **CELL 1** →	a_{62} → **CELL 2** →	a_{52} → **CELL 3** →
a_{42}		
$R=a_{12}$, $x=[a_{21},a_{31}]$, adr=3	up $R=a_{12}$, $x=[a_{41},a_{51}]$, adr=3	dn $R=a_{12}$, $x=a_{61}$, adr=1
p_c		
fc=1, co=1, ne=0	fc=1, co=1, ne=0	fc=0, co=1, ne=0
a_{23} → **CELL 1** →	a_{13} → **CELL 2** →	a_{62} → **CELL 3** →
a_{52}		
up $R=a_{13}$, $x=[a_{21},a_{31}]$, adr=1	p_r $R=a_{12}$, $x=[a_{41},a_{51}]$, adr=3	up $R=a_{12}$, $x=a_{61}$, adr=1
p_c		
fc=1, co=2, ne=1	fc=1, co=1, ne=0	fc=0, co=1, ne=0
a_{33} → **CELL 1** →	a_{23} → **CELL 2** →	a_{13} → **CELL 3** →
a_{62}		
up $R=a_{13}$, $x=[a_{21},a_{31}]$, adr=2	dn $R=a_{12}$, $x=[a_{41},a_{51}]$, adr=1	p_r $R=a_{12}$, $x=a_{61}$, adr=2
p_c		
fc=1, co=2, ne=0	fc=1, co=2, ne=1	fc=0, co=1, ne=0

a_{43} → **CELL 1** → a_{33} → **CELL 2** → a_{23} → **CELL 3** →
a_{13}
up R=a_{13}, x=[a_{21},a_{31}], adr=3 dn R=a_{12}, x=[a_{41},a_{51}], adr=1 dn R=a_{12}, x=a_{61}, adr=1
nil
fc=1, co=2, ne=0 fc=1, co=2, ne=0 fc=0, co=2, ne=1

a_{53} → **CELL 1** → a_{43} → **CELL 2** → a_{33} → **CELL 3** →
a_{23}
up R=a_{13}, x=[a_{21},a_{31}], adr=3 up R=a_{12}, x=[a_{41},a_{51}], adr=1 dn R=a_{12}, x=a_{61}, adr=1
p_r
fc=1, co=2, ne=0 fc=1, co=2, ne=0 fc=0, co=2, ne=0

a_{63} → **CELL 1** → a_{53} → **CELL 2** → a_{43} → **CELL 3** →
a_{33}
up R=a_{13}, x=[a_{21},a_{31}], adr=3 up R=a_{12}, x=[a_{41},a_{51}], adr=2 dn R=a_{12}, x=a_{61}, adr=1
up
fc=1, co=2, ne=0 fc=1, co=2, ne=0 fc=0, co=2, ne=0

Figure 5.21 : Operation of slice 1, n=6, x=2

5.3.5. Correctness of the array

Again, we can prove by induction on n that the array executes the Gaussian elimination algorithm. We discuss the operation of the first slice. Assume that a_{11} is input to the first cell at time t=0. Let n-1 = q x + r with $1 \le r \le x$. There are q+1 cells in slice 1.

We reproduce in figure 5.22a the input data for cell 1. Cell 1 generates the coefficient $a_{k1} := - a_{k1}/a_{11}$ at time t = k and stores it in its x-register at the address k-1 (register[k-1] := a_{k1}), for $2 \le k \le x+1$. At time t=x+2, the internal control *full_cell* takes the value *true* because *adr > x* and the cell receives an external control equal to *p_c*. At time t = (j-1)n+k, $2 \le j \le n$ and $2 \le k \le x+1$, cell 1 updates the coefficients a_{kj} into $a_{kj} := a_{kj} - a_{k1} * a_{1j}$. Otherwise cell 1 transmits unchanged its input data to the next cell. The output data from cell 1 is the input to cell 2, and is shown in figure 5.22b. If $q \ge 2$, cell 2 operates similarly, and we show its output data in figure 5.22c.

Cell q+1, the last cell of slice 1, generates the coefficient $a_{k1} := - a_{k1}/a_{11}$ at time t = q+k and stores it in its x-register at the address k-qx-1 (register[k-qx-1] := a_{k1}), for $qx+2 \le k \le n$. Because cell k only receives n-1-qx = r ≤ x coefficients with input control *p_c* , its internal control *full_cell* remains *false* , and it generates the new control for cell q+2. We show the output data from cell q+1 in figure 5.22d.

The input data for slice 2 is identical to that of slice 1 but corresponds to a matrix of size n-1. Valid inputs for cell 2 are interleaved with invalid inputs (for which $control_{in}$ *= nil*), but non-valid inputs have no influence on the operation of the cells. There is one exception, however: a_{11} is output from slice 1 with the control *pv* , which implies that all the cells of slice 2 will store a_{11} in their R-register. But this has no effect on the execution of the algorithm, because the first valid input to slice 2 after a_{11} is a_{22}, which also carries the control *pv* and therefore will reinitialize the cells in slice 2. More generally, the first k valid inputs to slice k are marked with *pv* , but only the last one, namely a_{kk}, will have an impact on the execution of step k of the algorithm.

a_{nn} ... a_{n3} ... a_{23} a_{13} a_{n2} ... a_{22} a_{12} a_{n1} ... a_{21} a_{11} → CELL 1 →
up ... up ... up p_r up ... up p_r p_c ... p_c pv → →

(a) input to cell 1

→ CELL 1 → ... a_{n2} ... $a_{x+2,2}$ $a_{x+1,2}$ ... a_{22} a_{12} a_{n1} ... $a_{x+2,1}$ $a_{x+1,1}$ ... a_{21} a_{11}
→ → ... up ... up dn ... dn p_r p_c ... p_c nil ... nil pv

(b) output from cell 1

→ CELL 2 → ... $a_{2x+2,2}$ $a_{2x+1,2}$ ... a_{22} a_{12} a_{n1} ... $a_{2x+2,1}$ $a_{2x+1,1}$ ... a_{21} a_{11}
→ → ... up dn ... dn p_r p_c ... p_c nil ... nil pv

(c) output from cell 2

→ CELL q+1 → ... a_{nn} ... a_{n3} ... a_{23} a_{13} a_{n2} ... a_{22} a_{12} a_{n1} ... a_{21} a_{11}
→ → ... up ... up ... p_r nil p_c ... p_c nil nil ... nil pv

(d) output from cell q+1

Figure 5.22 : Input and output data for the cells of slice 1

5.3.6. Design characteristics

The design consists of a unidirectional array of homogeneous elementary cells, and it is parametrized by the storage capacity of each cell. Since each cell has a fixed storage capacity, the array is completely modular and extendible. The input/output requirements of the array are also independent of the problem size. All the input coefficients of the matrix A to be triangularized are read on the same input channel, and all the data in the array flow in the same direction. These features make the array robust to design errors and very suitable for a VLSI implementation: acyclic implementations exhibit favourable characteristics with respect to fault-tolerance, two-level pipelining and problem decomposition in general: see Chuang and He [1984], Huang and Abraham [1984], Hwang and Cheng [1982] and Kung and Lam [1984].

The performance of the array is as follows: let $n-1 = q\,x + r$, $1 \le r \le x$. We have

$$S = q(q+1)x/2 + (q+1)r = n^2 / (2x) + O(n) \text{ cells}$$

and we compute the LU decomposition within

$$T = n^2 + S = n^2 (1+ 1/(2x)) + O(n) \text{ time steps}$$

Note that the period of the array is $P = n^2$, i.e. we can start the solution of a new problem instance every n^2 time steps. P is minimum since it corresponds to the time needed for the coefficients to enter the array.

5.4. Matrices over finite fields

In this section we deal with matrices whose coefficients are taken from finite fields. For the sake of simplicity we consider only GF(2), i.e. modulo 2 arithmetic, but the results can be straightforwardly extended to any prime number. First we consider pivoting issues over GF(2). Then we derive a new triangularization algorithm for matrices over GF(2). This algorithm is as robust as Gaussian elimination with partial pivoting (i.e. it fails to triangularize only if the matrix is singular) and it leads to a faster systolic implementation: 2n time steps instead of 3n for triangularizing an n x n matrix on a triangular array of n(n+1)/2 processors.

5.4.1. Pivoting issues

The key idea for pivoting in finite fields is that the first non-zero element in a column can be chosen as the pivot. There is no need for a global search for the maximum. Moreover, there is no need to process the rows which have already been scanned, since they already have a zero. As a consequence, it turns out that partial pivoting is equivalent to pairwise pivoting. An example will make things clear. Let A be a matrix of size n x (n+1), and suppose that we want to create a zero in position (2,1) combining row 1 and row 2:

• if $a_{11}=1$, row 1 will be chosen as the pivoting row, and the elimination of a_{21}, a_{31}, ..., a_{n1} will be done using the usual Gaussian elimination. In our example:
 - if $a_{21} = 0$, there is nothing to do
 - if $a_{21} = 1$, add row 1 to row 2 to zero out a_{21}
 Note that addition denotes here the addition in GF(2), i.e. the "exclusive or" operation XOR.

• if $a_{11} = 0$, we have to find a pivoting row. Two cases occur:
 - if $a_{21} = 0$, we do nothing
 - if $a_{21} = 1$, we interchange rows 1 and 2
 Row 2 then acts as the pivoting row for phase 1 of the elimination, which consists of zeroing out all elements of the first column of the matrix (A,b) but one.

Note that in the case $a_{11}=a_{21}=0$, row 2 will not be modified during the first step of the algorithm. Assume that a_{i1}, i>2, is the first non-zero element that we find: row i will be used as a pivoting row for phase 1, but since we already know that a_{11}, a_{21}, ..., $a_{i-1,1}$ are all zero, we do not have to combine row i with row 1, 2, ..., i-1. Finally, if we do not find any non-zero element in the column, the matrix is singular.

As indicated in figure 5.23, we can modify the program of the cells of the Ahmed-Delosme-Morf array (version with pairwise pivoting) so as to obtain an implementation of Gaussian elimination over GF(2) that will triangularize any non-singular matrix.

a_{in} a_{out}

Step t Step t+1

{ transfer data }
$a_{out} := a_{in}$;

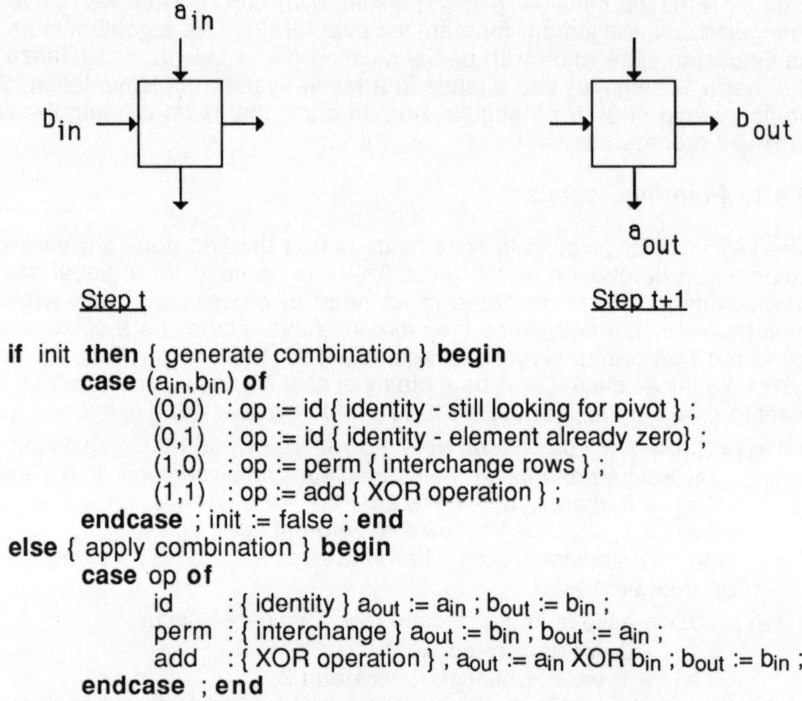


```
if init then { generate combination } begin
        case (a_in,b_in) of
                (0,0)   : op := id { identity - still looking for pivot } ;
                (0,1)   : op := id { identity - element already zero} ;
                (1,0)   : op := perm { interchange rows } ;
                (1,1)   : op := add { XOR operation } ;
        endcase ; init := false ; end
else { apply combination } begin
        case op of
                id      : { identity } a_out := a_in ; b_out := b_in ;
                perm    : { interchange } a_out := b_in ; b_out := a_in ;
                add     : { XOR operation } ; a_out := a_in XOR b_in ; b_out := b_in ;
        endcase ; end
```

Figure 5.23 : Program of the cells with partial pivoting over GF(2)

5.4.2. Faster triangularization over GF(2)

We propose here a new triangularization algorithm over GF(2). In the previous algorithm, we zeroed out the elements in a given column one after the other, because we needed to propagate the pivot row to all the following rows. To eliminate this propagation delay, we may try to perform many transformations in parallel for zeroing several elements of the same column simultaneously (this is the idea of the local pivot algorithm of section 4.6). Let LC(i,j,k) denote the linear Gaussian combination of row i and row j that creates a zero in position (i,k). For Gaussian elimination without pivoting, we always have j=k when performing a combination LC(i,j,k), since row k is used as pivot to zero out all elements a_{jk}, i>k, in column j.

Assume n= 5 and a linear array of macroscopic processors as in figure 5.1. But now assume that processor i initially holds the i-th row of (A,b). If each processor sends its row to its right neighbour, we can replace the five initial rows of the matrix A by the combinations:

Processor	Initially	Operation	Result
P_1	row 1	-	row 1
P_2	row 2	LC(2,1,1)	row 2 - a_{21}/a_{11} row 1
P_3	row 3	LC(3,2,1)	row 3 - a_{31}/a_{21} row 2
P_4	row 4	LC(4,3,1)	row 4 - a_{41}/a_{31} row 3
P_5	row 5	LC(5,4,1)	row 5 - a_{51}/a_{41} row 4

Of course in GF(2) all the four combinations above reduce to a sum (an XOR element by element). Anyway, this is an ideal situation, since all the elements in the first column must be non-zero. For instance if $a_{11}=1$, $a_{21}=0$, $a_{31} = 1$, it is not possible to zero out a_{31}, the first element of row 3, by a combination of the rows 2 and 3. But why should we always zero out the first element ? For instance if we have the situation

row 2	0	1	0	1	1
row 3	1	1	0	0	1

we can start the elimination in the second column and replace row 3 by the sum of the two rows:

row 3 + row 2	1	0	0	1	0

Of course in the next step, when zeroing out a_{31}, we will have to take care to preserve the zero created in position (3,2). This will be possible if P_2 does not automatically transmit row 1 to P_3, but rather a combination of rows 1 and 2 that has a zero in second position.

This short discussion gives the key idea of the following algorithm: when a processor holding a row i receives a row j from its left neighbour, it tries to create the leftmost possible zero in its row using the best possible combination of rows i and j. Moreover, it will transmit to its right neighbour a combination of row j and row i which will preserve the zero previously created using row i.

In order to exhibit the algorithm, we need the following two definitions:

- the weight W(r) of a row r is the index of its leftmost non-zero coefficient
- the best combination $BC(r_1,r_2)$ of a row r_1 and a row r_2 is the combination row $r_1 + \alpha$ row r_2, where $\alpha = r_1(W(r_2))$ is the value of the $W(r_2)$-th coefficient of r_1.

Coming back to the previous example:

r_1	1	1	0	0	1
r_2	0	1	0	1	1

we have $W(r_2) = 2$ and $\alpha = r_1(2) = 1$, hence $BC(r_1,r_2) = r_1 + r_2$. Intuitively, consider that r_1 and r_2 are n-bit numbers: the best combination of r_1 and r_2 is the smallest number that can be obtained by adding to r_1 some multiple of r_2. Note that the definition is not symmetric: here $BC(r_2,r_1) = r_2$. We easily check that $BC(r_1,r_2)$ is uniquely defined if r_1 and r_2 are two independent vectors.

We can express our algorithm as follows:

```
Processor Pi
current_row := row i ;
message_row := current_row ;
send current_row to Pi+1
for step := 2 to i do
    begin
        receive message_row from Pi-1 ;
        { replace current_row by its best combination with message_row
        and message_row by its best combination with current_row }
        current_temp := current_row ;
        message_temp := message_row ;
        current_row  := BC(current_temp,message_temp)
        message_row := BC(message_temp,current_temp)
        send message_row to Pi+1
    end ;
```

It seems that we compute two combinations of rows at each step in this algorithm, instead of one combination in the previous algorithm. However, we easily check that $BC(r_1,r_2) = r_1$ if $W(r_1)>W(r_2)$, and $BC(r_1,r_2) = BC(r_2,r_1) = r_1+r_2$ if $W(r_1)=W(r_2)$, so that we only perform one combination at each step (this will be clear when designing the systolic array).

Cosnard, Duprat and Robert [1988] prove that the previous algorithm triangularizes any nonsingular matrix over GF(2), up to a permutation of rows. In the algorithm, the elimination does not progress column by column, since we create zeros in the leftmost possible position. We make it clear in table 5.5, where (A,b) is a 5 x 6 matrix. At time t, processor P_i combines its current_row and the message_row from P_{i-1} to update its current_row and generate a new message_row to be transmitted to P_{i+1}. Thus table 5.5 reads as follows:

Time = t

Processor	**Current_row**	**Message_row**
P_{i-1}		ms(t)
P_i	cr(t)	

⇒ **Time = t+1**

Processor	**Current_row**	**Message_row**
P_i	cr(t+1)=BC(cr(t),ms(t))	ms(t+1)=BC(ms(t),cr(t))

We have marked out two characteristic operations in table 5.5:
(*) at step 2, P_2 does not modify its current_row, but it updates the message_row so as to preserve zeros in column 2 that might have been created further down in the matrix.
(**) at step 2, P_4 performs two combinations. But the weights of the current_row and the message_row are the same, and only one computation is carried out.

We check that we obtain a triangular matrix, up to a permutation of rows. The solution vector of the triangular system is $x = (1,1,1,1,1)^t$, which is the correct value from the original system.

Time = 1

Processor	Current_row	Message_row
P_1	1 1 0 0 0 0	1 1 0 0 0 0
P_2	0 1 0 1 1 1	0 1 0 1 1 1
P_3	1 1 0 0 1 1	1 1 0 0 1 1
P_4	1 0 1 0 1 1	1 0 1 0 1 1
P_5	0 0 1 0 0 1	0 0 1 0 0 1

Time = 2

Processor	Current_row	Message_row
P_1	1 1 0 0 0 0	-
P_2	0 1 0 1 1 1	1 0 0 1 1 1 (*)
P_3	1 0 0 1 0 0	0 1 0 1 1 1
P_4	0 1 1 0 0 0 (**)	0 1 1 0 0 0 (**)
P_5	0 0 1 0 0 1	1 0 0 0 1 0

Time = 3

Processor	Current_row	Message_row
P_1	1 1 0 0 0 0	-
P_2	0 1 0 1 1 1	-
P_3	0 0 0 0 1 1	0 0 0 0 1 1
P_4	0 0 1 1 1 1	0 0 1 1 1 1
P_5	0 0 1 0 0 1	0 1 0 0 0 1

Time = 4

Processor	Current_row	Message_row
P_1	1 1 0 0 0 0	-
P_2	0 1 0 1 1 1	-
P_3	0 0 0 0 1 1	-
P_4	0 0 1 1 0 0	0 0 0 0 1 1
P_5	0 0 0 1 1 0	0 0 0 1 1 0

Time = 5

Processor	Current_row	Message_row
P_1	1 1 0 0 0 0	-
P_2	0 1 0 1 1 1	-
P_3	0 0 0 0 1 1	-
P_4	0 0 1 1 0 0	-
P_5	0 0 0 1 0 1	0 0 0 0 1 1

Table 5.5 : Illustration of the algorithm for n=5

5.4.3. A new systolic array

Again, replacing each macroscopic processor by a linear array of cells leads to a 2D systolic architecture of n(n+1)/2 processors, which is shown in figure 5.24. The operation of the cells is detailed in figure 5.25. Any nonsingular matrix over GF(2) can be triangularized within 2n-1 time steps.

We point out that the operation of the cells is *not* more complicated than in the Ahmed-Delosme-Morf array for Gaussian elimination (in other words: hardware requirements are the same) although triangularization is now performed within fewer time steps. The program of the cells in figure 5.25

might appear much more complicated than the program for Gaussian elimination with partial pivoting. However, we have not optimized the control logic for the sake of clarity, and the key point is that we perform at most one combination of rows, i.e. one arithmetic operation per step, just as before. Of course arithmetic and control are of the same order of cost over GF(2), but this is no longer true over GF(p), p >2.

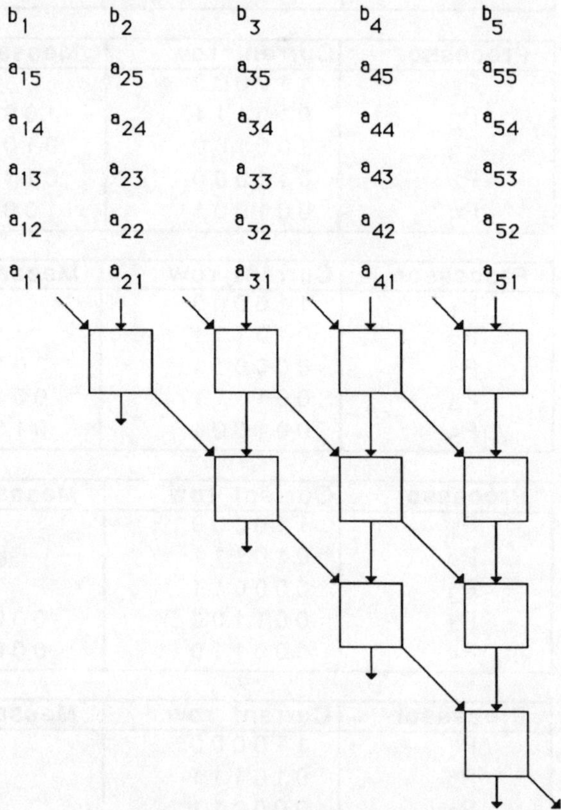

Figure 5.24 : The new systolic array for triangularization over GF(2)

To help the reader understand the program of figure 5.25, we follow the operation of a cell which receives a current_row *cr* and a message_row *ms* :

• as long as the two inputs are zero, we simply transmit them. The combination of *cr* and *ms* cannot yet be generated by the cell (*op=not_yet_decided*).

• the first time one of the inputs is non-zero, two cases occur:

- if both inputs are non-zero, W(message_row)=W(current_row), and the cell updates both rows (*op=upd_both*)

- if only one input is non-zero, e.g. cr_{in}=1 and ms_{in}=0, we already know that the message_row must not be modified (*op=id_ms*). But we have to wait for the first non-zero in *ms* to decide whether we must modify the current_row. The first time we receive ms_{in}=1, we will let *op=id* if cr_{in}=0 (because then BC(cr,ms)=cr), and *op=upd_cr* if cr_{in}=1 (because then BC(cr,ms)=cr XOR ms).

We assume that initially all cells have the instruction op=not_yet_decided.

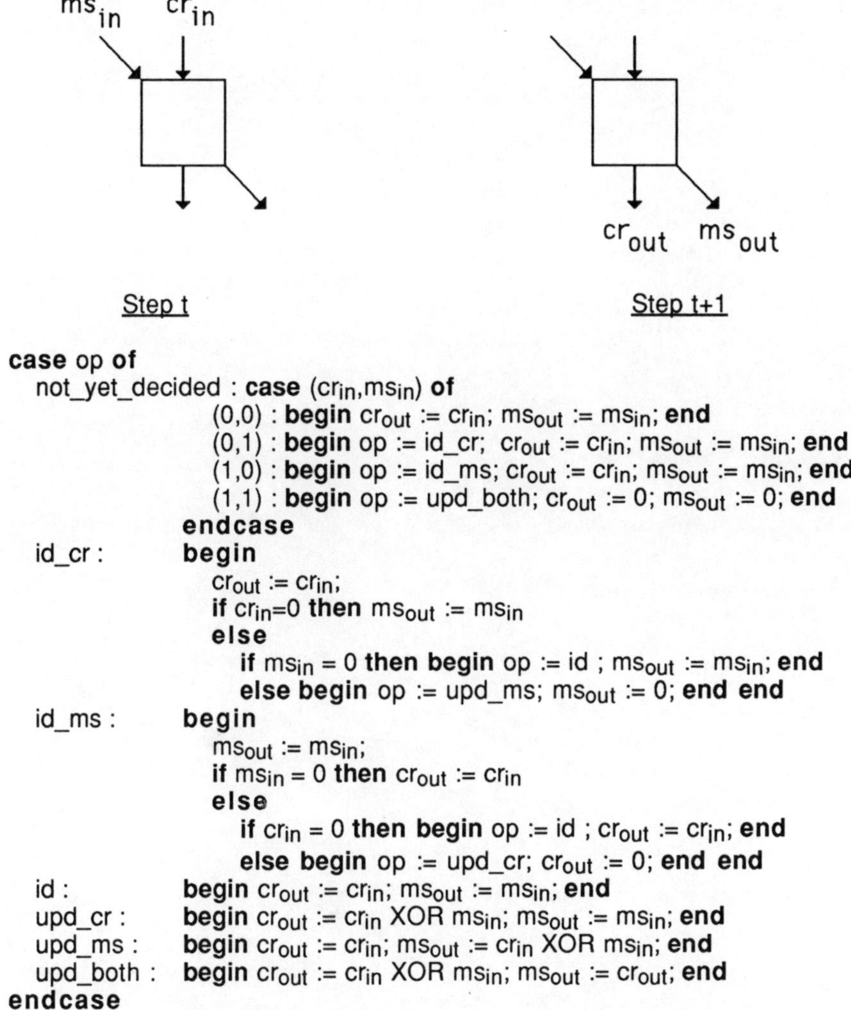


```
case op of
   not_yet_decided : case (cr_in,ms_in) of
                        (0,0) : begin cr_out := cr_in; ms_out := ms_in; end
                        (0,1) : begin op := id_cr;  cr_out := cr_in; ms_out := ms_in; end
                        (1,0) : begin op := id_ms; cr_out := cr_in; ms_out := ms_in; end
                        (1,1) : begin op := upd_both; cr_out := 0; ms_out := 0; end
                     endcase
   id_cr :           begin
                        cr_out := cr_in;
                        if cr_in=0 then ms_out := ms_in
                        else
                           if ms_in = 0 then begin op := id ; ms_out := ms_in; end
                           else begin op := upd_ms; ms_out := 0; end end
   id_ms :           begin
                        ms_out := ms_in;
                        if ms_in = 0 then cr_out := cr_in
                        else
                           if cr_in = 0 then begin op := id ; cr_out := cr_in; end
                           else begin op := upd_cr; cr_out := 0; end end
   id :              begin cr_out := cr_in; ms_out := ms_in; end
   upd_cr :          begin cr_out := cr_in XOR ms_in; ms_out := ms_in; end
   upd_ms :          begin cr_out := cr_in; ms_out := cr_in XOR ms_in; end
   upd_both :        begin cr_out := cr_in XOR ms_in; ms_out := cr_out; end
endcase
```

Figure 5.25 : Program of the cells
(new triangularization algorithm over GF(2))

5.5. Bibliographic notes

Section 5.1 is based on two classics, Ahmed, Delosme and Morf [1982] and Gentleman and Kung [1981]. See Robert [1987] for a survey of systolic algorithms in numerical linear algebra. For section 5.2, in addition to the references given in the text, see chapter 4 of Quinton and Robert [1989]. See Chuang and He [1984], Hwang and Cheng [1982] and Moldovan [1986] concerning partitioning techniques. Section 5.3 and 5.4 are respectively based on Benaini and Robert [1989] and Cosnard, Duprat and Robert [1988].

PART 2

Models and tools

CHAPTER
SIX

TASK GRAPH SCHEDULING

In this chapter, we deal with scheduling algorithms. We base our analysis of the parallel implementation on the task graph model. Informally, sequential algorithms are split into elementary tasks, whose execution ordering is directed by precedence constraints; independent tasks can be processed simultaneously. The task graph model, which can be constructed directly from these precedence constraints, is the basic tool of our theoretical analysis.

6.1. Task system for Gaussian elimination

In this section, we introduce the task graph model with the example of Gaussian elimination.

6.1.1. Task graph

We follow Coffman and Denning [1973] in employing the notion of task system as follows:

• a task is an indivisible unit of computational activity specified only in terms of its external behaviour: for example, inputs, outputs and execution time.

• a task system C = (J, «) is a set of tasks J = {T_1, T_2 , ..., T_n} together with an irreflexive, antisymmetric, transitive binary relation «. The relation « is called the precedence constraint and means that if T « T', then T must complete execution prior to T' commencing execution. We say that T' is a successor of T if T « T' and there is no task T" such that T « T" and T" « T'.

Selection of tasks is still in the realm of intuition. We can designate an entire procedure to be a task (large granularity, or coarse grain) or we can designate each computer operation to be a separate task (small granularity, or fine grain). For Gaussian elimination a natural choice is to select the routines introduced in chapter 1 (medium granularity). At step k, scaling the pivot column (with *prep(k)*) and updating each column j of index ≥ k+1 (with *update(k,j)*) are the kernels which we have already identified. The standard column-oriented KJI version with partial pivoting is thus split into tasks as follows:

```
for k = 1 to n-1 do
        task T_kk : prep(k)
                < find l such that |a_lk| = max { |a_kk|, ..., |a_nk| } ;
                pivot(k) := l ; swap(a_pivot(k),k, a_kk)
                for i = k+1 to n do a_ik := a_ik / a_kk >
        for j = k+1 to n do
                task T_kj : update(k,j)
                        < swap(a_pivot(k),j, a_kj)
                        for i = k+1 to n do a_ij := a_ij - a_ik * a_kj >
```

In the sequential algorithm, the set of tasks $J = \{T_{kj}, 1 \leq k \leq n-1, k \leq j \leq n\}$ is ordered by the relation $\rightarrow$, where

$$T_{kj} \rightarrow T_{ml} \quad \Leftrightarrow \quad k<m \text{ or } (k=m \text{ and } j<l)$$

The relation $\rightarrow$ induces a total order between the tasks. If we want to extract the parallelism from the sequential program, we have to identify the tasks that are independent and therefore can be executed in parallel. We already said in chapter 1 that the updating of the trailing columns at a given step k can be performed in parallel. We will retrieve this observation with a formal definition of independence between tasks.

A task T is defined by a quadruple $(D_T, R_T, f_T, W(T))$ where
• D_T is the domain of the task T, i.e. the set of its inputs
• R_T is the range of the task T, i.e. the set of its outputs
• f_T is an operator from D_T into R_T which represents the ordered list of the elementary operations performed inside the task T
• W(T) is the weight of task T, i.e. its execution time
For example with task T_{kk} of Gaussian elimination, we have the same domain and range $D(T_{kk}) = R(T_{kk}) = \{a_{ik}, k \leq i \leq n\}$, while for task T_{kj}, $j \neq k$, we have the domain $D(T_{kj}) = \{a_{ik}, k \leq i \leq n\} \cup \{a_{ij}, j \leq i \leq n\}$ and the range $R(T_{kj}) = \{a_{ij}, j \leq i \leq n\}$. We note that f_T is not very important in our context, as we assume that tasks are non-preemptive.

Let C = (J, «) be a task system. Two tasks T and T' are independent if and only if they do not modify a shared variable. This is expressed by the condition

$$R_T \cap R_{T'} = R_T \cap D_{T'} = D_T \cap R_{T'} = \emptyset$$

Note that two independent tasks T and T' can still share some variables in their domain. For Gaussian elimination, we check that the n-k tasks $\{T_{kj}; k<j \leq n\}$ are independent. On the other hand, we see that T_{kk} and T_{kj}, $j \neq k$, are not independent, because $R(T_{kk}) \cap D(T_{kj}) = \{a_{ik}, k \leq i \leq n\} \neq \emptyset$. Similarly, T_{kj} and $T_{k+1,j}$, $k+2 \leq j$, are not independent because $R(T_{kj}) \cap R(T_{k+1,j}) = \{a_{ij}, k+1 \leq i \leq n\} \neq \emptyset$.

Given a sequential algorithm $C = (J, \rightarrow)$, we extract the maximally parallel system C = (J,«) if we define the precedence relation so as to order the execution of non-independent tasks:

$$T \ll T' \Leftrightarrow T \rightarrow T' \text{ and } (R_T \cap R_{T'}) \cup (R_T \cap D_{T'}) \cup (D_T \cap R_{T'}) \neq \emptyset.$$

For Gaussian elimination, we can write the precedence relations (or constraints):

(Constraints A)	$T_{kk} \ll T_{kj}$	$1 \le k < j \le n$
(Constraints B)	$T_{kj} \ll T_{k+1,j}$	$1 \le k < j \le n$

For instance for relation (A), we know that T_{kk} and T_{kj}, $j \neq k$, are not independent. The precedence relation in the sequential algorithm ($T_{kk} \rightarrow T_{kj}$) lets us determine the precedence relation in the maximally parallel system ($T_{kk} \ll T_{kj}$).

Constraint (A) means that the processing of the pivot column at step k must be completed before the trailing columns can be updated. Constraint (B) means that the updating of column j at step k+1 can only begin when its updating from step k is terminated.

All precedence relations in C = (J,«) are obtained by repeatedly applying constraints (A) or (B). In other words, the precedence relation « is the transitive closure of the relation $X = \{(T_{kk}, T_{kj}),\ 1 \le k < j \le n\} \cup \{(T_{kj}, T_{k+1,j}),\ 1 \le k < j \le n\}$.

The task graph obtained from C = (J,«) is the oriented graph whose vertices are the elements of J and where (T,T') is an edge if T' is a successor of T for the relation «. The task graph for Gaussian elimination is shown in figure 6.1.

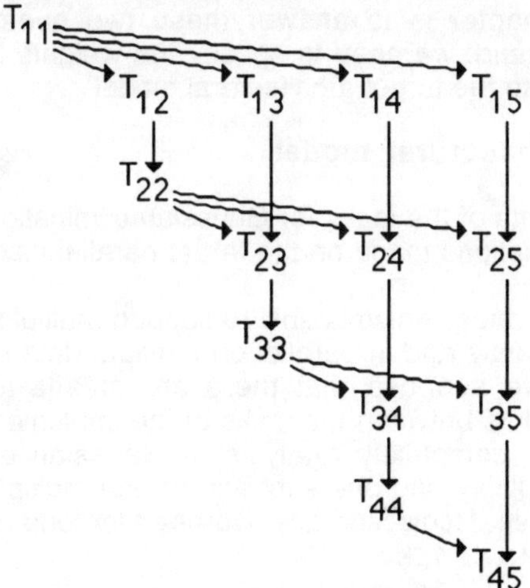

Figure 6.1 : Task graph for n=5

6.1.2. Scheduling algorithms

Let p be the number of processors available for executing our task system C = (J,«). Informally, we want to assign tasks to processors so that the total execution time is minimal and the precedence constraints are met. Formally, a scheduling is a mapping which associates to each task T of J

- a processor number proc(T) ∈ {1, 2, ..., p}; proc(T) is the index of the processor that will execute task T
- an execution date orig(T); orig(T) is the time at which the execution of T is initiated by processor proc(T).

The scheduling must satisfy the following two conditions:
(i) precedence constraints must be met: if $T \ll T'$, then T' cannot be initiated before T has completed; formally

$$orig(T) + W(T) \leq orig(T')$$

(ii) the same processor must not be assigned two different tasks at the same time; formally

$$proc(T) = proc(T') \Rightarrow (orig(T) + W(T) \leq orig(T')) \text{ or } (orig(T') + W(T') \leq orig(T))$$

Finally, the total execution time is $T_p = \max \{orig(T) + W(T);\ T \in J\}$.

Given p, the first question is:

(Q1)	determine the optimum execution time $T_{opt}(p)$, i.e. the minimum execution time over all possible schedules.

Let T_{opt} be the absolute minimum execution time, whatever the number of available processors: in other words, let $T_{opt} = \min \{T_{opt}(p);\ p \geq 1\}$. The second question is:

(Q2)	determine the minimum number of processors p_{opt} needed to achieve execution in time T_{opt}, i.e. $p_{opt} = \min \{p;\ T_{opt}(p) = T_{opt}\}$.

The aim of this chapter is to answer these two questions for Gaussian elimination. Beforehand, we need to specify the weights (execution times) of the tasks according to the target architectural model.

6.1.3. Target architectural model

Specifying the weights of the tasks for Gaussian elimination will reveal several unformulated assumptions made on the target parallel machine.

First we assume a system which is able to support multiple instruction streams executing independently and in parallel on multiple data streams (MIMD, see chapter 1). Next we suppose that there are means to impose temporal precedence constraints between the tasks of the implemented algorithms. We follow the classical complexity analysis of Gaussian elimination, and we assume that one multiply and one subtract, or one multiply and one compare constitutes a time step. Neglecting any overhead for loop control, we have

$$W(T_{kk}) = n+1-k \qquad 1 \leq k < n$$
$$W(T_{kj}) = n-k \qquad 1 \leq k < j \leq n$$

Elementary tasks are of length $O(n)$, so that overheads for loop control can effectively be neglected before the arithmetic. However, in the weight of the tasks we neglect everything concerned with communications: data transfers, synchronization and control overhead. A model where communication costs are neglected is certainly too crude.

To make the model more realistic, we assume that processors communicate via a central shared memory rather than through connections between their private memories. With this assumption, a given task can be allocated to any processor at the same cost. This would not be the case for a distributed memory machine, where the length of the communications between two processors depends upon their relative positions in the interconnection graph.

Now the transfer operations can be explained: the elements of the matrix A are accessed by columns. Only two transfer operations are allowed: loading a column of A from the central storage to a processor, and storing a column of A in memory. We allow for the simultaneous transfer of a given piece of data to several processors. In such a case, no processor will be authorized to modify this data. On the other hand, a processor can modify data only if it is resident in its own memory.

For T_{kk} there are n-k+1 data loads, and as many stores. For T_{kj}, $j \neq k$, there are 2(n-k+1) loads and n-k+1 stores. We multiply these quantities by the elementary communication time τ_c to include them into the execution time, so as to take communication into account. Let τ_a be the elementary arithmetic time. We have:

$$W(T_{kk}) = (n-k+1)\,\tau_a + 2(n-k+1)\,\tau_c \qquad 1 \le k < n$$

$$W(T_{kj}) = (n-k)\,\tau_a + 3(n-k+1)\,\tau_c \qquad 1 \le k < j \le n$$

Since the elements of A are accessed columnwise, another possibility for evaluating the weights of the tasks is to assume a stride-one accessing of data as prevalent in vector machines and cache-based architectures: then data loading and unloading can be pipelined, and overlapped with arithmetic. In all cases, since the number of data loads and stores in each task is proportional to the number of floating-point operations, we can let

$$W(T_{kk}) = a\,(n-k+1) + c_1 \qquad 1 \le k < n$$

$$W(T_{kj}) = b\,(n-k) + c_2 \qquad 1 \le k < j \le n$$

where a, b, c_1 and c_2 are 4 rational parameters. Many numerical algorithms lead to the task graph of figure 6.1, with various values for these parameters. This motivates the general study of this task graph.

In the following, we limit the number of processors p to be of the order of the problem size n: $p = O(n)$. We take the view that it is not realistic to assume that shared memory systems with $O(n^2)$ processors will soon be available to solve sizeable sets of equations. Also, Saad [1986a] shows that communication costs dominate the arithmetic to solve a matrix problem of order n with n^2 processors.

6.1.4. Static versus dynamic scheduling

Given the task system for Gaussian elimination, we will discuss only static schedulings, i.e. schedulings for which we explicitly compute *a priori* which processor will execute which task, and when. We could also use dynamic schedulings, for which processors dynamically pick up tasks in the queue Q of tasks ready for execution. The queue Q evolves dynamically as tasks are executed. Initially, Q is the set of tasks without predecessor. When a processor picks up a task T in Q, it is removed from Q. When this processor has completed the execution of T, Q is updated with the successors of T which are now ready for execution. Hence the principle of dynamic scheduling algorithms is as follows:

Q = { tasks without predecessor }
for all processors **do**
  pick up a task T in Q and let Q := Q \ {T}
  execute T
  for each successor T' of T
    remove T from the list of the predecessors of T'
  update Q := Q ∪ { successors of T which have no predecessor }

Each processor picks up a task in Q according to some scheduling strategy. The most widely used strategy is certainly critical path scheduling. For each task T in Q, we compute all paths in the dependence graph made up with tasks that depend on T: we start such a path with T, then comes a successor T' of T, then a successor T'' of T', and so on... The critical path cp(T) is defined as the weight of the longest path made in this way. Intuitively, the larger cp(T), the more urgent its execution. The pick-up strategy is then to select in Q a task of maximum critical path:

pick up a task T in Q such that $cp(T) = \max \{ cp(T'); T' \in Q\}$

To fully define the algorithm, we must add how we break ties, i.e. how we chose between tasks of the same critical path. We can use several criteria, such as the number of successors, or simply the lexicographical order on task indices.

For Gaussian elimination, it is easy to see that the critical path for task T_{kj} $1 \le k \le j \le n$, goes down and then along the diagonal. We obtain the path

$$T_{kj}, T_{k+1,j}, T_{k+2,j}, \ldots T_{jj}, T_{j,j+1} T_{j+1,j+1}, \ldots, T_{n-1,n}$$

whose length is $cp(T_{kj}) = \frac{(n-k)(n-k+1)}{2} - \frac{(n-j)(n-j+1)}{2} + (n-j)(n-j+2)$.

However, we do not know how to compute the execution time for the critical path scheduling.[1] Simulation results reported in Konig and Trystram [1989] show that it is very efficient, but no exact timing formula is available.

6.2. Bounds for parallel execution

Given a problem of size n, we let $p = \alpha n$, with $0<\alpha\le 1$ is a constant. Given α, we let n go to infinity. Our aim is to answer questions Q1 and Q2. We consider the task graph of figure 6.1, and we let $W(T_{kk}) = n+1-k$, $1\le k<n$ and $W(T_{kj}) = n-k$, $1\le k<j\le n$. In other words we concentrate on the case a = b = 1. We also let $c_1 = c_2 = 0$, which does not modify the asymptotic analysis.

---

1 Contrary to intuition, critical path scheduling is not always optimal. Consider the following task system: four tasks T_1, T_2, T_3 and T_4, with a single precedence relation $T_3 \ll T_4$. Let $W(T_1) = W(T_2) = 3$ and $W(T_3) = W(T_4) = 1$. Assume that we have p = 2 processors. We have $cp(T_1) = cp(T_2) = 3$, $cp(T_3) = 2$ and $cp(T_4) = 1$. Critical path scheduling would start executing T_1 and T_2 simultaneously, then T_3, then T_4, for a total execution time of 4 units, though we can design schedules executing in 3 units.

6.2.1. Determination of T_{opt}

From the definition of a time step (one multiply and one subtract, or one multiply and one compare), the sequential execution time is $T_1 = n^3/3 + O(n^2)$. See figure 6.1: the longest path s_1 of the graph is composed of the tasks $T_{11}, T_{12}, T_{22}, \ldots, T_{kk}, T_{k,k+1}, \ldots, T_{n-1,n-1}, T_{n-1,n}$. Its length $L(s_1)$ is

$$L(s_1) = n + 2 \sum_{k=2}^{n-1} (n-k+1) + 1 = n^2 - 1$$

Because tasks in path s_1 must be executed serially, $L(s_1)$ is a lower bound for the execution time of any parallel algorithm, whatever the number p of processors. Therefore:$T_{opt} \geq L(s_1)$. On the other hand, it is easy to design a parallel algorithm with $p = n-1$ processors whose execution time is T_{opt}. The construction is as follows. Processor 1 executes all the tasks in s_1. While processor 1 executes a task T_{kk}, the p-1 other processors remain idle. While processor 1 executes a task $T_{k,k+1}$, we let n-k processors execute in parallel the n-k independent tasks $T_{k,k+2}, T_{k,k+3}, \ldots, T_{kn}$, which all have the same weight as $T_{k,k+1}$. It follows that $T_{opt} = L(s_1)$, and also that $p_{opt} \leq n-1$.

Given a number of processors $p = \alpha$ n, a parallel algorithm will have a quadratic execution time $T_p = O(n^2)$. We let n go to infinity to derive asymptotic results. The asymptotic efficiency is defined as

$$e_{\infty,\alpha} = \lim_{n\to\infty} e_p, \text{ where } e_p = \frac{T_1}{p\ T_p}$$

In particular, an algorithm is said to be asymptotically optimal if $e_{\infty,\alpha}$ is maximum. With $p = n-1$ processors (α=1), we have $e_{\infty,1} = 1/3$. Finally, we let α_{opt} be the minimal value of α for which $T_{opt}(p=\alpha n)$ is equivalent to T_{opt}, i.e.

$$\alpha_{opt} = \min \{\alpha; \lim_{n\to\infty} T_{opt}(\alpha n)/T_{opt} = \}.$$

6.2.2. A schedule with $\lceil n/2 \rceil$ processors

Lord, Kowalik and Kumar [1983] propose a parallel algorithm with $p = \lceil n/2 \rceil$ processors (α = 1/2) which achieves the execution time T_{opt}. It is therefore optimal, and its efficiency is $e_{\infty,1/2} = 2/3$. We deduce that $\alpha_{opt} \leq 1/2$. The algorithm is explained now.

In the task graph of figure 6.1, we call level k, $1 \leq k \leq n-2$, the set of tasks $T_{k,k+1}, T_{k,k+2}, \ldots, T_{kn}$ plus the diagonal task $T_{k+1,k+1}$. Note that the first task T_{11} and the last task $T_{n-1,n}$ do not belong to any level. The first processor P_1 executes the tasks of the longest path s_1, as before. We see that P_1 executes two tasks per level, namely $T_{k,k+1}$ and $T_{k+1,k+1}$ at level k. While it executes these two tasks, the other processors can each execute two other tasks of the same level. For instance at level 2, P_1 executes T_{12} and T_{22}, P_2 will execute T_{13} and T_{14}, P_3 will execute T_{15} and T_{16}, and so forth. Since the maximum number of tasks per level is n (at level 1), $\lceil n/2 \rceil$ processors will do the job. The whole schedule is illustrated in table 6.1 for n=8. Formally, for $q \geq 2$, processor P_q executes the tasks $\{T_{1,2q-1}, T_{1,2q}, T_{2,2q}, T_{2,2q+1}, \ldots, T_{n-2(q-1),n}\}$.

Time step	Proc. 1	Proc. 2	Proc. 3	Proc. 4
t := 0	T_{11}			
t := t + n	T_{12}	T_{13}	T_{15}	T_{17}
t := t + n-1	T_{22}	T_{14}	T_{16}	T_{18}
t := t + n-1	T_{23}	T_{24}	T_{26}	T_{28}
t := t + n-2	T_{33}	T_{25}	T_{27}	
...	T_{34}	T_{35}	T_{37}	
	T_{44}	T_{36}	T_{38}	
	T_{45}	T_{46}	T_{48}	
	T_{55}	T_{47}		
	T_{56}	T_{57}		
	T_{66}	T_{58}		
	T_{67}	T_{68}		
t := t + 2	T_{77}			
t := t + 1	T_{78}			

Table 6.1 : Schedule with $\lceil n/2 \rceil$ processors (n=8)

6.2.3. A bound on α_{opt}

We now examine the question of whether a schedule of length (equivalent to) $T_{opt} = n^2 - 1$ exists with $p < \lceil n/2 \rceil$ processors ($\alpha < 1/2$). We have a very simple lower bound for α_{opt}:

Lemma 6.1 : $\alpha_{opt} \geq \frac{1}{3}$

Proof: We simply express the fact that with p processors, the parallel time T_p is greater than or equal to the sequential time T_1 divided by p (the efficiency is not greater than 1). If we want $\lim_{n\to\infty} T_p = T_{opt}$, then $n^3/(3p) \geq n^2 + O(n)$, hence $\alpha \geq 1/3$.

Using the structure of the task graph, we can derive a more accurate bound for the efficiency of a schedule with $p = \alpha n$ processors as follows:

Proposition 6.2 : $e_{\infty,\alpha} \leq \frac{1}{1+\alpha^3}$

Proof: We see from the task graph that task T_{11} is a predecessor to all tasks and has an execution time of n steps. As a consequence, any schedule will have only one processor doing work during the first n steps. Similarly, $T_{n-1,n}$ is the successor of all tasks, and thus during the last time step only one processor can be doing work.

Task $T_{n-2,n-1}$ is a successor of all tasks except itself, task $T_{n-1,n-1}$ (which is its successor), and the tasks of the last column $C_n = \{T_{kn};\ 1 \leq k \leq n-1\}$. Furthermore, at most one task of the last column can be executed at a given time, since C_n is totally ordered by the precedence relation «. Therefore for any schedule, from the time that $T_{n-2,n-1}$ commences execution, no more than two processors can be doing work. By a similar argument, once $T_{n-j,n-j+1}$ commences execution, no more than j processors can be doing work. During each interval of length $2j = W(T_{n-j,n-j+1}) + W(T_{n-j+1,n-j+1})$, at most j processors are working, and at least p-j are necessarily idle.

Let LA denote the lost area, i.e. the sum of the times during which processors are necessarily idle at the end of the execution:

$$LA = 1.n + (p-1).1 + \sum_{j=2}^{p-1} (p-j).2j = \frac{p^3}{3} + O(n^2)$$

We have the following inequality:

$$p\,T_p \geq T_1 + LA$$

which expresses that the number of processors p times the length of the schedule T_p (i.e. the computational power of all processors) must be greater than the total work to be done T_1 plus the lost area LA. Letting $p = \alpha n$:

$$e_p = \frac{T_1}{p\,T_p} \leq \frac{T_1}{T_1 + LA} = \frac{1}{1 + \frac{LA}{T_1}} \Rightarrow e_{\infty,\alpha} \leq \frac{1}{1+\alpha^3}.$$

Corollary 6.3 : $\alpha_{opt} \geq \alpha_0$, where $\alpha_0 \approx 0.347$ is a solution to the equation
$3\alpha - \alpha^3 = 1$

Proof: We simply let $T_p = T_{opt}$ in the inequality $p\,T_p \geq T_1 + LA$.

In the next section, we prove that indeed $\alpha_{opt} = \alpha_0$. We design a schedule with $p = \alpha_0 n$ processors whose length is (equivalent to) T_{opt}. This is a definitive answer to question Q2.

6.3. An optimal schedule

In this section, we design a schedule whose length is (equivalent to) T_{opt} and which requires $\alpha = \alpha_0$ processors. First we state this result:

Theorem 6.4 : $\alpha_{opt} = \alpha_0$, where $\alpha_0 \approx 0.347$ is a solution to the equation
$3\alpha - \alpha^3 = 1$.

Note that the efficiency of this asymptotically optimal schedule is very good:

$$e_{\infty,\alpha_0} = \frac{1}{1+\alpha_0^3} = \frac{1}{1 + 3\alpha_0} \approx 0.959.$$

6.3.1. Global description of the schedule

We first introduce the algorithm informally, pointing out the key-ideas of the design. Let $\beta_0 = 1 / \alpha_0$. We partition the task graph into five regions, as indicated in figure 6.2.

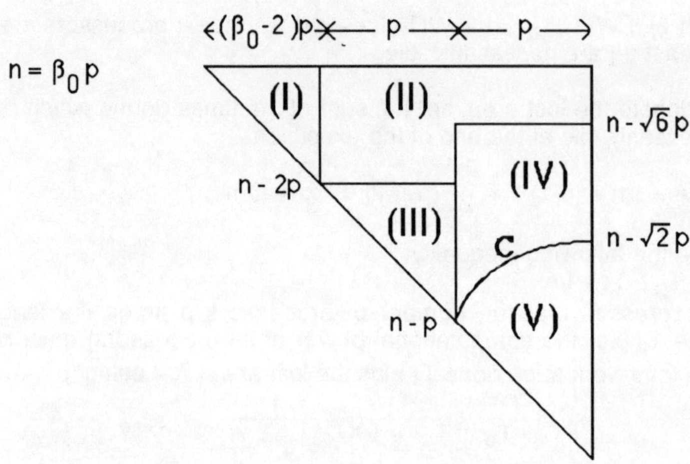

Figure 6.2 : Partitioning the task graph when $p = \alpha_0 n$

When designing a parallel algorithm, one would like to keep all the processors active as long as possible. However, this is clearly impossible in the bottom part of the graph. When $T_{n-p,n-p}$ has been executed (at time t, say), there are less than p tasks in the graph that can be executed in parallel, so that some processors will necessarily be inactive. All the tasks of the path $\{T_{n-p+1,n-p}, T_{n-p+1,n-p+1}, \ldots, T_{n-1,n-2}, T_{n-1,n-1}, T_{n-1,n}\}$ have to be executed sequentially. Let τ be the length of this path. It will take at least a time τ to complete the execution. The idea is to maximize the work that the p processors can do in these τ units of time. This corresponds exactly to region (V) in figure 6.2.

The challenge is to execute all the other regions (I) to (IV) in full parallelism, with all the processors being active. Then we lose some parallelism when executing region (V), but we lose the minimum. As a consequence, the resulting algorithm will be optimal.

The boundary curve C between regions (IV) and (V) is the equipotential curve which contains task $T_{n-p,n-p}$: it is composed of the tasks $T_{i(j),j}$, $n-p \le j \le n$, $i(j) = \max \{ i \,/\, cp(T_{ij}) \ge cp(T_{n-p,n-p+1}) \}$, where $cp(T_{ij})$ is the length of the critical path from task T_{ij}, defined as the longest path in the graph from T_{ij} to $T_{n-1,n}$.

The algorithm proceeds in three sequential phases:

1. in the first phase, tasks of regions (I) and (II) are executed. $\lceil (\beta_0-2)p/2 \rceil$ processors start the execution of region (I), and the other ones start the execution of region (II). As the execution of region (I) progresses, some processors are released and start executing tasks of region (II). Tasks of region (II) are executed in a greedy manner, level by level.
2. in the second phase, tasks of regions (III) and (IV) are executed. We assign one pair of columns in region (III) and another pair of columns in region (IV) to each pair of processors.
3. in the third phase, for the execution of region (IV), we simply assign one column to each processor.

For each region X, let TW(X) be the total weight of X, i.e. the sum of the weights of the tasks in X. Let $s_{1,1}$, $s_{1,2}$ and $s_{1,3}$ be the subsets of the longest path s_1 in regions (I), (III) and (V) respectively. We want the whole algorithm to execute in time (equivalent to) $T_{opt} = L(s_1)$. Phase 1 will be executed in time $L(s_{1,1})$, phase 2 in time $L(s_{1,2})$ and phase 3 in time $L(s_{1,3})$. We also want regions (I) to (IV) to be executed with full efficiency. During phase 1, the processors execute a global amount of work equal to p $L(s_{1,1})$, which implies the relation $p.L(s_{1,1}) = TW(I) + TW(II)$. Similarly, we must have $p.L(s_{1,2}) = TW(III) + TW(IV)$. We will show later that these relations do hold.

6.3.2. Phase 1

We do not consider T_{11}, which only affects the execution by a linear quantity O(n), thereby not modifying the asymptotic result. There are two pools P and Q of processors: processors of pool P are assigned to region (I), processors of pool Q to region (II). P and Q evolve dynamically. At the beginning, $q = \lceil(\beta_0-2)p/2\rceil$ processors belong to P, and p-q to Q. At the end all processors are in Q. More precisely, one processor moves from P to Q each time two new levels in (I) are processed.

Pool P for region (I)

An example will makes things clear. Assume q=4 and that execution of phase 1 starts at time t=0. We have the following situation (figure 6.3):

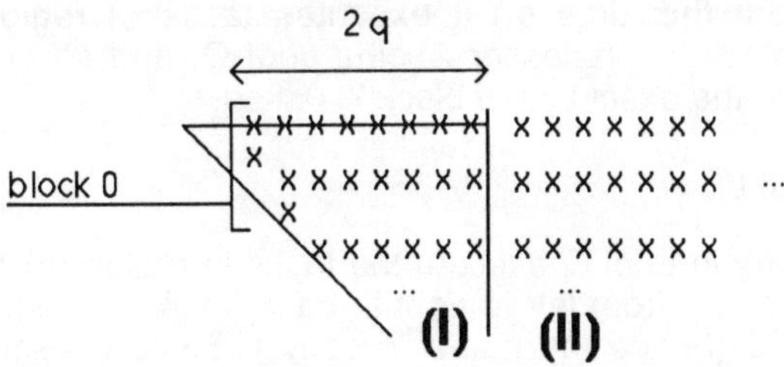

Figure 6.3 : First phase of the algorithm, region (I)

Block 0 consists of the first two levels of region (I). It is executed as depicted in table 6.2. The tasks successively executed by processor 1 are numbered in figure 6.4.

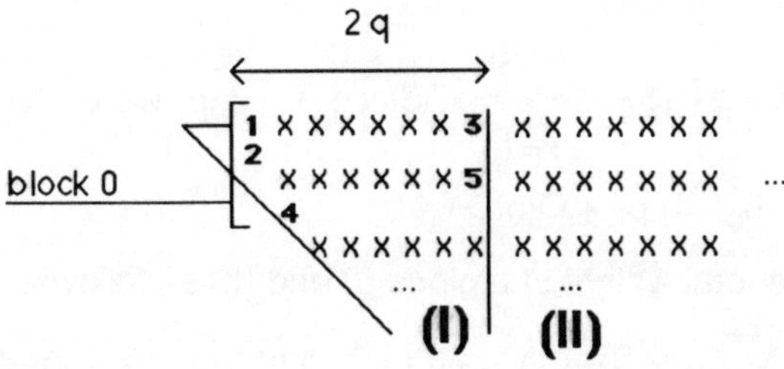

Figure 6.4 : Tasks executed by processor 1 for block 0 of region (I)

first level

processor	1	2	3	4	2	3	4	1
task	T_{12}	T_{13}	T_{14}	T_{15}	T_{16}	T_{17}	T_{18}	T_{19}
time	0	0	0	0	t_1	t_1	t_1	t_2-1
processor	1							
task	T_{22}							
time	t_1							

second level

processor	2	3	4	2	3	4	1
task	T_{23}	T_{24}	T_{25}	T_{26}	T_{27}	T_{28}	T_{29}
time	t_2	t_2	t_2	t_3	t_3	t_3	t_4
processor	1						
task	T_{33}						
time	t_3						

Table 6.2 : Execution of the first block of region (I)

We report the times when processors begin execution in table 6.2, where $t_1 = W(T_{1,2})$, $t_2 = 2t_1$, $t_3 = 3t_1-1$ and $t_4=4t_1-3$.

At time t_4, all the q processors except the first one proceed to the next two levels (block 1). Note that they all start the execution of this new block at the same time. When processor 1 has executed the last task of level 2, it joins pool Q and from this time on it executes tasks of region (II). After the processing of block 1, processor 2 joins pool Q, and so on (processor k+1 joins pool Q after the execution of block k, $0 \le k \le q-1$).

Pool Q for region (II)

All the processors in pool Q execute the tasks in region (II) from one level of the graph to another, from left to right in each level, starting the execution as soon as possible (hence the name "greedy"). Since in region (II) there are more than p tasks in each level, it is guaranteed that all processors always have some task to execute. However, we must check that precedence constraints are satisfied. This is obvious for constraints (B), but we must check that a new level k+1 in region (II) is not started before the diagonal task T_{kk} is completed (constraints (A)).

Lemma 6.5 : $p\, L(s_{1,1}) = TW(I) + TW(II) + O(n^2)$

Proof: We have $L(s_{1,1}) = 2 \sum_{x=1}^{n-2p} n-x$. Since $n = \beta_0 p$, we derive

$$L(s_{1,1}) = (\beta_0^2 - 4)\, p^2 + O(n)$$

We compute the total weight of regions (I) and (II) as follows:

$$TW(I) = \sum_{x=1}^{n-2p} (n-2p-x)(n-x) = p^3\, (\beta_0^3 - 3\beta_0^2 + 4)/3 + O(n^2)$$

$$= p^3 + O(n^2) \text{ since } \beta_0 \text{ is solution of the equation } \beta^3 - 3\beta^2 + 1 = 0$$

$$TW(II) = \sum_{x=1}^{n-2p} p(n-x) + \sum_{x=1}^{n-\sqrt{6}p} p(n-x) = p^3 (\beta_0^2 - 5) + O(n^2)$$

We check that $p\ L(s_{1,1}) = TW(I) + TW(II) + O(n^2)$. This relation means that when the last processor of pool P finishes the execution of region (I), the execution of region (II) will be completed within a linear number of time steps O(n) by processors of pool Q.

Lemma 6.6 : Precedence constraints are satisfied during phase 1 of the algorithm.

Proof: It is clear that precedence constraints (A) and (B) are met during the execution of region (I). For region (II), constraints (B) are obviously verified. It is also clear that constraints (A) are satisfied for the execution of levels 1 to $n-\sqrt{6}p$, since the width of region (II) is 2p in this part: each processor active in pool Q will have to execute at least two tasks per level, thereby the execution will progress downwards more slowly than in region (I). To prove constraints (A) apply in the bottom part of region (II), refer to figure 6.5 below:

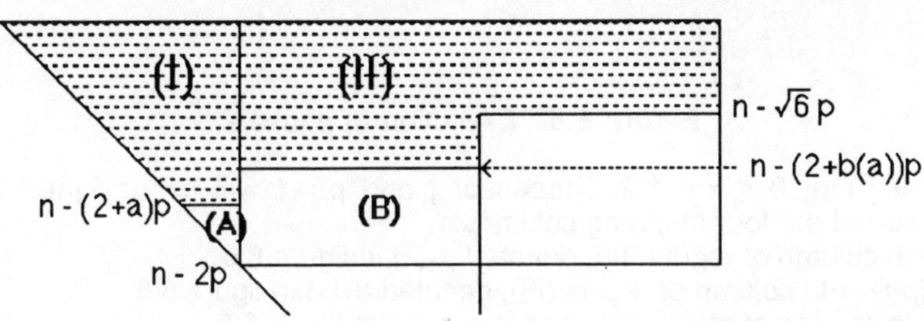

Figure 6.5 : Verifying constraints (A) in phase 1

We have executed region (I) up to level n-(2+a)p, $0 \le a \le \sqrt{6}-2$, and we want to compute the level n-(2+b(a))p that we have reached at that time in region (II). If we obtain $b(a) \ge a$, the result will follow.

With the notations of figure 6.5, lemma 1 implies that

$$p\ L(s_{1,1} \cap (A)) = TW(A) + TW(B) + O(n^2)$$

which leads to

$$p^3 (4a + a^2) = p^3 (a^3/3 + a^2) + p^3 (b(a)^2/2 + 2b(a)) + O(n^2)$$

Therefore

$$+ 2b(a) = 4a - a^3/3$$

from which we easily derive $b(a) \ge a$ for $0 \le a \le \sqrt{6}-2$.

We resynchronize all the processors at the end of phase 1, at the price of a linear factor, which does not affect the asymptotic computation of the execution time.

6.3.3. Phase 2

Assume that the number p of processors is even, and assume the existence of an extra processor numbered 0 which executes only the diagonal tasks in $s_{1,2}$ as soon as possible (this does not affect the asymptotic analysis). The basic idea for phase 2 is to assign to each pair of processors a pair of columns in region (III) and a pair of columns in region (IV). We shall explain the motivation for such an allocation after setting some notation. Consider figure 6.6:

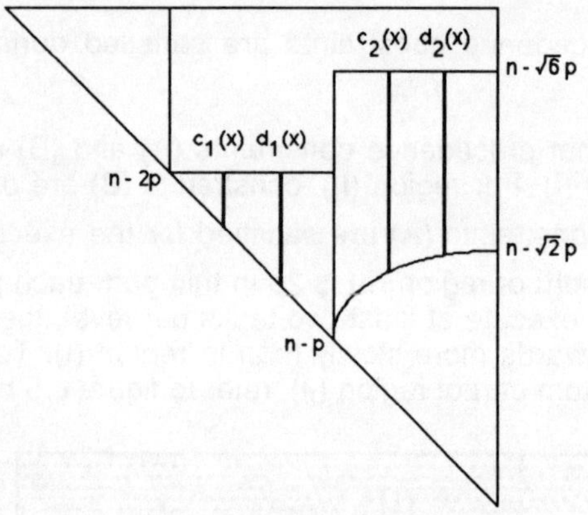

Figure 6.6 : Execution of phase 2

Let $x = j / p$, $0 \leq x \leq 1/2$. Processor j and p-j+1 will be assigned to the execution of the four following columns:
- the j-th column of region (III), denoted $c_1(x)$ in figure 6.6
- the (p-j+1)-th column of region (III), denoted $d_1(x)$ in figure 6.6
- the j-th column of region (IV), denoted $c_2(x)$ in figure 6.6
- the (p-j+1)-th column of region (IV), denoted $d_2(x)$ in figure 6.6

We want to execute phase 2 in time $L(s_{1,2})$, and with full efficiency, which imply that the relation $p.L(s_{1,2}) = TW(III) + TW(IV)$ holds. But we can have something more precise here: the sum of the execution of the tasks of the four columns above is independent of x and equal to $2L(s_{1,2})$, which motivates our allocation:

Lemma 6.7 : For all x such that $0 \leq x \leq 1/2$, we have

$$L(s_{1,2}) = TW(c_1(x)) + TW(d_1(x)) + TW(c_2(x)) + TW(d_2(x)) + O(n)$$

Proof: Let $0 \leq x \leq 1/2$ and $j = x\,p$. We easily compute $TW(c_1(x))$ and $TW(d_1(x))$:

$$TW(c_1(x)) = \sum_{i=1}^{j} 2p\text{-}j = [2 - (2\text{-}x)^2/2]\, p^2 + O(n)$$

Similarly, $TW(d_1(x)) = [2 - (1+x)^2/2]\, p^2 + O(n)$.

For $c_2(x)$ and $d_2(x)$, we must compute the level at which the columns of region (IV) intersect curve (C). Let n-c(j) be the level at which the j-th column of region (IV) intersects curve (C): it is such that the lengths of the two paths identified in bold on the figure 6.7 are equal.

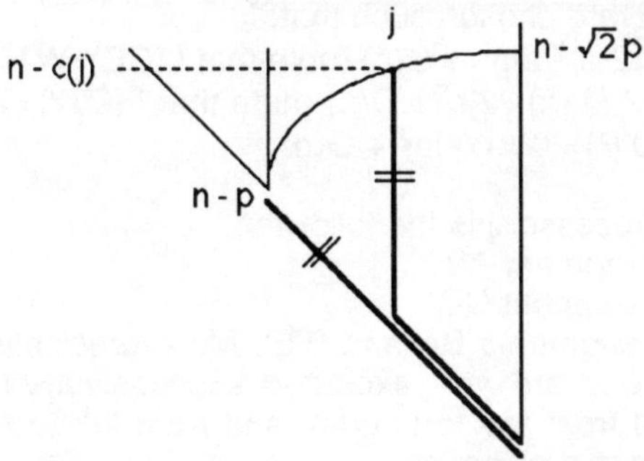

Figure 6.7 : Determining curve (C) analytically

Hence, we have $c(j)^2/2 - (p-j)^2/2 = L(s_{1,3}) - (p-j)^2 + O(n)$, where $L(s_{1,3}) = p^2 + O(n)$. We derive $c(j) = \sqrt{2p^2 - (p-j)^2} + o(n)$.

Now, we easily compute for $0 \le x \le 1/2$:

$$TW(c_2(x)) = [2 + (1-x)^2/2]\, p^2 + O(n) \text{ and } TW(d_2(x)) = [2 + x^2/2]\, p^2 + O(n)$$

We check that $TW(c_1(x)) + TW(d_1(x)) + TW(c_2(x)) + TW(d_2(x)) = 6p^2 + O(n)$. Since $L(s_{1,2}) = 3p^2 + O(n)$, lemma 6.7 is proven.

Of course it is not sufficient to say that we assign four columns to each pair of processors. We have to explicitly determine the schedule for each processor and to ensure that precedence constraints are met. First we check that $TW(c_1(x)) + TW(c_2(x)) \le TW(d_1(x)) + TW(d_2(x))$ for $0 \le x \le 1/2$. Processor j (with $j = xp$) will execute the whole columns $c_1(x)$ and $c_2(x)$, and some additional tasks in the other two columns. Processor p-j+1 will execute parts of columns $d_1(x)$ and $d_2(x)$. Consider figure 6.8:

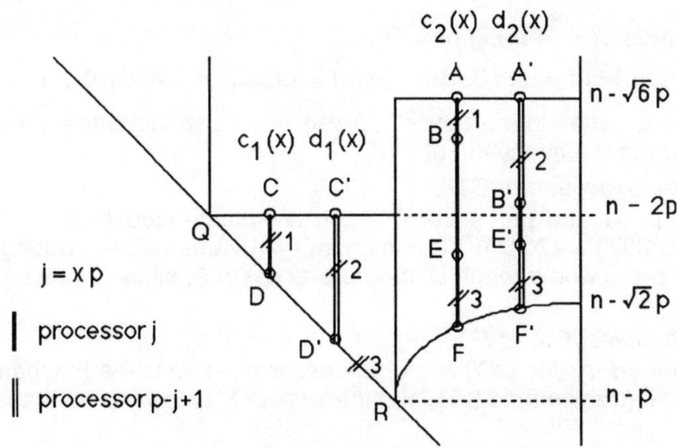

Figure 6.8 : Precise scheduling for phase 2

In figure 6.8, two segments marked //.i, $1 \le i \le 3$, have the same length. Given $x \le 1/2$, B,B',E and E' are chosen such that:

- $L(AB)=L(CD)= [2-(2-x)^2/2]p^2 + O(n)$ (note that $L(CD)=WT(c_1(x))=L(QD)/2$)
- $L(A'B')=L(C'D')= [2-(1+x)^2/2]p^2+ O(n)$ (note that $L(C'D')=WT(d_1(x))=L(QD')/2$)
- $L(EF)=L(E'F')=L(D'R)= (2x+x^2)p^2 + O(n)$

The schedule for processor j is the following:

(i) execute segment AB
(ii) execute segment CD
(iii) execute segments BE and B'E'. More precisely, the two segments BE and B'E' are *not* executed successively, but rather tasks are executed from top to bottom, and from left to right when there are two tasks in a given level.
(iv) execute segment EF

and for processor p-j+1:

(i) execute segment A'B'
(ii) execute segment C'D'
(iii) execute segment E'F'

Since L(AB) + L(CD) = L(QD), processor j meets its deadline: processor 0 will be able to execute the diagonal task in column $c_1(x)$ in due time for a global execution of phase 2 in time $L(s_{1,2})$. A similar observation can be made for processor p-j+1.

Lemma 6.8 : Precedence constraints are satisfied during phase 2 of the algorithm.

Proof: Constraints (B) are obviously verified. Let $0 \le x \le 1/2$ and j = xp. We first check constraints (A) for processor p-j+1:

- *during the execution of A'B':*

when processor p-j+1 reaches level n-u.p, processor 0 is at level n-f(u)p such that the path from level n-2p to level n-u.p in column $d_2(x)$ is equal to the length of the subset of $s_{1,2}$ comprised between levels n-2p and n-f(u)p. This leads to

$$(3-u^2/2)\ p^2 = (4-f(u)^2)\ p^2 + O(n)$$

from which $f(u) \ge u$ for $u \ge \sqrt{2}$. But $L(A'B') = L(C'D') \le TW(d_1(0)) = 3p^2/2 + O(n)$, from which u varies in the range $[\sqrt{3},\sqrt{6}]$. As a consequence, constraints (A) are met during the execution of A'B'.

- *during the execution of C'D':*

processor p-j+1 and processor 0 reach D' simultaneously (from the relation L(A'B') + L(C'D') = L(QD')) . If constraints (A) were violated during C'D', then processor p-j+1 would reach D' before processor 0, since it executes only one task per level.

- *during the execution of E'F':*

same argument as for C'D', since processor p-j+1 reaches F' when processor 0 reaches R (from lemma 6.7), and the level of F' is lower than that of R.

For processor j, we prove constraints (A) as follows:

- *during the execution of AB:*

same proof as for processor p-j+1, which can be made simpler here: observe that B is higher than level n-2p.

• *during the execution of CD:*
same argument as for processor p-j+1 during C'D'.

• *during the execution of segments BE and B'E':*
- as long as processor j executes only one task per level, from B to the level of B', we use the same proof as for processor p-j+1 during A'B'. When there are two tasks per level (from the level of B' to that of F'), processor j progresses downwards at the same speed as processor 0, hence constraints (A) are still met.
- from the level of F' to F, we use the fact that processor j reaches F when processor 0 reaches R (from lemma 6.7), and the level of F is lower than that of R.

At the end of phase 2, processors are resynchronized, at the price of a linear factor O(n) in the execution time.

6.3.4. Phase 3

We assign a column to each processor: processor j executes tasks of column n-j, and at the end the diagonal task $T_{n-j,n-j}$.

To show briefly that precedence constraints (A) are satisfied, let the processors start the execution of region (V) at time t=0. From the definition of C, we see that processor j reaches level n-j at time $t_{j,j} = cp(T_{n-p,n-p}) - (n-j)^2$. For all i>j, processor i reaches level n-j at time

$$t_{i,j} = cp(T_{n-p,n-p}) - (n-i)^2 - [(n-j)^2/2 - (n-i)^2/2].$$

Hence $t_{ij} \geq t_{jj} + W(T_{n-j,n-j})$, and the precedence constraints are fulfilled.

As a consequence, region (V) is executed in time $cp(T_{n-p,n-p}) = L(s_{1,3}) = p^2 + O(n)$. The description of the algorithm is now complete. The execution time is $T_{opt} = L(s_1)$ up to a linear factor, hence the algorithm is asymptotically optimal. Its asymptotic efficiency is equal to $e_{\infty,\alpha} = \frac{1}{3\alpha_0} \simeq 0.959$.

6.4. With an arbitrary number of processors

Assume that $p = \alpha n$ processors are available, where $0 \leq \alpha \leq 1$. If $\alpha \geq \alpha_0$, we use the same algorithm as with $\alpha_0 n$ processors, which is optimal since it executes in T_{opt}. Its asymptotic efficiency is $e_{\infty,\alpha} = \frac{1}{3\alpha}$.

For $\alpha \leq \alpha_0$, things are more complicated, since we do not know the execution time of an optimal algorithm. But from proposition 6.2 we know that the asymptotic efficiency $e_{\infty,\alpha}$ of any parallel algorithm with $p=\alpha n$ processors is less than $1/(1+\alpha^3)$. For $\alpha \leq \alpha_0$, we now design a parallel algorithm whose asymptotic efficiency is equal to $1/(1+\alpha^3)$: hence the bound is tight, and the algorithm is (asymptotically) optimal.

6.4.1. Optimal algorithm

Let $\beta = 1/\alpha$. We simply add one phase 0 corresponding to the execution of region (0) composed of the levels 1 to n - β_0p: see figure 6.9.

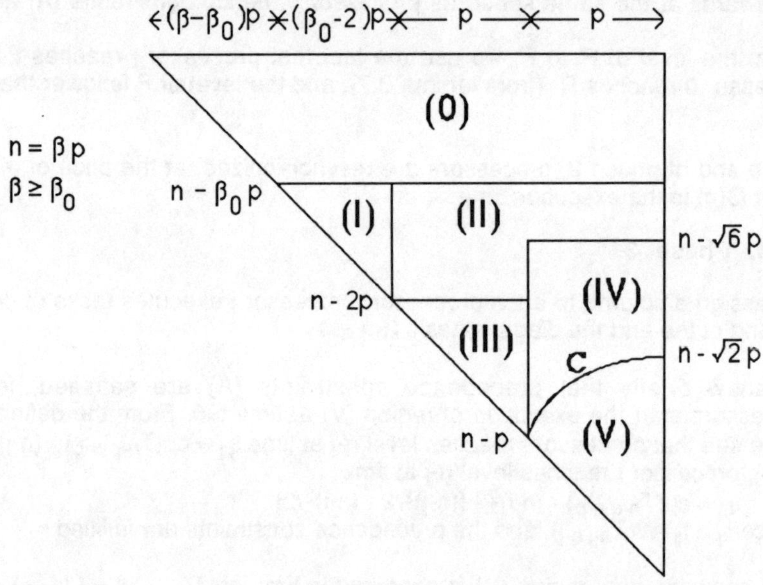

Figure 6.9 : Partitioning the task graph when $p = \alpha n$, $\alpha \leq \alpha_0$

For the execution of region (0), we do not consider T_{11}, which only affects the execution by a linear quantity O(n), thereby not modifying the asymptotic result. For the sake of simplicity, we assume the existence of an extra processor which performs only the diagonal tasks T_{22}, T_{33}, ... as soon as possible. Again, this does not affect the asymptotic analysis.

All the processors execute the non-diagonal tasks from one level of the graph to another, from left to right in each level, in a greedy manner. Precedence constraints are satisfied because each processor executes at least two tasks in each level (in region (0) the number of tasks per level is at least twice the number of processors), which gives enough time to the extra processor to perform the diagonal task before the other processors start the execution of the next level.

We synchronize all the processors at the end of phase 0, losing a linear quantity O(n). Region (0) is executed in full parallelism, and phase 0 is executed in time (asymptotically) equal to the sequential time TW(0) divided by p. We proceed as before for regions (I) to (V).

Lemma 6.9 : For $\alpha \leq \alpha_0$, the asymptotic efficiency of the algorithm is

$$e_{\infty,\alpha} = 1/(1+\alpha^3).$$

Proof: The sequential execution time is $T_1 = n^3/3 + O(n^2)$. The parallel execution time is equal to the sum Σ of the surfaces of regions (0), (I), (II), (III) and (IV) divided by p (since these regions are processed with full parallelism) plus $cp(T_{n-p,n-p})$, the execution time of region (IV):

$$T_p = \Sigma / p + cp(T_{n-p,n-p}).$$

The surface of region (V) is $TW(V) = 2p^3/3$ (direct computation from the definition of C), and $cp(T_{n-p,n-p}) = p^2 + O(p)$. We have $\Sigma = T_1 - TW(V)$, hence $T_p = (n^3+p^3) / (3p)$, and the value of $e_{\infty,\alpha}$ follows.

Note the continuity of $e_{\infty,\alpha}$ for $\alpha = \alpha_0$.

6.4.2. Geometrical interpretation of α_0

Consider the partitioning of the task graph which we have used. We point out that the subdivision into regions (0) to (IV) is only for technical purposes. What is intrinsic in the problem is curve (C) and region (V): region (V) can be viewed as the maximal region which can be processed within the time $L(s_{1,3})$, where $s_{1,3} = s_1 \cap (V)$, and s_1 is the longest path of the task graph. Let LA denote the lost area, as introduced in proposition 6.2. We check that

$$p\,L(s_{1,3}) = TW(V) + LA + O(n^2)$$

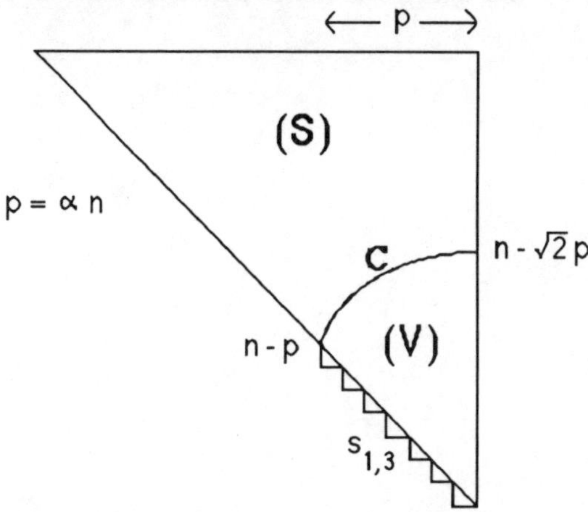

Figure 6.10 : A geometrical interpretation of α_0

Consider figure 6.10, and let $p = \alpha n$. We know that we can execute in time $T_{opt} = L(s_1)$ for α large enough (e.g. $\alpha=1/2$). To execute in $L(s_1)$, we must execute all tasks in region (S) in time $L(s_1 \cap S)$, since we can execute only tasks of region (V) in time $L(s_{1,3})$. This implies the relation $TW(S) \le p\,L(s_1 \cap S)$, i.e. $n^3 - 2p^3/3 \le p(n^2-p^2) + O(n^2)$, hence $3\alpha - \alpha^3 - 1 \ge 0$, or $\alpha \ge \alpha_0$. We have derived the following characterization of α_0:

Proposition 6.10 : $\alpha_0 = \min \{ \alpha \,/\, TW(S) \le p\,L(s_1 \cap S) \}$

6.5. Conclusion

Given a dense nonsingular n x n matrix A and $p = \alpha n$ processors, $\alpha \leq 1$, we have designed parallel algorithms for the LU decomposition of A with partial pivoting on a multiprocessor system. Our parallel algorithms are asymptotically optimal for all values of α, and achieve a very good efficiency. In particular, we have met the bound stated by Lord, Kowalik and Kumar [1983] for the minimum number of processors required to achieve execution in time $T_{opt} = n^2 + O(n)$: a definitive answer to question Q2.

6.6. Bibliographic notes

The design of optimal scheduling algorithms for Gaussian elimination has been studied by several authors. Following the pioneering work of Lord, Kowalik and Kumar [1983], Cosnard et al. [1988a], Missirlis and Tjaferis [1988], Robert and Trystram [1989], Gerasoulis and Nelken [1988], Veldhorst [1989], Marrakchi and Robert [1989] have successively developed new algorithms. Sections 6.3 and 6.4 are based on Marrakchi and Robert [1989].

CHAPTER

SEVEN

ANALYSIS OF DISTRIBUTED ALGORITHMS

In this chapter we deal with complexity results for the implementation of Gaussian elimination on distributed memory machines. We focus on the oriented ring as a target machine. Section 7.2 discusses speedup evaluation.

7.1. Data allocation strategies

We want to derive an analytical model for evaluating the performances of the data allocation strategies which we have considered in section 4.4 when discussing local pipelined algorithms.

7.1.1. Model of computation

As in chapter 4, we consider an oriented ring of p processors numbered from 0 to p-1. Each processor has a private memory and can communicate by a message passing protocol with its two neighbours. Processor P_i receives messages from P_{i-1} and sends messages to P_{i+1} (the subscripts are taken modulo p). The machine operates in an asynchronous MIMD mode. Communications are by rendezvous, and there is no overlap between computations and communications. Moreover, for the sake of convenience, we now assume that a processor cannot simultaneously receive data from its left neighbour and send (different) data to its right neighbour. This assumption, although not mandatory, will facilitate our derivation of lower bounds.

In our analytical analysis, we do not take pivoting into consideration. We consider the pipelined ring algorithm for the KJI-inside version:

```
{ program of processor P_i }
for k=1 to n-1 do
    if alloc(k) = i then
            send column k to P_i+1
    else
            receive column k from P_i-1
            if (i+1 mod p) ≠ alloc(k) then send column k to P_i+1
    endif
    perform the eliminations:
    execute T_kj for all columns j≥k+1 such that alloc(j) = i
endfor
```

where T_{kj} is the following task: < $a_{kj} := a_{kj} / a_{kk}$
for i = k+1 **to** n **do** $a_{ij} := a_{ij} - a_{ik} * a_{kj}$ >

Let τ_a be the time for an arithmetic operation such as a multiply-add. The time to transfer L words between two neighbour processors is modelled as $\beta + L\,\tau_c$, where β is the communication start-up and τ_c the elemental transfer time. We consider block-r allocation functions, i.e. we distribute blocks of r consecutive columns to the processors in a wraparound fashion. Column j, $1 \le j \le n$, is allocated to processor q=alloc(j), $0 \le q < p$, such that

$$\text{alloc}(j) = \lceil \frac{j}{r} - 1 \rceil \bmod p$$

The problem is to determine the allocation function which minimizes the total execution time, defined as the sum of the arithmetic time T_a, and of the communication time T_c (which includes idle time).

Clearly, we have restricted the problem to a special case. We have imposed constraints both on the algorithm and on the allocation function. This is only a first step towards full complexity results for the distributed implementation of Gaussian elimination. Our hypotheses are consistent with the following assumptions specified by Gerasoulis and Nelken [1988] and Saad [1986a]:

• equidistribution of the data: the number of processors p is a divisor of the problem size n, and each of the p processors holds exactly n/p columns of the system matrix in its local memory

• locality assumption: a processor may modify only the data which are stored in that processor

• completion assumption: a processor must complete all computations involving the most recently received message before beginning computations involving the next received message.

7.1.2. Relationship between processor number and problem size

What is the relation between the processor number p and the problem size n ? The space requirement for the sequential algorithm is equal to the size of the matrix, that is n^2 words. Given a single processor with a memory of size M words, this implies that the maximal problem size that can be dealt with is $n_{max,1} \approx \sqrt{M}$. Consider now a ring of p processors. We have p memories of size M, so that we can solve in parallel a problem of size at most $n_{max,p} \approx \sqrt{pM}$. Note that we neglect here any additional storage required by the parallel implementation, such as the need for communication buffers. In fact, the value $n_{max,p}$ above is an upper bound. For most existing parallel architectures, we have $p \le M$ (Intel iPSC, FPS T Series, Ncube) or at least p and M of the same order of magnitude.[1]

As a consequence, in most practical situations we have $p \le n$, and in the following asymptotic analysis, we assume that the number of processors is proportional to the size of the problem: we let $p = \alpha\, n$, where $\alpha \in]0,1]$ is a fixed number, and we let n go to infinity. The reason for choosing p proportional to n is as follows: we know from Saad [1986a] that

---

[1] Note that for the largest configurations of the Connection Machine, or of the AMT DAP, we do have p > M, see Hwang [1987].

communications predominate if $p = O(n^2)$, so that we should not use a number of processors greater than the problem size. On the other hand, if p is negligible compared to n, communications have no influence on the asymptotic execution time. The situation under consideration is when p and n are proportional, since the costs of the computations and of the communications are then of the same order $O(n^2)$: we have $T_a = O(n^3/p)$ and $T_c = O(n^2)$.

Finally, for our asymptotic analysis, we assume $\beta = 0$, as in Ipsen, Saad and Schultz [1986] and Saad [1986a]. Even though β can be in practice much higher than τ_c, we still have messages of length O(n), so that the contribution from the start-ups is negligible.

Given the ratio $\alpha = p/n$ and the machine-dependent parameters τ_a and τ_c, we want to derive the value of the block size r which maximizes the efficiency.

7.1.3. Arithmetic time

Let τ_a be the time for one arithmetic operation. The sequential time is $T_{seq} = 2n^3/3 + O(n^2)$. The weight of a task T_{kj}, $1 \le k < j$, is $W(T_{kj}) = [2(n-k)+1]\tau_a$. Since column j is updated through steps 1 to j-1 during the algorithm, the processor which holds it will perform

$$= \sum_{k=1}^{j} W(T_{kj}) = (j-1)(2n-j+1)\tau_a \text{ operations.}$$

We see that W(j) is a non-decreasing function of j (see figure 7.1)

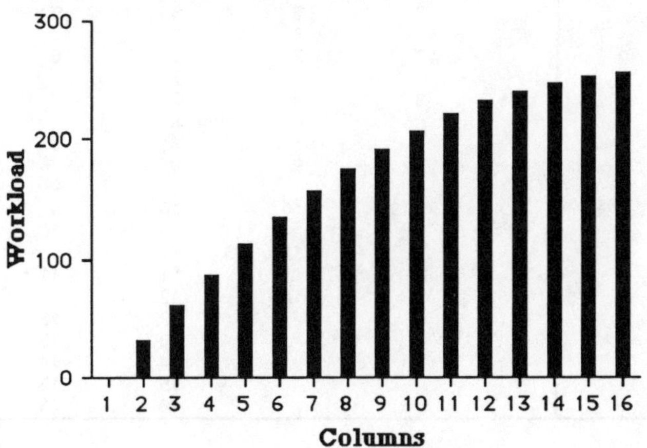

Figure 7.1 : Arithmetic workload for each column (n=16)

The workload of processor number q, $0 \le q < p$, is

$$WL(q) = \sum_{alloc(j)=q} W(j).$$

The parallel arithmetic time is then $T_a = \max_{0 \le i < p} WL(q)$. We find that

$$T_a = \frac{n}{6p}\left(4n^2 + 3rpn - r^2p^2\right)\tau_a + o(pn)$$

Note that T_a is a non-decreasing function of r (differentiate T_a with respect to r). The larger the blocks, the less balanced the workload distribution.

7.1.4. Communication time

To determine T_c, see figures 7.2 to 7.4, where only communications are considered, and are all assumed to be one unit of time. In figure 7.2 we consider the full block allocation strategy (r=n/p). In figure 7.3 we consider the wrap allocation strategy (r=1). We see that a lot of overhead is added for the wrap allocation compared to the full block allocation. In fact, each time that two consecutive pivot columns (for step k and k+1) are not held by the same processor, idle time is introduced for synchronization. This could already be observed in figures 4.11 and 4.12.

	P_0	P_1	P_2	P_3	P_4
Columns	1,2, 3,4	5,6, 7,8	9,10, 11,12	13,14, 15,16	17,18, 19,20
Time-step					
t = 1	1	1			
t = 2		1	1		
t = 3	2	2	1	1	
t = 4		2	2	1	1
t = 5	3	3	2	2	
t = 6		3	3	2	2
t = 7	4	4	3	3	
t = 8		4	4	3	3
t = 9			4	4	
t = 10		5	5	4	4
t = 11			5	5	
t = 12		6	6	5	5
t = 13			6	6	
t = 14		7	7	6	6
t = 15			7	7	
t = 16		8	8	7	7
t = 17			8	8	
t = 18				8	8
t = 19			9	9	
t = 21				9	9
t = 22			10	10	9
t = 23				10	10
t = 24			11	11	
t = 25				11	11
t = 26			12	12	
t = 27				12	12
t = 28				13	13
t = 29				14	14
t = 30				15	15
t = 31				16	16

Figure 7.2 : Communication scheme for Gauss, full block repartition (n=20, p=5, r=4)

	P_0	P_1	P_2	P_3	P_4
Columns	1,6, 11,16	2,7, 12,17	3,8, 13,18	4,9, 14,19	5,10, 15,20
Time-step					
t = 1	1	1			
t = 2		1	1		
t = 3			1	1	
t = 4		2	2	1	1
t = 5			2	2	
t = 6				2	2
t = 7	2		3	3	2
t = 8				3	3
t = 9	3				3
t = 10	3	3		4	4
t = 11	4				4
t = 12	4	4			
t = 13	5	4	4		5
t = 14	5	5			
t = 15		5	5		
t = 16	6	6	5	5	
t = 17		6	6		
t = 18			6	6	
t = 19		7	7	6	6
t = 20			7	7	
t = 21				7	7
t = 22	7		8	8	7
t = 23				8	8
t = 24	8				8
t = 25	8	8		9	9
t = 26	9				9
t = 27	9	9			
t = 28	10	9	9		10
t = 29	10	10			
t = 30		10	10		
t = 31	11	11	10	10	
t = 32		11	11		
t = 33			11	11	
t = 34		12	12	11	11
t = 35			12	12	
t = 36				12	12
t = 37	12		13	13	12
t = 38				13	13
t = 39	13				13
t = 40	13	13		14	14
t = 41	14				14
t = 42	14	14			
t = 43	15	14	14		15
t = 44	15	15			
t = 45		15			
t = 46	16	16	15	15	12
t = 47		16	16		
t = 48			16	16	
t = 49		17	17	16	16
t = 50			17	17	
t = 51				17	17
t = 52			18	18	
t = 53				18	18
t = 54				19	19

Figure 7.3 : Communication scheme for Gauss, wrap repartition (n=20, p=5, r=1)

To analyse the general case, consider figure 7.4 where r=2. In each rectangular box in figure 7.4, there are 2r units of time for sending and receiving r columns, plus one additional unit of time due to synchronization constraints.

	P_0	P_1	P_2	P_3	P_4
Columns	1,2, 11,12	3,4, 13,14	5,6, 15,16	7,8, 17,18	9,10, 19,20
Time-step					
t = 1	1	1			
t = 2		1	1	•	
t = 3	2	2	1	1	
t = 4		2	2	1	1
t = 5			2	2	
t = 6		3	3	2	2
t = 7			3	3	•
t = 8		4	4	3	3
t = 9	3		4	4	3
t = 10				4	4
t = 11	4		5	5	4
t = 12	•			5	5
t = 13	5		6	6	5
t = 14	5	5		6	6
t = 15	6				6
t = 16	6	6		7	7
t = 17	7	•			7
t = 18	7	7		8	8
t = 19	8	7	7		8
t = 20	8	8			
t = 21	9	8	8		9
t = 22	9	9	•		
t = 23	10	9	9		10
t = 24	10	10	9	9	
t = 25		10	10		
t = 26	11	11	10	10	
t = 27		11	11	•	
t = 28	12	12	11	11	
t = 29		12	12	11	11
t = 30			12	12	
t = 31		13	13	12	12
t = 32			13	13	•
t = 33		14	14	13	13
t = 34			14	14	
t = 35				14	14
t = 36			15	15	
t = 37				15	15
t = 38			16	16	
t = 39				16	16
t = 40				17	17
t = 41				18	18

Figure 7.4 : Communication scheme for Gauss, block-r repartition (n=20, p=5, r=2)

We derive from figure 7.4 the following expression:

$$T_c = (p-2)n\tau_c \qquad \text{\{initialization: send column 1 of length n\}}$$

$$+ \quad 2\sum_{k=1}^{n-r}(n-k+1)\tau_c \qquad \text{\{receive and send column k of length n-k+1\}}$$

$$+ \quad \sum_{k=0}^{\frac{n}{r}-p+1}(n-kr+1)\tau_c \qquad \text{\{idle time due to synchronization in rectangular boxes\}}$$

which leads to

$$T_c = \left(pn + n^2 + \frac{n^2}{2r} - \frac{p^2 r}{2}\right)\tau_c + o(np)$$

We check that T_c is a non-increasing function of r (differentiate T_c with respect to r). The larger the blocks, the more reduced the volume of communications; this corroborates figures 7.2 to 7.4.

7.1.5. Best block size

We know from the previous results that, given $\alpha = n/p$, T_a is an increasing function of r whereas T_c is a decreasing one. In other words, T_a is minimum for the wrap allocation (r=1), while T_c is minimum for the full block allocation (r=n/p). The smaller r, the more balanced the computations, but the more expensive the communications. We can summarize our results:

Theorem 7.1 : Let $\alpha = p/n$ be the ratio of the processor number to the problem size, and let $\rho = \tau_c / \tau_a$ be the ratio of the elemental costs of communication to arithmetic. The efficiency for a block-r allocation is

$$e_{\alpha,r} = \frac{1}{1 + \lambda_1 \alpha + \lambda_2 \alpha^2 + \lambda_3 \alpha^3} + o(1)$$

where $\lambda_1 = \frac{3r}{4} + \frac{3\rho}{2} + \frac{3\rho}{4r}$, $\lambda_2 = \frac{3\rho}{2} - \frac{r^2}{4}$, and $\lambda_3 = -\frac{3\rho r}{4}$

Given α and ρ, it is easy to compute the value of r which maximizes the efficiency. Note that for small α, the efficiency can be approximated as

$$e_{\alpha,r} \approx \frac{1}{1 + \left(\frac{3r}{4} + \frac{3\rho}{2} + \frac{3\rho}{4r}\right)\alpha}$$

(we drop the terms in α^2 and α^3). The efficiency is then maximum for $r_{opt} \approx \sqrt{\rho}$. This is a key result for all situations where the number of processors is significantly less than the size of the problem that we want to solve, a situation very likely to happen in practice.

Now we state a lower bound both for the arithmetic and for the communication time:

Proposition 7.2 : For Gauss on a ring of $p = \alpha\, n$ processors, $0<\alpha\le 1$,

$$\frac{2\, n^2 \tau_a}{3\alpha} + o(np) \le T_a$$

$$n^2 (1+\alpha)\, \tau_c + o(np) \le T_c$$

Proof : The bound for T_a is simple: $T_a \ge T_{seq} / p$. The bound for T_c is derived as follows: let P_m be the left neighbour of the processor which holds the first column. It takes $(p-1)(n-1)\tau_c = \alpha n^2 \tau_c + o(np)$ units of time for P_m to receive column 1 at step 1. Then P_m must receive at least n-n/p-1 columns from its left neighbour, since it has only n/p columns in its local memory. P_m will need $\tau_c n^2/2 + o(np)$ units of time for receiving these columns (remember that n/p is negligible when compared to n). Finally, the right neighbour of P_m also needs to receive n-n/p-1 columns from P_m (these are not necessarily the same as the ones received by P_m), and P_m will spend $\tau_c n^2/2 + o(np)$ units of time for sending.

We already know that the full block distribution meets the lower bound on T_c. However, the wrap distribution does not meet the lower bound on T_a. In fact for the wrap distribution, $T_a = T_{bound} + \tau_a n^2(3-\alpha)/6 + o(np)$, where $T_{bound} = \frac{2n^2\tau_a}{3\alpha}$. Clearly the bound is not tight for large α, but T_a does not tend to T_{bound} for small α. If we want to achieve a better load balancing of the arithmetic, we can use the reflection mapping of Geist and Heath [1986] if $\alpha < 1/2$: processor i, $0 \le i < p$, has columns 2mp+i+1 and 2(m+1)p-i, $0 \le m \le \frac{n}{2p} - 1$. Then

$$T_a = T_{bound} + \alpha n^2 \tau_a/3 + o(np)$$

We can also use a bi-reflection mapping if $\alpha < 1/4$: processor i, $0 \le i < p$, has columns 4mp+i+1, 4mp+2p-i, 4mp+3p-i and 4mp+3p+i+1, $0 \le m \le \frac{n}{4p}$ 1. Then

$$T_a = T_{bound} + \alpha n^2 \tau_a/12 + o(np)$$

Both the reflection and the bi-reflection mapping tend to T_{bound} for small α.

7.1.6. Connection with chapter 5

We have studied the performances of various data allocations for the implementation of Gaussian elimination on a ring of processors. We have derived the best block size to be used as a function of the ratio α of the number of processors to the problem size and of the ratio ρ of the elemental costs of communication to arithmetic.

We point out the good adequacy of these theoretical results with numerical experiments run on a hypercube. Let n=480 and use various numbers of processors, from 4 to 16, so that α varies from 1/120 to 1/30. The best experimental value of r is always r=4. We report in table 7.1 the execution times for r=3, 4 and 5. On the other hand, we estimate $\rho = 14.13$ for the FPS hypercube and messages of average length 240. We report this value in the expression of the efficiency e_α, and we compute the value of r which maximizes it. This is the "optimal value" reported in table 7.1. Note that for small α, the theory predicts that $r_{opt} = \sqrt{\rho} \approx 3.76$.

Block size r	**p = 4**	**p = 8**	**p = 16**
3	35.58	19.97	12.37
4	35.53	19.96	12.26
5	35.71	20.14	12.56
optimal value of r	3.80	3.85	3.97

Table 7.1: Time (seconds) for n = 480

7.2. Speedup evaluation on distributed memory machines

Our aim in this section is to compare two different ways of evaluating the speedup of parallel algorithms on a distributed memory machine. The usual way for computing speedups is to consider a fixed-size problem and to evaluate the ratio of the time spent by a single processor to the time spent with several processors. According to Amdahl's law (see section 1.3), this ratio is bounded by the inverse of the sequential fraction of the program, thereby prohibiting massive parallelism.

However, solving a fixed-size problem, independent of the number of processors, has little sense using a distributed memory machine. Gustafson [1988] has proposed another way to compute speedups, which we have used in section 4.5: for each number of processors, we consider the largest instance of the problem that can be solved and compute the time it would have taken on a single processor. The ratio between these times is Gustafson's speedup.

In order to make it clear that Gustafson's speedup is best suited to distributed memory architectures, we consider our previous performance analysis model for Gaussian elimination (without pivoting) on an oriented ring. We discuss two implementations of the algorithm, the pipelined ring algorithm which we have already described, and the reverse ring algorithm, for which communications will be shown to destroy the performances when solving large problems.

7.2.1. Reverse ring algorithm

For the sake of simplicity, we choose the wrap allocation for allocating columns to processors. At step k in the pipeline ring (PR) algorithm, the processor holding column k, i.e. P_i, where i = (k-1) mod p, sends it to its right neighbour P_{i+1}, which in turn sends it to P_{i+2}, and so on until the pivot column reaches P_{i-1}, the left neighbour of P_i. The main advantage of this asynchronous strategy is that communications and computations can be overlapped. Each processor starts updating its internal columns as soon as it has received the pivot column and transmitted it to its neighbour.

On the other hand, we can design an algorithm where arithmetic and communications do not overlap. To synchronize *de facto* the processors at each step of the algorithm, we transmit the pivot column backwards in the ring. At step k in the reverse ring (RR) algorithm, processor P_i, i = (k-1) mod p, sends the pivot column to its left neighbour P_{i-1}, which in turn sends it to P_{i-2}, and so on until the pivot column reaches P_{i+1}, the right neighbour of P_i. Now processor P_{i+1} is the last one to receive column k. Hence computations for step k+1 cannot begin before the end of step k. The RR algorithm is as follows:

```
{ RR algorithm - program of processor P_i }
for k=1 to n-1 do
    if alloc(k) = i then
        send column k to P_{i-1}
    else
        receive column k from P_{i+1}
        if (i-1 mod p) ≠ alloc(k) then send column k to P_{i-1}
    endif
    { perform the eliminations }
    execute T_kj for all columns j≥k+1 such that alloc(j) = i
endfor
```

7.2.2. Performance modelling

The RR algorithm is simple to analyse, because arithmetic and communications do not overlap. The time $T_{RR}(n,p)$ for factoring a matrix of size n on a ring of p processors is the sum of the time $T_{a,RR}(n,p)$ needed for the arithmetic and of the time $T_{c,RR}(n,p)$ needed for the communications. The arithmetic is the same as for the PR algorithm, so that

$$T_{a,RR}(n,p) = T_{a,PR}(n,p) = \left(\frac{2n^3}{3p} + \frac{n^2}{2} - \frac{np}{6}\right)\tau_a + o(np)$$

For the communications, we propagate at step k the pivot column of length n-k across the ring, so that $T_{c,RR}(n,p) = \sum_{k=1}^{n-1}(p-1)(n-k)\tau_c = (p-1)\frac{n^2\tau_c}{2} + o(np)$. Recall that $T_{c,PR}(n,p) = \left(\frac{3n^2}{2} + pn - \frac{p^2}{2}\right)\tau_c + o(np)$. We can conceptually view the PR algorithm as a non-overlapped algorithm where the communications have a cost independent of the size of the ring: the factor (p-1) coming from $T_{c,RR}(n,p)$ is replaced by the constant 3 in $T_{c,PR}(n,p)$.

Given a number p of processors, we consider the largest problem size $n_{max,p} \approx \sqrt{pM}$ that can be solved using the available memory. On today's machines, M is very large (from one to ten Mwords), and the ratio $\alpha = p/n$ will be small. Neglecting low order terms in our expressions for $T_{PR}(n,p)$ and $T_{RR}(n,p)$, we get

$$T_{PR}(n,p) = \left(\frac{2n^3}{3p} + \frac{n^2}{2}\right)\tau_a + \frac{3n^2}{2}\tau_c$$

$$T_{RR}(n,p) = \left(\frac{2n^3}{3p} + \frac{n^2}{2}\right)\tau_a + \frac{(p-1)n^2}{2}\tau_c$$

We can express $\tau_{max}(p)$, the average time needed for one arithmetic operation, as

$$\tau_{max}(p) = \frac{T(n_{max}(p),p)}{\frac{2}{3}n_{max}(p)^3}, \text{ with } n_{max}(p) = \sqrt{pM}.$$

We obtain respectively:

PR algorithm

$\tau_{max}(p) = (\gamma + \gamma') \, p^{-1/2} + \delta \, p^{-1}$ for p>1 for p>1

$\tau_{max}(1) = \gamma + \delta$

RR algorithm

$\tau_{max}(p) = \varepsilon \, p^{1/2} + (\gamma + \gamma'') \, p^{-1/2} + \delta \, p^{-1}$ for p>1

$\tau_{max}(1) = \gamma + \delta$

where $\delta = \tau_a$

$\gamma = 0.75 \, \tau_a \, M^{-1/2}$

$\gamma' = 2.25 \, \tau_c \, M^{-1/2}$ $\gamma'' = -\,0.75 \, \tau_c \, M^{-1/2}$

$\varepsilon = 0.75 \, \tau_c \, M^{-1/2}$

We plot in figure 7.5 the theoretical values of $\tau_{max}(p)$ for both algorithms, assuming a (typical ?) machine for which $\tau_a = 10^{-7}$, $\tau_c = 10^{-6}$ and $M = 10^6$. The theoretical values are computed up to 64K processors.

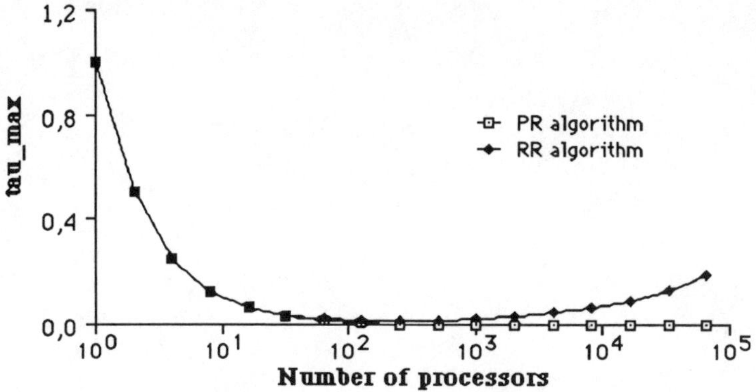

Figure 7.5 : τ_{max} as a function of p (theoretical values)

We believe that $\tau_{max}(p)$ is the variable which gives the best insight of the performances of a distributed memory machine, because it measures the actual yield of the machine. The formulae above show that the asymptotic behaviour of $\tau_{max}(p)$ essentially depends on the performance of the algorithm regarding communications. For the PR algorithm, $\tau_{max}(p) = O(p^{-1/2})$, hence the larger p, the better $\tau_{max}(p)$: we do not lose any efficiency using a massively parallel machine. This somehow contradicts Amdahl's law !

On the contrary for the RR algorithm, the value of $\tau_{max}(p)$ is minimum for p=192; for a larger number of processors, the communications swamp the arithmetic: $\tau_{max}(p) = O(p^{1/2})$ for large p. We perform better with 8 processors than with 64K processors, because the intrinsic time needed for each flop is greater. Of course we solve a larger problem with 64K processors ...

Even for parallel algorithms whose execution time does not obey a simple analytical formula, computing $\tau_{max}(p)$ is easy and really shows the increase in performances that can be achieved with the multiplication of the hardware (processor, memory, communication links).

7.3. Bibliographic notes

As we said, results presented in this chapter are only a first step towards the analysis of the distributed complexity of Gaussian elimination. Few results are available in the literature: see Gentleman [1978], Ipsen, Saad and Schultz [1986] and Saad [1986b]. Section 7.1 is based on Robert, Tourancheau and Villard [1989]. Section 7.2 is based on Cosnard, Robert and Tourancheau [1989].

CHAPTER
EIGHT

DESIGN METHODOLOGIES FOR SYSTOLIC ARRAYS

In this chapter, we deal with the systematic design of systolic arrays. First we review the dependence mapping method for the automatic synthesis of systolic algorithms based on uniform recurrence equations. Then we move to complexity results for the mapping of Gaussian elimination onto 2D systolic arrays. Finally we describe several systolic solutions whose space-time complexity are better than those of the arrays described in chapter 5.

8.1. Dependence mapping method

In this section, we systematically derive 2D systolic arrays for Gaussian elimination. Our aim is to retrieve the arrays described in chapter 5. We use the dependence mapping method introduced by Quinton [1987]. We informally explain the key steps of the method using the simple example of matrix-matrix multiplication before moving to Gaussian elimination.

8.1.1. Matrix product

Consider two n x n dense matrices A and B, and let C = AB. We have

$$c_{ij} = \sum_{k=1}^{n} a_{ik} \, . \, b_{kj}, \quad 1 \le i \le n, 1 \le j \le n \qquad (8.1)$$

A natural way to serialize this accumulation is to put:

$$\begin{array}{ll} c(i,j,0) = 0 & 1 \le i,j \le n \\ c(i,j,k) = c(i,j,k\text{-}1) + a_{ik} \, . \, b_{kj} & 1 \le i,j,k \le n \\ c_{ij} = c(i,j,n) & 1 \le i,j \le n \end{array} \qquad (8.2)$$

The c(i,j,k), 1≤k≤n, are the partial accumulated values for c(i,j). For any coordinate triple (i,j,k) lying in the domain $D^n = \{(i,j,k);\ 1\le i\le n,\ 1\le j\le n,\ 1\le k\le n\}$ of $\mathbb{Z}^3$, we have to compute a function $c_{out} := c_{in} + a_{in}.b_{in}$, which will deliver c(i,j,k) provided that c_{in}, a_{in} and b_{in} are given correct values c(i,j,k-1), a_{ik} and b_{kj}. We observe that in equation (8.2) each computation makes use of two data items a_{ik} and b_{kj} which are common to several computations. In order to avoid reading the same data several times, it is possible to make a_{ik} and b_{kj} circulate from computation node to computation node. Clearly, a_{ik} is used by all coefficients c(i,j,k) where j ranges from 1 to n. Therefore we can assume that input value a_{ik} of node (i,j,k) is provided by node (i,j-1,k). Similarly, b_{kj} is used by all coefficients c(i,j,k), 1≤i≤n. So we can assume that input value b_{kj} of node (i,j,k) is provided by node (i-1,j,k). Such a scheme can be formally expressed as the following system of equations:

Input equations

$1 \le i \le n,\ 1 \le k \le n \quad \rightarrow \quad A(i,j,k) = a_{ik}$

$1 \le j \le n,\ 1 \le k \le n \quad \rightarrow \quad B(i,j,k) = b_{kj}$

$1 \le i \le n,\ 1 \le j \le n \quad \rightarrow \quad C(i,j,k) = c_{ij}$

Computation equations

$$1 \le i \le n,\ 1 \le j \le n,\ 1 \le k \le n \quad \rightarrow \quad \begin{cases} C(i,j,k) = C(i,j,k-1) + A(i,j-1,k).B(i-1,j,k) \\ A(i,j,k) = A(i,j-1,k) \\ B(i,j,k) = B(i-1,j,k) \end{cases} \qquad (8.3)$$

Output equations

$1 \le i \le n,\ 1 \le j \le n \quad \rightarrow \quad c_{ij} = C(i,j,n)$

Such a system of recurrent equations is said to be *uniform* , since computation at node (i,j,k) depends only on values computed at points that are obtained by a translation which does not depend upon the values of i, j and k. The space-time diagram associated with these recurrence equations is a directed graph G called the dependence graph. The set of vertices is the computation domain D^n which contains the domain of the integer triples (i,j,k) associated with the computation of the variables C(i,j,k). There is an arc in G from vertex u to vertex v if the computation in v uses a variable computed in u. The dependence graph G is shown in figure 8.1 for n=3.

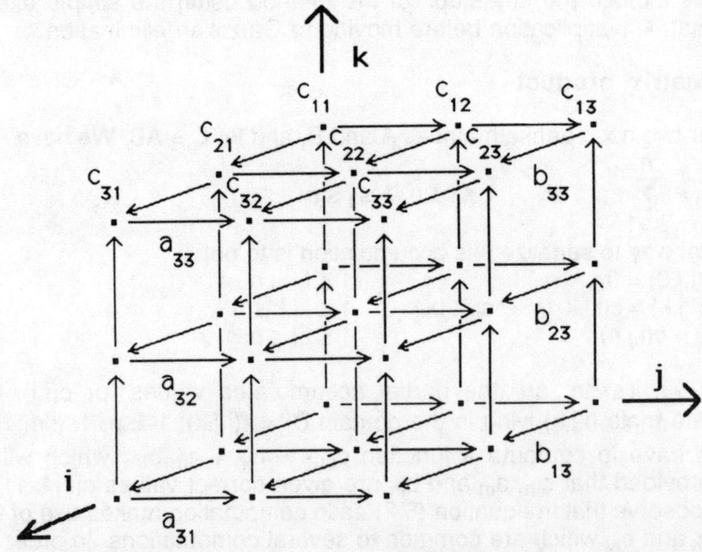

Figure 8.1 : Dependence graph for the matrix product

Since the recurrent equations are uniform, we have a finite set of dependence vectors $\Theta = \{\theta_a, \theta_b, \theta_c\}$ that defines where node (i,j,k) has to take its input values. For instance $\theta_a = (0,1,0)$ because node (i,j,k) reads its A-input from node (i,j-1,k). Similarly, θ_b = (1,0,0), and θ_c = (0,0,1). We call these vectors dependence vectors because the computation in vertex (i,j,k) depends upon the result of the computation in the vertices (i,j,k)-θ, $\theta \in \Theta$.

The next step of the method is to define a schedule for the computation, by means of a timing function. A timing function is a mapping t: $D^n \rightarrow \mathbb{Z}$ such that if computation at vertex x $\in D^n$ depends upon those at vertex y then t(x) > t(y). In order to have a regular scheduling for the computations, we look for an affine function t: let t(i,j,k) = λ_1 i + λ_2 j + λ_3 k + α, with λ_1, λ_2, λ_3 and α integers. Let t' be the linear part of t. Let x, y be two vertices such that x depends upon y: we have x = y + θ for some $\theta \in \Theta$. The condition t(x) > t(y) amounts to t'(θ) > 0. We obtain the following conditions:

$\lambda_1 \geq 1, \lambda_2 \geq 1, \lambda_3 \geq 1$

The global execution time will be equal to T = max {t(x); x $\in D^n$}. We choose the λ_i so that this time is minimum, i.e. we take $\lambda_1 = \lambda_2 = \lambda_3 = 1$. Finally we choose α so that every vertex x $\in D^n$ is scheduled at a positive time: the minimum of t over D^n is for node (1,1,1), and we get α = -2. Now we have completely defined the timing function:

t(i,j,k) = i+j+k-2 for (i,j,k)$\in D^n$

According to this timing function, it is possible to solve (8.3) by successively executing computations for nodes x $\in D^n$ whose timing value t(x) is 1,2, ..., 3n-2. See figure 8.2 where the time steps of each vertex are shown.

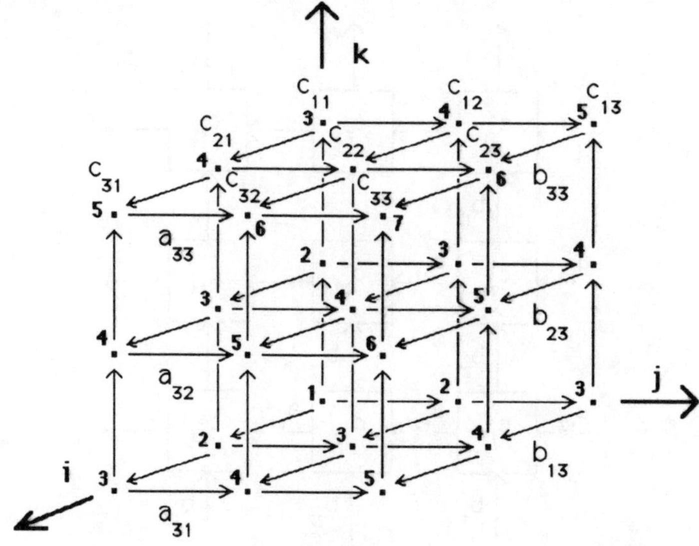

Figure 8.2 : Timing function for the matrix product

The last step of the method is to define an architecture that supports these calculations. This is obtained by defining an allocation function which maps D^n onto a *finite* set E: we want the number of processors |E| of the target architecture to be finite. Let alloc: $D^n \rightarrow$ E be the allocation function. We do not want to map on the same processor the computations of two distinct vertices that are scheduled at the same time; in other words:

$$\text{alloc}(x) = \text{alloc}(y) \Rightarrow t(x) \neq t(y) \text{ for all } x, y \in D^n, x \neq y \qquad (8.4)$$

In order to obtain designs with a good regularity and local interconnections, we take the allocation function to be linear: more precisely, we take alloc to be an orthogonal projection along a direction u, where u is a vector non-collinear to λ, so that condition (8.4) holds: if alloc(x) = alloc(y), then x-y $\in$ Ker(alloc), and x-y is collinear to u. Hence x-y is not collinear to the time vector $\lambda = (\lambda_1, \lambda_2, \lambda_3)$, therefore x-y $\notin$ Ker t' and $t(x) \neq t(y)$.

Once the timing function t and the allocation function a have been defined, the architecture is completely defined. Each processor π of alloc(D^n) executes the computation attached to the nodes of D^n that are mapped onto it. Communication among the processors is also completely defined: processor π executes at time t(i,j,k) the computation of node (i,j,k) $\in D^n$: $c_{out} := c_{in} + a_{in} * b_{in}$. It receives

- a_{in} = A(i,j-1,k) from processor alloc(i,j-1,k) = alloc((i,j,k)-θ_a) = π - alloc(θ_a)
- b_{in} = B(i-1,j,k) from processor π - alloc(θ_b)
- c_{in} = C(i,j,k-1) from processor π - alloc(θ_c).

The delays along the communication links are also determined: for instance a_{in} is computed at time t(i,j-1,k) = t(i,j,k) - t'(θ_a) by processor π - alloc(θ_a), so that there are t'(θ_a) delays for propagating the a-values between π - alloc(θ_a) and π.

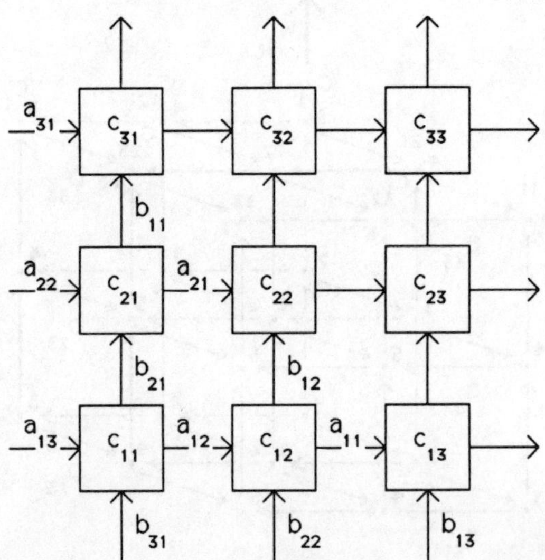

Figure 8.3 : Systolic array for the matrix product

Maybe the most natural projection here is to choose u = (0,0,1), i.e. to project the domain D^n along the k-axis: alloc(i,j,k) = (i,j,0). Then alloc(D^n) contains n^2 processors: this is the smallest value that can be obtained from D^n with a projection. The corresponding systolic architecture is shown in figure 8.3. The only drawback to this solution is that the results are not output naturally from the array: the C-values do not move during the computation. More precisely, c_{ij} is repeatedly updated in processor (i,j), since alloc(θ_c) = 0.

8.1.2. Gaussian elimination

We are now ready to tackle the more complicated example of Gaussian elimination. Let Ax= b be a linear system of size n. We transform it into the triangular system Ux = c using Gaussian elimination without pivoting. A is overwritten by its LU decomposition A = LU (see section 1.2). The triangularization scheme can be formally expressed as the following system of equations:

Input equations (8.5)

$1 \le i \le n,\ 1 \le j \le n \quad \rightarrow \quad A(i,j,k) = a_{ij}$

$1 \le i \le n,\ j=n+1 \quad \rightarrow \quad A(i,j,k) = b_i$

Computation equations (8.6)

$1 \le k \le n,\ j=k,\ k+1 \le i \le n \quad \rightarrow \quad A(i,j,k) = A(i,j,k-1)/A(k,k,k)$

$1 \le k \le n,\ i=k,\ k \le j \le n+1 \quad \rightarrow \quad A(i,j,k) = A(i,j,k-1)$

$1 \le k \le n,\ k+1 \le i \le n,\ k+1 \le j \le n+1 \quad \rightarrow \quad A(i,j,k) = A(i,j,k-1) - A(i,k,k)*A(k,j,k)$

Output equations (8.7)

$1 \le k \le n-1,\ k+1 \le i \le n \quad \rightarrow \quad l_{ik} = A(i,k,k)$

$1 \le k \le n,\ k \le j \le n \quad \rightarrow \quad u_{kj} = A(k,j,k)$

$1 \le k \le n,\ j=n+1 \quad \rightarrow \quad c_k = A(k,n+1,k)$

The computation domain is D^n = { (i,j,k), $1 \le k \le n$, $k \le i \le n$, $k \le j \le n+1$ }. The dependence graph G is represented in figure 8.4 for n=4.

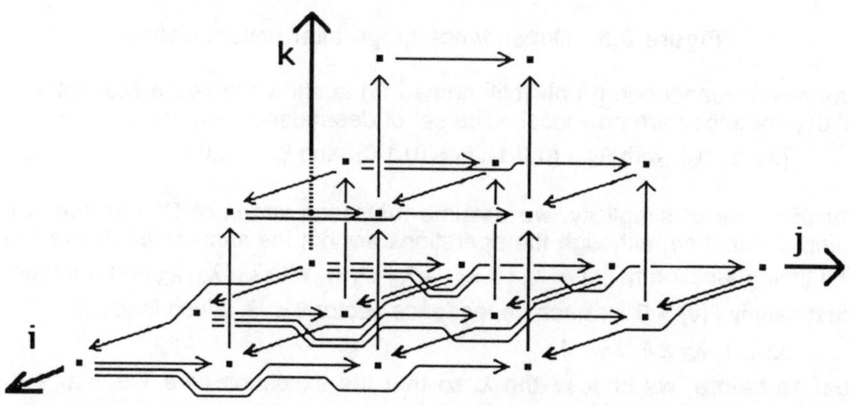

Figure 8.4 : Non-uniform dependence graph for Gaussian elimination

Contrarily to the matrix-matrix product, the dependences in the recurrence equations are not uniform: for instance vertex (i,k,k) depends upon vertex (k,k,k) for all i>k. In other words θ = (i-k,0,0) is a dependence vector for all i>k.

We would like to uniformize the equations to avoid non-local dependences. A natural idea is to pipeline the circulation of the variables A(i,k,k) along the direction (0,1,0). In this way A(i,k,k) will start at vertex (i,k,k) and successively visit vertices (i,k+1,k), (i,k+2,k), ..., (i,n,k). Similarly, we pipeline the circulation of the variables A(k,j,k) along direction (1,0,0).[1] This leads to the new system of recurrence equations (input and output equations are left unchanged):

Computation equations (8.8)

$1 \le k \le n$, $j=k$, $k+1 \le i \le n$	$\rightarrow$	$A(i,j,k) = A(i,j,k-1)/U(i,j,k)$
$1 \le k \le n$, $i=k$, $k \le j \le n+1$	$\rightarrow$	$A(i,j,k) = A(i,j,k-1)$
$1 \le k \le n$, $k+1 \le i \le n$, $k+1 \le j \le n+1$	$\rightarrow$	$L(i,j,k) = L(i,j-1,k)$
$1 \le k \le n$, $j=k$, $k+1 \le i \le n$	$\rightarrow$	$L(i,j,k) = A(i,k,k)$
$1 \le k \le n$, $k \le j \le n+1$, $k+1 \le i \le n$	$\rightarrow$	$U(i,j,k) = U(i-1,j,k)$
$1 \le k \le n$, $i=k$, $k \le j \le n+1$	$\rightarrow$	$U(i,j,k) = A(k,j,k)$
$1 \le k \le n$, $k+1 \le i \le n$, $k+1 \le j \le n+1$	$\rightarrow$	$A(i,j,k) = A(i,j,k-1) - L(i,j,k)*U(i,j,k)$

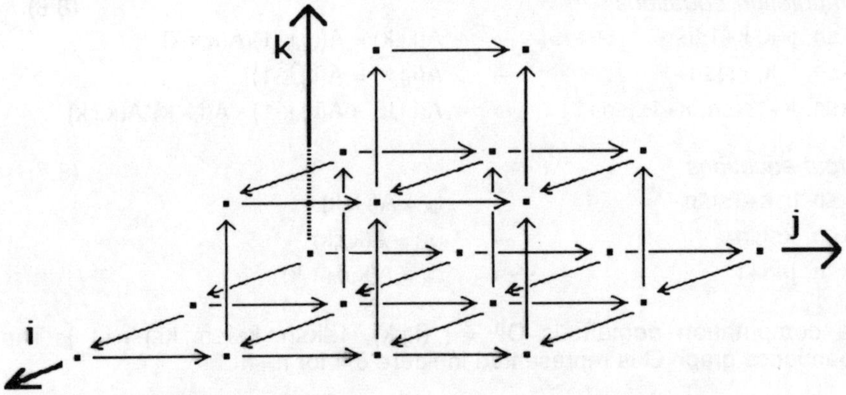

Figure 8.5 : Dependence graph after uniformization

The new dependence graph (still named G) is shown in figure 8.5. Note that all dependences are now local. The set of dependence vectors is

$$\{\theta_a, \theta_l, \theta_u\}, \text{ with } \theta_a = (0,0,1),\ \theta_l = (0,1,0), \text{ and } \theta_u = (1,0,0)$$

For the sake of simplicity, we assume that each vertex of D^n has the same computation time, although the operations are not the same in all the vertices. The timing function $t(i,j,k) = \lambda_1 i + \lambda_2 j + \lambda_3 k + \alpha$, with $\lambda_1, \lambda_2, \lambda_3$ and α integers, must satisfy $t'(\theta) > 0$ for each dependence vector $\theta \in \Theta$, which leads to

$$\lambda_1 \ge 1,\ \lambda_2 \ge 1,\ \lambda_3 \ge 1$$

Just as before, we choose the λ_i so that the execution time $T = \max\{ t(x);\ x \in D^n \}$ is minimum, i.e. we take $\lambda_1 = \lambda_2 = \lambda_3 = 1$. Finally we choose α so that every vertex $x \in D^n$ is scheduled at a positive time: the minimum of t over D^n is

[1] There are systematic ways of uniformizing equations whose domains are convex polyhedra, see van Dongen and Quinton [1988].

for node (1,1,1), and we get $\alpha = -2$. We obtain the same timing function as for the matrix product: $t(i,j,k) = i+j+k-2$ for $(i,j,k) \in D^n$.

For the allocation function, we can choose $u = (0,1,0)$, that is $alloc(i,j,k) = (i,0,k)$. We obtain the Ahmed-Delosme-Morf array of figure 5.5. We can also choose $u = (1,0,0)$, that is $alloc(i,j,k) = (0,j,k)$. Then we obtain the Gentleman-Kung array of figure 5.8.

8.2. Complexity results

In this section, we prove complexity results for systolic Gaussian elimination. More precisely, we consider the previous system of uniform recurrence equations whose dependence graph is shown in figure 8.5. We want to determine optimal timing and allocation functions for these equations. Note that this is only a partial result: the original system of equations (8.5, 8.6, 8.7) that specifies Gaussian elimination has been transformed through the uniformization of the recurrences, and we only deal with the complexity of the resulting uniform system (8.5, 8.8, 8.7).

8.2.1. Optimal timing function

Again, we assume that each vertex of $D^n = \{ i,j,k), 1 \le k \le n, k \le i \le n, k \le j \le n+1\}$ has the same computation time, although the operations are not the same in all the vertices.

Proposition 8.1 : The timing function $t(i,j,k) = i+j+k-2$ is optimal.

Proof : We already know that $t(i,j,k) = i+j+k-2$ is a timing function, since $t'(\theta)>0$ for each dependence vector $\theta \in \Theta$. We also know that this timing function is optimal among all linear timing functions. What we want to prove is that it is optimal among all possible timing functions.

Any sequence of computations located on a path of the dependence graph G must be done sequentially. Therefore the execution time is always greater than the length of the longest path in G.[1] For all $x \in D^n$, $t(x) \le t(n,n+1,n) = 3n-1$. It thus suffices to exhibit a path in the dependence graph G of length 3n-1 to show that t is optimal. The path $s = \{v_1, v_2, ..., v_{3n-1}\}$ is one such path, where
• $v_i = (i,1,1)$ for $1 \le i \le n$: first n vertices in direction (1,0,0), starting at vertex (1,1,1) up to vertex (n,1,1)
• $v_i = (n,i-n+1,1)$ for $n+1 \le i \le 2n$: then n vertices in direction (0,1,0) up to vertex (n,n+1,1)
• $v_i = (n,n+1,i-2n+1)$ for $2n+1 \le i \le 3n-1$: finally n-1 vertices in direction (0,0,1) up to (n,n+1,n).

As a consequence, the optimal time for systolic Gaussian elimination is $t_{opt} = 3n-1$. We now prove that $t(i,j,k) = i+j+k-2$ is the *only* optimal timing function:

Proposition 8.2 : There is a unique optimal timing function.

---

[1] We have also used this argument in section 6.2.

Proof : Let x = (i,j,k) be a vertex of D^n. First we prove that x is the (i+j+k-2)-th vertex of a longest path in G, constructed as follows: start at vertex (1,1,1), then do i-1 steps in direction (1,0,0), j-1 steps in direction (0,1,0), and k-1 steps in direction (0,0,1). At this point we are at vertex x, and this is the (i+j+k-2)-th vertex of the path. Then do n-i steps in direction (1,0,0), n+1-j steps in direction (0,1,0), and n-k steps in direction (0,0,1) to reach vertex y =(n,n+1,n).

Let t be an optimal timing function: $t(u) \leq 3n-1$ for all $u \in D^n$. Since there are 3n-1 vertices in the path, then t(y) = 3n-1 for the last vertex y, and the timing of each vertex is necessarily equal to its index in the path. In particular t(x) = i+j+k-2.

8.2.2. Complexity in terms of processors

Both the Ahmed-Delosme-Morf and the Gentleman-Kung arrays are scheduled with the optimal timing function, hence their execution time 3n-1 is optimal. We have compared their respective numbers of processors in section 5.1: n(n+1)/2 for the Ahmed-Delosme-Morf solution and n(n+3)/2 for the Gentleman-Kung one. A natural question arises: what is the minimum number of processors that requires a systolic solution with the optimal scheduling ?

When discussing allocation functions, we have insisted that the target design should be regular and locally connected, and therefore we have considered linear allocation functions. If we find a non-linear allocation function that requires fewer processors, then the resulting solution is not guaranteed to be as regular as the "pure" systolic schemes. However, finding the minimum number of processors for any allocation function will give us a lower bound of what can be achieved, and this will give us an indication of how efficient are our favourite solutions.

Proposition 8.3 : The minimum number of processors M_n for the systolic triangularization of an n x (n+1) matrix [A,b] in optimal time $t_{opt} = 3n-1$ is $M_n = n^2/4 + O(n)$. More precisely $M_{2p-1} = p^2$ and $M_{2p} = p(p+1)$ for all $p \geq 1$.

Proof : Proposition 8.3 is due to Bermond et al. [1988], and we follow their proof. For $1 \leq t \leq 3n-1$, let $D^n(t) = \{(i,j,k) \in D^n, i+j+k=t+2\}$, and $m_n(t) = | D^n(t) |$. Then $m_n(t)$ is the number of vertices of D^n which are executed at time t, and $M_n = \max \{ m_n(t); 1 \leq t \leq 3n-1\}$ is the maximum number of vertices executed at the same time, hence the minimum number of processors required.

We partition $D^n(t)$ into $D^n(t) = \cup_{1 \leq k \leq n} D^{n,k}(t)$ where $D^{n,k}(t) = \{(i,j,z) \in D^n(t) \,/\, z=k\}$

and we let $m_{n,k}(t) = | D^{n,k}(t) |$. Clearly $m_n(t) = \sum_{k=1}^{n} m_{n,k}(t)$. See table 8.1 for an example with n=5: at least $M_5 = 9$ processors are required to execute the scheme in time 3n-1=14.

t	1	2	3	4	5	6	7	8	9	10	11	12	13	14
$m_{5,1}(t)$	1	2	3	4	5	5	4	3	2	1				
$m_{5,2}(t)$				1	2	3	4	4	3	2	1			
$m_{5,3}(t)$							1	2	3	3	2	1		
$m_{5,4}(t)$										1	2	2	1	
$m_{5,5}(t)$													1	1
$m_5(t)$	**1**	**2**	**3**	**5**	**7**	**8**	**9**	**9**	**8**	**7**	**5**	**3**	**2**	**1**

Table 8.1: Values of $m_{n,k}(t)$ for n=5

We see in table 8.1 that, given n and k, the sequence $m_{n,k}(t)$ is a palindrome. We also see that, given n, the sequence $m_n(t)$ is a palindrome. We prove this in the following lemmas:

Lemma 8.4 :

$m_{n,k}(t) = 0$ if $t \le 3k-3$ or $t \ge n+2k-1$
$m_{n,k}(t) = t-3k+3$ if $3k-2 \le t \le n+2k-2$
$m_{n,k}(t) = 2n+k-t$ if $n+2k-1 \le t \le 2n+k-1$

Proof : $m_{n,k}(t)$ is the number of solutions of the equation $i+j = t-k+2$, with $k \le i \le n$ and $k \le j \le n+1$. Let $i' = i-k+1$, $j' = j-k+1$; $m_{n,k}(t)$ is the number of solutions of the equation $i'+j' = t-3k+4$, with $1 \le i' \le n-k+1$, $1 \le j' \le n-k+2$, and the result follows.

Lemma 8.5 :

$m_{n+1}(t) = m_n(t-3)+t$ if $1 \le t \le n+1$
$m_{n+1}(t) = m_n(t-3)+2n+3-t$ if $n+1 \le t \le 2n+2$
$m_{n+1}(t) = m_n(t-3)+3n+3-t$ if $2n+3 \le t \le 3n+2$

Proof : $D^{n+1}(t)$ is the union of $D^{n+1,1}(t)$ and the image of $D^n(t-3)$ by the translation $i \to i+1$, $j \to j+1$ and $k \to k+1$. Therefore

$$m_{n+1}(t) = m_{n+1,1}(t+1) + m_n(t-3)$$

We get the result by applying lemma 8.4.

Lemma 8.6 :

$m_{n+1}(t) = m_n(t)$ if $1 \le t \le n$
$m_{n+1}(t) = m_n(t)+t-n$ if $n+1 \le t \le 2n+1$
$m_{n+1}(t) = m_n(t)+3n+3-t$ if $2n+2 \le t \le 3n+2$

Proof : $D^{n+1}(t)$ is the union of $D^n(t)$ and the set of vertices (i,j,k) such that $i+j+k=t+2$ and at least one of the following conditions is satisfied: $i=n+1$ or $j=n+2$ or $k=n+1$:

• the number of vertices of $D^{n+1}(t)$ with $j=n+2$ is equal to the number of couples (i,k) such that $i+n+2+k=t+2$ and $k \le i \le n+1$, that is 0 for $t \le n+1$, $\lfloor \frac{t-n}{2} \rfloor$ for $n+2 \le t \le 2n+1$ and $\lceil \frac{3n+3-t}{2} \rceil$ for $2n+2 \le t \le 3n+2$

• the number of vertices of $D^{n+1}(t)$ with $i=n+1$ ($j \ne n+2$) is equal to the number of couples (j,k) such that $n+1+j+k=t+2$ and $k \le j \le n+1$, that is 0 for $t \le n$, $\lceil \frac{t-n}{2} \rceil$ for $n+2 \le t \le 2n+1$ and $\lfloor \frac{3n+3-t}{2} \rfloor$ for $2n+2 \le t \le 3n+2$

• if $(i,j,k) \in D^{n+1}(t)$ with $k=n+1$, then $i=n+1$

The lemma follows easily.

Lemma 8.7 : (i) the sequence $m_n(t)$ for $1 \le t \le 3n-1$ is a palindrome: $m_n(t) = m_n(3n-t)$ for $1 \le t \le 3n-1$

(ii) the sequence $m_n(t)$ is strictly increasing for $t \le \lceil \frac{3n}{2} \rceil - 1$

(iii) $m_n(\lceil \frac{3n}{2} \rceil - 2) = M_n - 1$ and $m_n(\lceil \frac{3n}{2} \rceil - 1) = m_n(\lceil \frac{3n}{2} \rceil) = M_n$

(iv) $M_{n+1} = M_n + \lceil \frac{n+1}{2} \rceil$

Proof : We prove (i) by induction on n. If n=1, $m_1(1)=m_1(2)=1$. Assume that $m_n(t) = m_n(3n-t)$ for a given $n \ge 1$.

- if $t \le n$, then $m_{n+1}(3n+3-t) = m_n(3n-t)$ by lemma 8.5 and $m_{n+1}(t) = m_n(t)$ by lemma 8.6. By induction hypothesis, $m_{n+1}(3n+3-t) = m_{n+1}(t)$.
- if $n+1 \le t \le \lfloor \frac{3n+3}{2} \rfloor$, then $m_{n+1}(3n+3-t) = m_n(3n-t)+2n+3-(3n+3-t) = m_n(3n-t)+t-n$ by lemma 8.5 and $m_{n+1}(t) = m_n(t)+t-n$ by lemma 8.6. Therefore $m_{n+1}(3n+3-t) = m_{n+1}(t)$.

Now we prove (ii) to (iv) by induction on n. If n=1, $m_1(1)=m_1(2)=1$ and $M_2 = 2$. Assume that conditions (ii) to (iv) hold for a given $n \ge 1$.

- by lemma 8.6, $m_{n+1}(t+1) - m_{n+1}(t) \ge m_n(t+1) - m_n(t)$. Therefore the sequence $m_{n+1}(t)$ is strictly increasing for $t \le \lceil \frac{3n}{2} \rceil - 1$
- by lemma 8.6, we also have

$$m_{n+1}(\lceil \tfrac{3(n+1)}{2} \rceil - 2) = M_n + \lceil \tfrac{3(n+1)}{2} \rceil - 2 - n = M_n + \lceil \tfrac{n-1}{2} \rceil$$

$$m_{n+1}(\lceil \tfrac{3(n+1)}{2} \rceil - 1) = M_n + \lceil \tfrac{3(n+1)}{2} \rceil - 1 - n = M_n + \lceil \tfrac{n+1}{2} \rceil$$

$$m_{n+1}(\lceil \tfrac{3(n+1)}{2} \rceil) = M_n - 1 + \lceil \tfrac{3(n+1)}{2} \rceil - n = M_n + \lceil \tfrac{n+1}{2} \rceil.$$

Proposition 8.3 now comes directly using the relation $M_{n+1} = M_n + \lceil \frac{n+1}{2} \rceil$ with $M_1 = 1$.

Finding a "pure" systolic solution for Gaussian elimination in t_{opt} and with M_n processors is an unsolved problem. Note that the Ahmed-Delosme-Morf and Gentleman-Kung arrays require approximately twice this number of processors. In the next section, we first present a solution which works in t_{opt} and uses only $3n^2/8$ processors. Then we show how to modify this solution in order to derive an optimal array ... which is nearly "purely" systolic.

8.3. Folding

In this section, we modify the linear array algorithm described in section 5.1 by folding it around its horizontal axis. The space-time extension of the resulting ring algorithm will lead to a systolic solution requiring fewer processors than the Ahmed-Delosme-Morf and Gentleman-Kung arrays.

8.3.1. From a linear array algorithm to a ring algorithm

We take here a macroscopic point of view, as in figure 5.1. We look carefully at table 5.1 (n=5) which we reproduce below for the sake of convenience:

Step	P_1	P_2	P_3	P_4	P_5
1	T_{11}				
2	T_{12}				
3	T_{13}	T_{22}			
4	T_{14}	T_{23}			
5	T_{15}	T_{24}	T_{33}		
6	T_{16}	T_{25}	T_{34}		
7		T_{26}	T_{35}	T_{44}	
8			T_{36}	T_{45}	
9				T_{46}	T_{55}
10					T_{56}

Here a task represents a combination of columns and is assumed to last one time step. We see that processor P_1 executes its last task at time 6, that is one step before P_4 initiates its first computation T_{44}. So we can fold the array around its horizontal axis and assign to processor P_1 the set of tasks that were previously assigned to P_4 (in addition to its own tasks). Similarly, P_2 is given the set of tasks of P_5. In the general case, let n = 2p+1 be odd for the sake of simplicity. Then P_i, $1 \le i \le p$, is assigned the set of tasks $\{T_{ij};\ i \le j \le n+1\} \cup \{T_{i+p+1,j};\ i+p+1 \le j \le n+1\}$, and the last processor P_{p+1} is assigned the set of tasks $\{T_{p+1,j};\ p+1 \le j \le n+1\}$. This leads to the parallel algorithm illustrated in figure 8.6. Processor i, $1 \le i \le p$, executes task T_{ij} at time i+j-1, $i \le j \le n+1$, and task $T_{i+p+1,j}$ at time i+j+p, $i+p+1 \le j \le n+1$

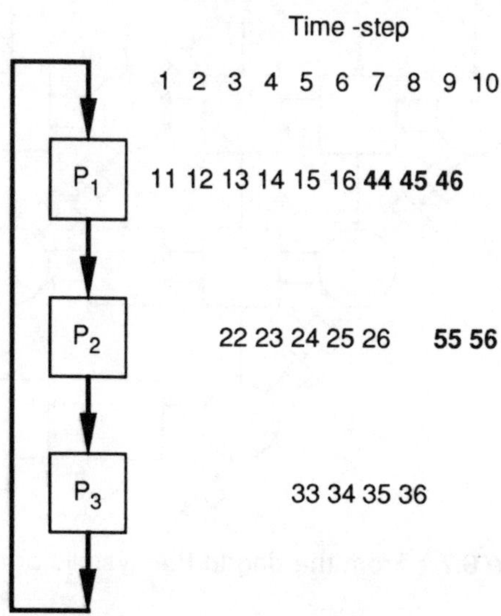

Figure 8.6 : Solving a problem of size n on a ring of ⌈n/2⌉ processors (n=5)

We move to a systolic design by the same space-time extension as in chapter 5. We obtain the array represented in figure 8.7. For the sake of clarity, we have particularized the action of some cells: these are the circular cells of figure 8.7, and they correspond to the circular cells in figure 5.5. This distinction between circular and square cells is a violation of the modularity property in that, for instance, the fourth cell of the first row of the array (cell p+2 if n=2p+1) should not be different from its neighbours if we want to extend the array in order to solve larger problems. It is not difficult, however, to keep a unique type of cell: just let the diagonal control have priority over the horizontal control, and all cells can operate the same way.The program of the cells is given in figure 8.8.

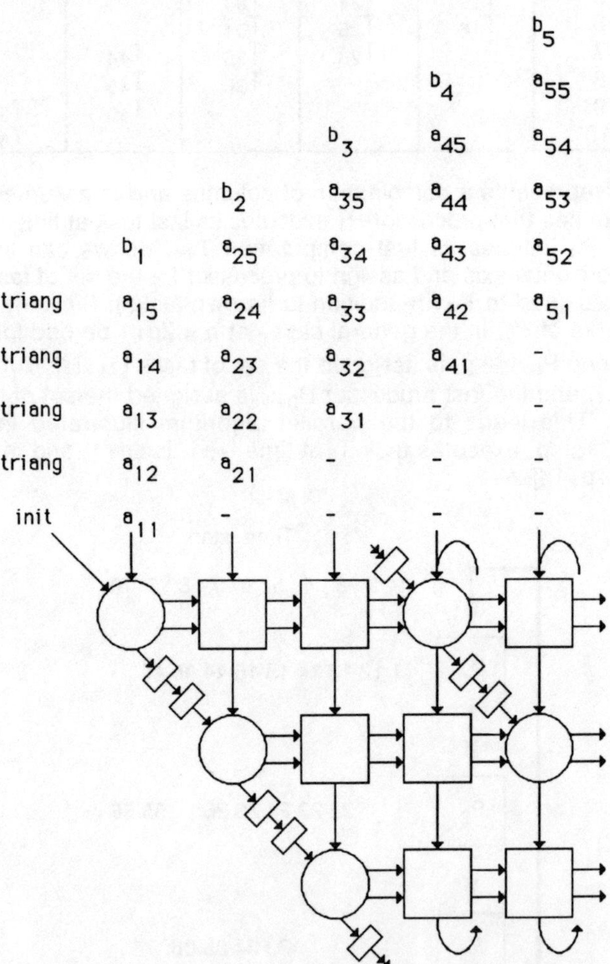

Figure 8.7 : From the ring to the systolic array

diag_ctrl in
a in
b out
h_ctrl out
diag_ctrl out

Step t
Step t+1

case diag_ctrl$_{in}$ **of**
init : **begin** b$_{out}$:= a$_{in}$; h_ctrl$_{out}$:= diag_ctrl$_{in}$; **end**
triang : **begin** b$_{out}$:= a$_{in}$; h_ctrl$_{out}$:= diag_ctrl$_{in}$; **end**
nil : act as square cell controlled by horiz_control$_{in}$
endcase
diag_ctrl$_{out}$:= diag_ctrl$_{in}$;

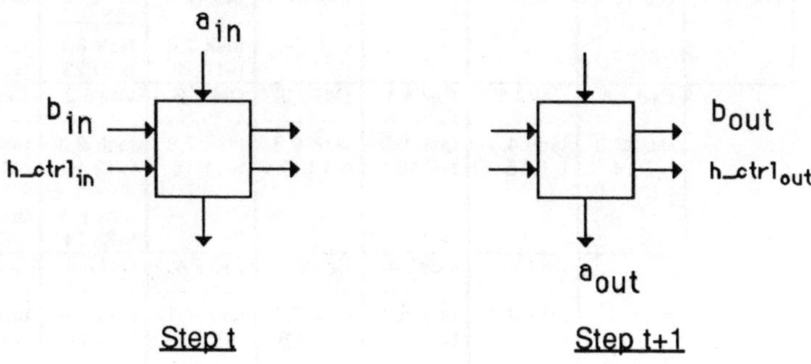

case h_ctrl$_{in}$ **of**
init : { initialize register } **begin** r := - a$_{in}$ / b$_{in}$; b$_{out}$:= b$_{in}$; **end**
triang : { update a$_{in}$ } **begin** a$_{out}$:= a$_{in}$ + b$_{in}$ * r ; b$_{out}$:= b$_{in}$; **end**
endcase
h_ctrl$_{out}$:= h_ctrl$_{in}$;

Figure 8.8 : Operation of the processors

Let n = 2p+1: the new array has $\frac{(3p+2)(p+1)}{2} \approx \frac{3n^2}{8}$ cells as claimed. Note, however, that this saving of around 25% over the arrays of chapter 5 does not come for free: the period[1] of the array is now P = n+p+1 rather than P = n+1 for the Ahmed-Delosme-Morf array, or P = n for the Gentleman-Kung array. Also, there are now cycles in the dependence graph of the array, and partitioning issues become more involved.

8.3.2. An optimal array

We are now ready for the design of the optimal solution. As the design is rather technical, we only outline the derivation process. In table 8.2, we

[1] The period of the array is the minimum time between the solution of two consecutive instances of the problem (see chapter 5).

consider again the array of figure 8.7, but we choose a larger example: we let n=9, and we represent the tasks assigned to the processors. For each task, we indicate as $t=t_1,t_2$ the time step t_1 at which execution begins, and the time step t_2 at which the last computation is performed. Two tasks T and T' can be assigned to the same processor if the first one completes execution before the second one is initiated, i.e. if $t_2(T) < t_1(T')$. We check in table 8.2 that our mapping was safe: this condition always holds when two tasks are assigned to the same cell.

Cell 1,1 task 1,1 t=1,10	Cell 2,1 task 2,1 t=2,11	Cell 3,1 task 3,1 t=3,12	Cell 4,1 task 4,1 t=4,13	Cell 5,1 task 5,1 t=5,14	Cell 6,1 task 6,1 t=6,15 task 6,6 t=16,20	Cell 7,1 task 7,1 t=7,16 task 7,6 t=17,21	Cell 8,1 task 8,1 t=8,17 task 8,6 t=18,22	Cell 9,1 task 9,1 t=9,18 task 9,6 t=19,23
	Cell 2,2 task 2,2 t=4,12	Cell 3,2 task 3,2 t=5,13	Cell 4,2 task 4,2 t=6,14	Cell 5,2 task 5,2 t=7,15	Cell 6,2 task 6,2 t=8,16	Cell 7,2 task 7,2 t=9,17 task 7,7 t=19,22	Cell 8,2 task 8,2 t=10,18 task 8,7 t=20,23	Cell 9,2 task 9,2 t=11,19 task 9,7 t=21,24
		Cell 3,3 task 3,3 t=7,14	Cell 4,3 task 4,3 t=8,15	Cell 5,3 task 5,3 t=9,16	Cell 6,3 task 6,3 t=10,17	Cell 7,3 task 7,3 t=11,18	Cell 8,3 task 8,3 t=12,19 task 8,8 t=22,24	Cell 9,3 task 9,3 t=13,20 task 9,8 t=23,25
			Cell 4,4 task 4,4 t=10,16	Cell 5,4 task 5,4 t=11,17	Cell 6,4 task 6,4 t=12,18	Cell 7,4 task 7,4 t=13,19	Cell 8,4 task 8,4 t=14,20	Cell 9,4 task 9,4 t=15,21 task 9,9 t=25,26
				Cell 5,5 task 5,5 t=13,18	Cell 6,5 task 6,5 t=14,19	Cell 7,5 task 7,5 t=15,20	Cell 8,5 task 8,5 t=16,21	Cell 9,5 task 9,5 t=17,22

Table 8.2 : Assigning tasks to processors in the previous solution

Looking more carefully at table 8.2, we try to reduce the number of cells to derive an array of size $M_n = (p+1)^2 = 20$ for n = 2p+1 = 9. Table 8.2 can be divided into two parts: the left triangle T made of cells C_{ij} with $1 \le i \le p$ and $1 \le j \le p$, and the rightmost rectangle R made of cells C_{ij} with $i \ge p+1$ or $j \ge p+1$. A natural idea is to keep R, which has the good number of cells M_n. We do not change the allocation of the tasks that are already assigned to R, and we try to assign to R the tasks that were assigned to T. For our example with n=9, we see that there is only one possibility for allocating task T_{44}, namely cell C_{95}. Having made this choice, cell C_{85} is the only candidate for task T_{43}. Similarly, cell C_{94} is assigned task T_{33}. We are led to the allocation represented in table 8.3:

Cell 5,1 task 5,1 t=5,14	Cell 6,1 task 6,1 t=6,15 task 6,6 t=16,20	Cell 7,1 task 7,1 t=7,16 task 7,6 t=17,21	Cell 8,1 task 8,1 t=8,17 task 8,6 t=18,22	Cell 9,1 task 9,1 t=9,18 task 9,6 t=19,23
Cell 5,2 task 5,2 t=7,15	Cell 6,2 task 6,2 t=8,16	Cell 7,2 task 7,2 t=9,17 task 7,7 t=19,22	Cell 8,2 task 8,2 t=10,18 task 8,7 t=20,23	Cell 9,2 task 1,1 t=1,10 task 9,2 t=11,19 task 9,7 t=21,24
Cell 5,3 task 5,3 t=9,16	Cell 6,3 task 6,3 t=10,17	Cell 7,3 task 7,3 t=11,18	Cell 8,3 task 2,1 t=2,11 task 8,3 t=12,19 task 8,8 t=22,24	Cell 9,3 task 2,2 t=4,12 task 9,3 t=13,20 task 9,8 t=23,25
Cell 5,4 task 5,4 t=11,17	Cell 6,4 task 6,4 t=12,18	Cell 7,4 task 3,1 t=3,12 task 7,4 t=13,19	Cell 8,4 task 3,2 t=5,13 task 8,4 t=14,20	Cell 9,4 task 3,3 t=7,14 task 9,4 t=15,21 task 9,9 t=25,26
Cell 5,5 task 5,5 t=13,18	Cell 6,5 task 4,1 t=4,13 task 6,5 t=14,19	Cell 7,5 task 4,2 t=5,14 task 7,5 t=15,20	Cell 8,5 task 4,3 t=7,15 task 8,5 t=16,21	Cell 9,5 task 4,4 t=10,16 task 9,5 t=17,22

Table 8.3 : Optimal allocation of tasks to processors

Is the allocation regular enough for the solution to deserve the label *systolic* ? We represent the array in figure 8.9, without detailing its operation further. Some hints for the reader:

• rows 1 to 4 enter the array as indicated: they are not skewed as in the previous design. They progress leftwards until they are reflected by the anti-diagonal AD2 (see figure 8.9). Then they move rightwards up to the right border, then they go down along the anti-diagonal direction. Such a scheme can be easily implemented with a few boolean control signals.

• rows 5 to 9 move exactly as in the previous solution of figure 8.7. They are input with a skewed scheme. There is a toroidal connection between the first and last rows of the array.

• the only problem is for the connections marked /1/ to /4/ in the figure. Rows 1 to 4 use these connections to meet rows 5 to 9 as they did in the design of figure 8.7. These connections are not local. A possible solution to make them local is to fold the array twice, once along the main anti-diagonal AD1 and once around the vertical axis (third column in the example).

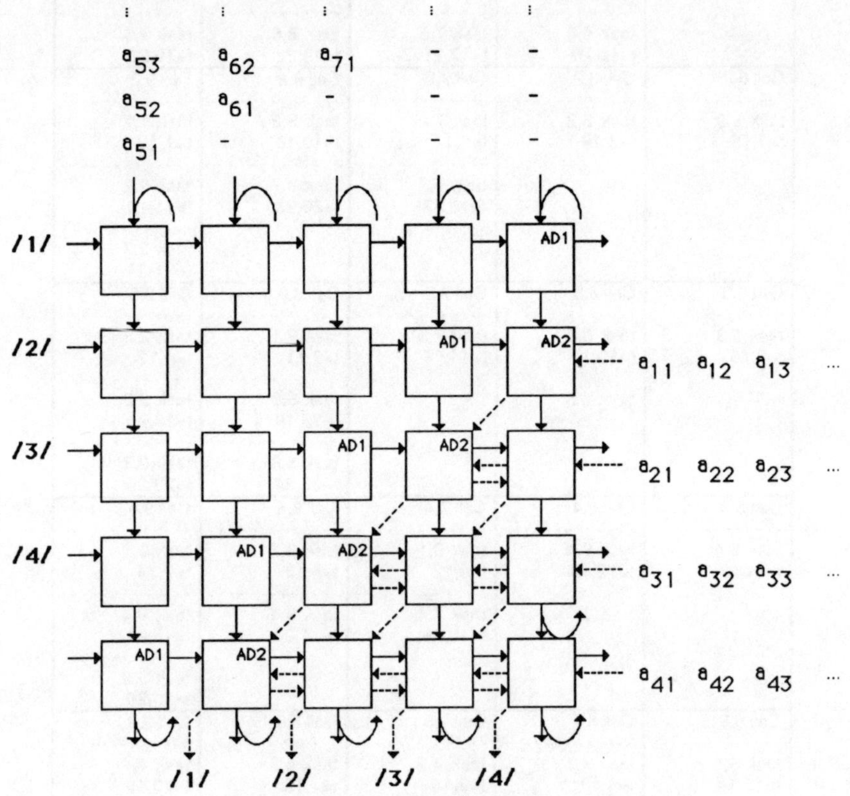

Figure 8.9 : The optimal systolic array

8.4. Bibliographic Notes

See Quinton [1987, 1988] or chapters 12 and 13 of Quinton and Robert [1989] for an in-depth presentation of the dependence method. Section 8.2 is based upon Bermond et al. [1988]. Section 8.3 is derived from Benaini, Robert and Tourancheau [1989] and Benaini and Robert [1990].

BIBLIOGRAPHY

Ahmed, H.M., Delosme, J.M. & Morf, M., "Highly concurrent computing structures for matrix arithmetic and signal processing", *Computer* **15**, 1 (1982), 65-82

Akl, S.G., *The design and analysis of parallel algorithms*, Prentice-Hall (1989)

Alliant FX/Series, *Product summary*, Alliant Computer Systems Corp. (1987)

Almasi, G.S. & Gottlieb, A., *Highly parallel computing*, The Benjamin Cummings Publishing Company (1989)

Amdahl, G.M., "Validity of the single-processor approach to achieving large-scale computing capabilities", in *AFIPS Conference Proceedings* **30**, Thompson Books (1967), 483-485

André, F. & Verjus, J.P. (eds), *Hypercube and distributed computers*, North-Holland (1989)

Annaratone, M., Arnould, E., Gross, T., Kung, H.T., Lam, M., Menzilcioglu, O. & Webb, J.A., "The Warp computer: architecture, implementation and performance", *IEEE Trans. Computers* **36**, 12 (1987), 1523-1538

Arlauskas, R., "iPSC/2 system: a second generation hypercube", in *The Third Conference on Hypercube Computers and Applications*, G. Fox ed., ACM Press (1988), 38-42

Athas, W.C. & Seitz, C.L., "Multicomputers: message-passing concurrent computers", *Computer* **21**, 8 (1988), 9-24

Benaini, A. & Robert, Y., "A modular systolic linear array for Gaussian elimination", Technical Report 89-08, LIP-IMAG, Ecole Normale Supérieure de Lyon (1989)

Benaini, A. & Robert, Y., "Spacetime-minimal systolic arrays for Gaussian elimination and the algebraic path problem", Technical Report 90-09, LIP-IMAG, Ecole Normale Supérieure de Lyon (1990)

Benaini, A., Robert, Y. & Tourancheau, B., "A new systolic architecture for the algebraic path problem", in *Systolic array processors*, J. McCanny et al. eds, Prentice-Hall (1989), 73-82

Bermond, J.C., Peyrat, C., Sakho, I. & Tchuente, M., "Parallelization of Gauss elimination algorithm on systolic arrays", Technical Report 430, Laboratoire de Recherche en Informatique, Université de Paris-Sud (1988)

Berry, M., Gallivan, K., Harrod, W., Jalby, W., Lo, S., Meier, U., Philippe, B. & Sameh, A.H., "Parallel algorithms on the CEDAR system", in *CONPAR 86*, G. Goos and J. Hartmanis eds., Lecture Notes in Computer Science 237, Springer Verlag (1986), 25-39

Bertsekas, D.P. & Tsitsiklis, J.N., *Parallel and distributed computation: numerical methods*, Prentice-Hall (1989)

Bromley, K., Kung, S.Y. & Swartzlander, E. (eds), *International conference on systolic arrays*, IEEE Computer Society Press (1988)

Buchholz, W., "The IBM System/370 vector architecture", *IBM Systems Journal* **25**, 1 (1986), 51-62

Calahan, D.A., "Block-oriented, local memory-based linear equations on the CRAY-2: uniprocessor algorithms", in *Int. Conf. Parallel Processing ICPP 86*, The Pennsylvania State University Press (1986), 375-378

Chandy, S.C. & Misra, J., *Parallel program design: a foundation*, Addison-Wesley (1988)

Chen, S.C., Dongarra, J.J. & Hsiung, C.C., "Multiprocessing linear algebra algorithms on the Cray X-MP-2: experiences with small granularity", *J. Parallel and Distributed Computing* **1** (1984), 22-31

Chuang, H.Y.H. & He, H., "Design of problem-size independent systolic arrays systems", in *Int. Conf. Computer Design ICCD 84*, IEEE Press (1984), 152-156

Coffman, E.G. & Denning, P.J., *Operating system theory*, Prentice-Hall (1973)

Comon, P. & Robert, Y., "A systolic array for computing BA^{-1}", *IEEE Trans. ASSP* **35**, 6 (1987), 717-723

Cosnard, M., Duprat, J. & Robert, Y., "Parallel triangularization in modular arithmetic", in *Parallel Processing*, M. Cosnard et al. eds., North-Holland (1988), 207-220

Cosnard, M., Marrakchi, M., Robert, Y. & Trystram, D., "Parallel Gaussian elimination on an MIMD Computer", *Parallel Computing* **6** (1988a), 275-296

Cosnard, M., Quinton, P., Raynal, M. & Robert, Y. (eds), *Parallel and distributed algorithms*, North-Holland (1988b)

Cosnard, M., Quinton, P., Robert, Y. & Tchuente, M. (eds), *Parallel algorithms and architectures*, North-Holland (1986)

Cosnard, M. & Robert, Y., "Implementing the nullspace algorithm over GF(p) on a ring of processors", in *2nd Int. Symposium on Computer and Information Sciences*, E. Gelenbe & A.Riza Kaylan eds., Bogazici University, Istanbul (1987), 92-110

Cosnard, M., Robert, Y. & Tourancheau, B., "Evaluating speedups on distributed memory architectures", *Parallel Computing* **10** (1989), 247-253

Cosnard, M., Tourancheau, B. & Villard, G., "Gaussian elimination on message passing architectures", in *Supercomputing*, E.N. Houstis et al. eds., Lecture Notes in Computer Science 297, Springer Verlag (1988), 611-628

Daly, C. & Du Croz, J., "Performance of a subroutine library on vector processing machines", *Computer Physics Communications* **37** (1985), 181-186

Dongarra, J.J., "The LINPACK benchmark: an explanation", in *Supercomputing*, E.N. Houstis et al. eds., Lecture Notes in Computer Science 297, Springer Verlag (1988), 456-474

Dongarra, J.J., Bunch, J.R., Moler, C.B. & Stewart, G.W., *LINPACK users' guide*, SIAM Press (1979)

Dongarra, J.J., Du Croz, J., Duff, I. & Hammarling, S., "A proposal for a set a Level 3 basic linear algebra subprograms", Argonne National Laboratory Report MCS-TM-88 (1987)

Dongarra, J.J., Du Croz, J, Hammarling, S. & Hanson, R., "An extended set of FORTRAN basic linear algebra subprograms", Argonne National Laboratory Report MCS-TM-41 (1986)

Dongarra, J.J. & Eisenstat, S.C., "Squeezing the most out of an algorithm in Cray FORTRAN, *ACM Trans. Math. Software* **10**, 3 (1984), 221-230

Dongarra, J.J., Gustavson, F.G. & Karp, A., "Implementing linear algebra algorithms for dense matrices on a vector pipeline machine", *SIAM Review* **26**, 1 (1984), 91-112

Dongarra, J.J. & Hinds, A.R., "Unrolling loops in FORTRAN", *Software - Practice and Experience* **9** (1979), 219-229

Dongarra, J.J. & Sorensen, D.C., "Linear algebra on high-performance computers", in *Parallel Computing 85*, M. Feilmeier et al. eds., North-Holland (1986), 221-230

van Dongen, V. & Quinton, P., "Uniformization of linear recurrence equations: a step towards the automatic synthesis of systolic arrays", in *International Conference on Systolic Arrays*, K. Bromley et al. eds., IEEE Computer Society Press (1988), 473-482

Dunigan, T.H., "Hypercube performance", in *Hypercube Multiprocessors 1987*, H.T. Heath ed., SIAM Press (1987), 178-192

Faber, V., Lubeck, O.M. & White, A.B.Jr., "Superlinear speedup of an efficient sequential algorithm is not possible", *Parallel Computing* **3** (1986), 259-260

Faber V., Lubeck, O.M. & White, A.B.Jr., "Comments on the paper "Parallel efficiency can be greater than unity"", *Parallel Computing* **4** (1987), 209-210

Flatt, H.P. & Kennedy, K, "Performance of parallel processors", *Parallel Computing* **12** (1989), 1-20

Flynn, M, "Some computer organisations and their effectiveness", *IEEE Trans. Computers* **21**, 9 (1972), 948-960

Fogelman-Soulie, F., Robert, Y. & Tchuente, M. (eds), *Automata networks in computer science*, Manchester University Press (1987)

Fong, K.W. & Jordan, T.L., "Some linear algebra algorithms and their performance on Cray 1", Technical Report LA-6774, Los Alamos National Laboratory (1977)

Fox, G. (ed), *The third conference on hypercube computers and applications*, ACM Press (1988)

Fox, G., Johnson, M., Lyzenga, G., Otto, S., Salmon, J. & Walker, D., *Solving problems on concurrent processors*, Prentice-Hall (1988)

Gajski, D.D. & Peir, J.K., "Essential issues in multiprocessors systems", *Computer* **18**, 6 (1985), 9-27

Gallivan, K, Jalby, W., Meier, U. & Sameh A., "The impact of hierarchical memory systems on linear algebra algorithmic design", *Int. J. of Supercomputer Applications* **2**, 3 (1988), 37-57

Geist, G.A. & Heath, M.T., "Matrix factorization on a hypercube multiprocessor", in *Hypercube Multiprocessors 1986*, M.T. Heath ed., SIAM Press (1986), 161-180

Gentleman, W.M., "Some complexity results for matrix computations on parallel processors", *J.. ACM* **25**, 1 (1978), 112-115

Gentleman, W.M. & Kung, H.T., "Matrix triangularisation by systolic arrays", in *Proceedings SPIE* (Society of Photo-Optical Instrumentation Engineers) **298**, Real-time Signal Processing IV (1981), 19-26

Gerasoulis, A. & Nelken, I., "Gaussian elimination and Gauss-Jordan on MIMD architectures", Report LCSR-TR-105, Department of Computer Science, Rutgers University (1988)

Gibbons, A. & Rytter, W., *Efficient parallel algorithms*, Cambridge University Press (1988)

Golub, G.H. & van Loan, C.F., *Matrix computations*, The Johns Hopkins University Press (1983)

Gustafson, J.L., "Reevaluating Amdahl's law", *Comm. A.C.M.* **31**, 5 (1988), 532-533

Gustafson, J.L., Hawkinson, S. & Scott, K., "The architecture of a homogeneous vector supercomputer", in *Int. Conf. Parallel Processing ICPP 86*, The Pennsylvania State University Press (1986), 649-652

Heath, M.T. (ed), *Hypercube multiprocessors 1986*, SIAM Press (1986)

Heath, M.T. (ed), *Hypercube multiprocessors 1987*, SIAM Press (1987)

Heller, D., "Partitioning big matrices for small systolic arrays", in *VLSI and Modern Signal Processing*, S.Y. Kung et al. eds. (1985), 185-199

Helmbold, D.P. & McDowell, C.E., "Modeling speedup(n) greater than n", in *Int. Conf. Parallel Processing ICPP 89*, The Pennsylvania State University Press (1989), III 219-225

Hockney, R.W., "Classification and evaluation of parallel computer systems", in *Parallel Computing in Science and Engineering*, R. Dierstein et al. eds., Lecture Notes in Computer Science 295, Springer Verlag (1987), 13-25

Hockney, R.W. & Jesshope, C.R., *Parallel computers 2: architecture, programming and algorithms*, Adam Hilger (1988)

Huang, K.H. & Abraham, J.A., "Algorithm based fault-tolerance for matrix operations", *IEEE Trans. Computers* **33**, 6 (1984), 518-528

Hwang, K., *Computer arithmetic: principles, architecture and design*, John Wiley & Sons (1979)

Hwang, K., "Advanced parallel processing with supercomputer architectures", *Proceedings of the IEEE* **75**, 10 (1987), 1348-1379

Hwang, K & Briggs F., *Computer architecture and parallel processing*, McGraw-Hill (1984)

Hwang, K. & Cheng, Y.H., "Partitioned matrix algorithm for VLSI arithmetic systems", *IEEE Trans. Computers* **31**, 12 (1982), 1215-1224

Ipsen, I.C.F., Saad, Y. & Schultz, M.H., "Complexity of dense linear system solution on a multiprocessor ring", *Lin. Alg. Appl.* **77** (1986), 205-239

Jalby, W. & Meier, U., "Optimizing matrix operations on a parallel multiprocessor with a hierarchical memory system", in *Int. Conf. Parallel Processing ICPP 86*, The Pennsylvania State University Press (1986), 429-432

Janssen, R., "A note on superlinear speedup", *Parallel Computing* **4** (1987), 211-213

Johnsson, S.L. & Ho, C.T., "Optimum broadcasting and personalized communication in hypercubes", *IEEE Trans. Computers* **38**, 9 (1989), 1249-1268

Karp, A.H., "Programming for parallelism", *Computer* **20**, 5 (1987), 43-57

Kogge, P.M., *The architecture of pipelined computers*, McGraw-Hill (1981)

Konig, J.C. & Trystram, D., "Ordonnancement du graphe à deux pas pour le calcul parallèle", *C.R. Acad. Sci. Paris* **309**, I (1989), 569-572

Kronsjö, L., *Computational complexity of sequential and parallel algorithms*, Wiley (1985)

Kung, H.T., "Why systolic architectures?", *Computer* **15**, 1 (1982), 37-46

Kung, H.T. & Lam, M.S., "Fault-tolerance and two-level pipelining in VLSI systolic arrays", *J. Parallel and Distributed Computing* **1**, 1 (1984), 32-63

Kung, H.T. & Leiserson, C.E., "Systolic arrays for (VLSI)", in *Introduction to VLSI systems*, C.A. Mead and L.A. Conway, Addison-Wesley (1980), chapter 8.3

Kung, S.Y., *VLSI array processors*, Prentice-Hall (1988)

Kung, S.Y., Whitehouse, H.J. & Kailath T. (eds), *VLSI and modern signal processing*, Prentice-Hall (1985)

Lawson, C., Hanson, R., Kincaid, D. & Krogh, F., "Basic linear algebra subprograms for FORTRAN usage", *ACM Trans. Math. Software* **5** (1979), 308-371

Lee, R.B., "Empirical results on the speed, efficiency, redundancy and quality of parallel computations", in *Int. Conf. Parallel Processing ICPP 80*, The Pennsylvania State University Press (1980), 91-96

Liu, B. & Strother, N., "Programming in VS FORTRAN on the IBM 3090 for maximum vector performance", *Computer* **21**, 8 (1988), 65-76

Lord, R.E., Kowalik, J.S. & Kumar, S.P., "Solving linear algebraic equations on an MIMD computer", *J. ACM* **30**, 1 (1983), 103-117

McCanny, J., McWhirter, J. & Swartzlander, E.E. Jr. (eds), *Systolic array processors*, Prentice-Hall (1989)

Marrakchi, M. & Robert, Y., "Optimal algorithms for Gaussian elimination on an MIMD computer", *Parallel Computing* **12** (1989), 183-194

Mead, C.A. & Conway, L.A., *Introduction to VLSI systems*, Addison-Wesley (1980)

Minsky, M. & Papert, S., "On some associative parallel and analog computations", in *Associative Information Techniques*, E.J. Jacks ed., American Elsevier (1971)

Missirlis, M.N. & Tjaferis, F., "Parallel matrix factorization on a shared memory MIMD computer", in *Supercomputing,* E.N. Houstis et al. eds., Lecture Notes in Computer Science 297, Springer Verlag (1988), 926-938

Modi, J.J., *Parallel algorithms and matrix computation*, Oxford University Press (1988)

Moldovan, D.I., "Mapping an arbitrarily large QR algorithm into fixed size systolic arrays", *IEEE Trans. Computers* **35**, 1 (1986), 1-12

Moler, C., "Matrix computation on distributed memory multiprocessors", in *Hypercube Multiprocessors 1986*, M.T. Heath ed., SIAM Press (1986), 181-195

Moore, W., McCabe, A. & Urquhart, R. (eds), *Systolic arrays*, Adam Hilger (1987)

Nagel, W.E. & Szelényi, F., "Multitasking on CRAY and IBM multiprocessors: concepts and experiences", in *High Performance Computing*, J.L. Delhaye and E. Gelenbe eds., North-Holland (1989), 133-142

Nugent, S.F., "The iPSC/2 direct-connect communications technology", in *The Third Conference on Hypercube Computers and Applications*, G. Fox ed., ACM Press (1988), 51-60

Oppe, T.C. & Kincaid, D.R., "Parallel LU-factorization algorithms for dense matrices", in *Supercomputing,* E.N. Houstis et al. eds., Lecture Notes in Computer Science 297, Springer Verlag (1988), 576-594

Ortega, J.M., "The ijk forms of factorization methods I. Vector computers", *Parallel Computing* **7** (1988), 135-147

Ortega, J.M. & Romine, C.H., "The ijk forms of factorization methods II. Parallel systems", *Parallel Computing* **7** (1988), 149-162

Parkinson, D., "Parallel efficiency can be greater than unity", *Parallel Computing* **3** (1986), 261-262

Parkinson, D. & Wunderlich, M., "A compact algorithm for Gaussian elimination over GF(2) implemented on highly parallel computers", *Parallel Computing* **1** (1984), 65-73

Quinn, M.J., *Designing efficient algorithms for parallel computers*, McGraw-Hill (1987)

Quinton, P., "The systematic design of systolic arrays", in *Automata Networks in Computer Science*, F. Fogelman-Soulie et al. eds., Manchester University Press (1987), 229-260

Quinton, P., "Mapping recurrences on parallel architectures", in *Int. Conf on Supercomputing ICS 88*, L.P. Kartashev and S.I. Kartashev eds., International Supercomputing Institute (1988), III 1-8

Quinton, P. & Robert, Y., *Algorithmes et Architectures Systoliques*, Masson (1989)

Radicati, G. & Robert, Y., "Parallel conjugate gradient-like algorithms for solving nonsymmetric linear systems on a vector multiprocessor", *Parallel Computing* **11** (1989), 223-239

Radicati, G., Robert, Y. & Sguazzero, P., "Dense linear systems FORTRAN solvers on the IBM 3090 vector multiprocessor", *Parallel Computing* **8** (1988a), 377-384

Radicati, G., Robert, Y. & Sguazzero, P., "Block algorithms for linear algebra on the IBM 3090 Vector Multiprocessor", *Supercomputer* **5**, 1 (1988b), 15-25

Robert, Y., "Systolic algorithms and architectures", in *Automata Networks in Computer Science*, F. Fogelman-Soulie et al. eds., Manchester University Press (1987), 187-228

Robert, Y. & Sguazzero, P., "The LU decomposition algorithm and its efficient FORTRAN implementation on the IBM 3090 vector multiprocessor", Technical Report ICE-0006, IBM ECSEC Rome (1987)

Robert, Y. & Tchuente, M., "Résolution systolique de systèmes linéaires denses", *RAIRO Modélisation et Analyse Numérique* **19**, 2 (1985), 315-326

Robert, Y. & Tourancheau, B., "Block Gaussian elimination on a hypercube vector multiprocessor", *Revista de Matematicas Aplicadas* **10** (1989), 49-69

Robert Y., Tourancheau B. & Villard, G., "Data allocation strategies for the Gauss and Jordan algorithms on a ring of processors", *Information Processing Letters* **31**, 1 (1989), 21-29

Robert, Y & Trystram, D., "Optimal scheduling algorithms for parallel Gaussian elimination", *Theoretical Computer Science* **64** (1989), 159-173

Saad, Y., "Communication complexity of the Gaussian elimination algorithm on multiprocessors", *Lin. Alg. Appl.* **77** (1986a), 315-340

Saad, Y., "Gaussian elimination on hypercubes", in *Parallel Algorithms and Architectures*, M. Cosnard et al. eds., North-Holland (1986b), 5-18

Saad, Y., & Schultz, M.H., "Topological properties of hypercubes", *IEEE Trans. Computers* **37**, 7 (1988), 867-872

Saad, Y. & Schultz, M.H., "Data communication in parallel architectures", *Parallel Computing* **11** (1989), 131-150

Samukawa, H., "Programming style on the IBM 3090 Vector Facility considering both performance and flexibility", *IBM Systems Journal* **27**, 4 (1988), 453-474

Schendel, U., *Introduction to numerical methods for parallel computers*, Ellis Horwood (1984)

Schönauer, W., *Scientific computing on vector computers*, North-Holland (1987)

Sorensen, D.C., "Analysis of pairwise pivoting in Gaussian elimination", Technical Report MCS-TM-26, Argonne National Laboratory (1984)

Stewart, G.W., *Introduction to matrix computations*, Academic Press (1973)

Stone, H.S., "Problems of parallel computation", in *Complexity of sequential and parallel numerical algorithms*, J.F. Traub ed., Academic Press (1973)

Stone, H.S., *High-performance computer architecture*, Addison-Wesley (1987)

Toomey, L.J., Plachy, E.G., Scarborough, R.G., Sahulka, R.J., Shaw, J.F. & Shannon, A.W., "IBM parallel FORTRAN", *IBM Systems Journal* **27**, 4 (1988), 416-435

Tucker, S.G., "The IBM 3090 system: an overview", *IBM Systems Journal* **25**, 1 (1986), 4-19

Veldhorst, M., "Gaussian elimination with partial pivoting on an MIMD computer", *J. Parallel and Distributed Computing* **6** (1989), 62-68

INDEX